Blurred Zones: Investigations of the Interstitial

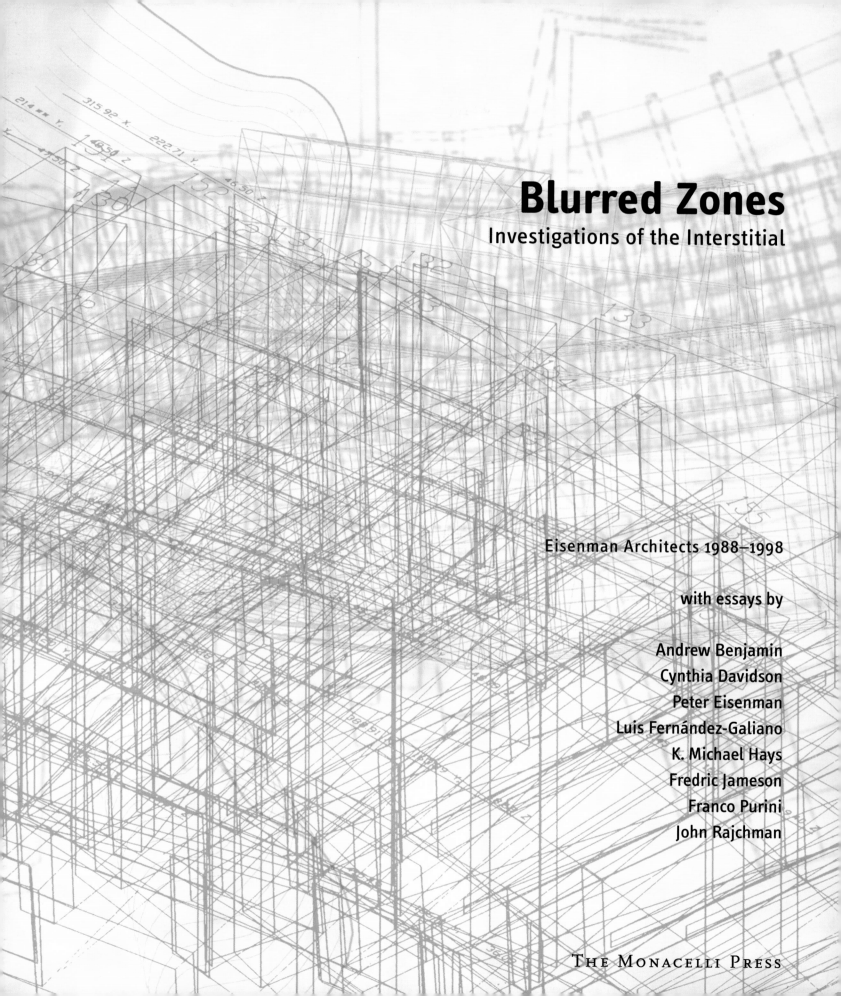

Blurred Zones
Investigations of the Interstitial

Eisenman Architects 1988–1998

with essays by

Andrew Benjamin

Cynthia Davidson

Peter Eisenman

Luis Fernández-Galiano

K. Michael Hays

Fredric Jameson

Franco Purini

John Rajchman

THE MONACELLI PRESS

Acknowledgments

Given the number of people involved in producing not only this book but also the ten years of work that it represents, it is impossible to acknowledge everyone adequately. The list of names that appears at the end of this volume is only the tip of an iceberg. It is important, however, to especially acknowledge my partner Richard Rosson; the project designers and architects who helped to shape and realize our work from 1988 to 1998, including Thomas Leeser, Hiroshi Maruyama, Greg Lynn, Frédéric Levrat, Ed Mitchell, Michael McInturf, Donna Barry, Sergio Bregante, Ingeborg Rocker; and two artists who consulted on projects included here, Silvia Kolbowski and Richard Serra. Making this book was an undertaking of another sort, but equally dependent on the contributions of others. For this I am grateful to the writers whose essays appear here, especially to Fredric Jameson, Franco Purini, Luis Fernández-Galiano, and Andrew Benjamin, who wrote pieces specifically for **Blurred Zones,** and to Cynthia Davidson for editing all of the texts. Finally, Juliette Cezzar persevered through all of the odds to produce a beautiful design, which Gianfranco Monacelli patiently waited to publish it at The Monacelli Press.   —P.E.

Photography Credits

Model photographs: Dick Frank, with the exception of Max Reinhardt Haus (Jochan Littkemann) and wooden model for Memorial to the Murdered Jews of Europe
Greater Columbus Convention Center, Aronoff Center for Design and Art: Jeff Goldberg (ESTO)
Koizumi Sangyo Office Building: Masao Ueda, Peter Aaron (ESTO)
Nunotani Headquarters Building: Shigeo Ogawa

First published in the United States of America in 2002 by
The Monacelli Press, Inc.
902 Broadway, New York, NY 10010.

Library of Congress Cataloging-in-Publication Data
Blurred zones : investigations of the interstitial : Eisenman Architects, 1988–1998 /
with essays by Andrew Benjamin . . . [et al.]
p. cm.
Includes bibliographical references.
ISBN 1-58093-049-2
1. Eisenman, Peter, 1932– – Criticism and interpretation. 2. Eisenman Architects.
3. Architecture, Modern – 20th century – Designs and plans. I. Benjamin, Andrew E.
NA737.E33 B58 2003
720'.92 – dc21   2002022658

Designed by Juliette Cezzar
Printed and bound in Italy

Blurred Zones
Peter Eisenman

Author's Note: Since I first conceived of the term blurring *in architecture and the concept for a book called* Blurred Zones *some thirteen years ago, the term has become quite popular – so much so that my editors argued for changing the title of this book. Architects such as Toyo Ito and Diller + Scofidio now use the term, but in an entirely different manner than it is used here. For example, Diller + Scofidio use the term quite literally, as in their Blur Building. I continue to use* blurring *and* blurred *in the context of the work in this book because the idea of blurring has not been argued in the conceptual sense that it is presented here.*
—P.E., September 2001

According to the French thinker Michel Foucault, everything exists as between the visible and the articulate. This condition of between assumes that these two poles – the visible and the articulate – are more or less stable. In the mediated world of today, however, even the visible is becoming articulate. As a consequence, there is an excess of articulation. When the articulate is increasingly compressed into shorter and shorter time spans, like twenty-second sound bites, the visual becomes more and more a question of image rather than substance. Another consequence of our mediated age is the loss of the immediate relation between the visible and the body, that is, the tactile and the affective. Architecture can provide affect – a form of articulation that appeals to both the somatic and the articulate: to the body, the mind, and the eye at the same time. This is something that other media do not do.

Blurring, or the blurred zones that characterize the work presented here, deals with the world of affect, rather than effect, as presenting a strategy for a different mind/body relationship in architecture. Affect is concerned with the way particular forms of architectural effects, tropes, rhetoric, can displace our conventional or expected experience of space. If, as Walter Benjamin said, architecture is viewed in a state of distraction, then such affects might provoke a different awareness of a space/time experience. For example, figure/ground is an effect that concentrates on the aesthetic materiality of form; shape produces a clarity of affects. Blurring reduces the affect of these effects, producing a need for different effects. It must be understood that blurring in this context is never literal; one never sees blurring.

Affect operates from the way the upright body moves in and around space; it recalibrates the subject's somatic experience of both presence and information, as well as one's fundamental desire for these experiences. This desire generates an unconscious, somatic expectancy on the part of the subject. For example, when one goes down an unfamiliar set of stairs in the pitch dark, say a flight of steps to a basement, a somatic expectancy occurs vis-à-vis each next step. Hence at the last stair at the bottom, the body automatically takes another step. When the foot comes down unexpectedly on the floor, one often feels as if one has lost one's balance. This is a somatic expectancy, a desire on the part of the body to repeat what it has learned to anticipate. Benjamin calls this reaction a matter of habit. Habits are rooted in desire, and desire is often motivated by habit. For example, we often take the same route to destinations we repeatedly return to.

Most architecture is the concretization of habit. There are primitive and unconscious motivations that become conscious in architecture: the desire for ground or to be rooted; the desire for shelter; the desire for meaning. These desires, more than the objects of their desire, seem to motivate a more or less status quo in architecture. If architecture can begin to dislocate this motivation, then the desire manifested in the habitual or somatic expectancy can perhaps be reoriented.

The word *architecture* conjures up an enormous range of meanings that embraces everything from home to building, symbol to function. But while it includes these things, it also assumes certain conditions beyond the bounds of what is necessary and sufficient to define architecture's particular discourse. In turn, these assumptions repress other possibilities. Blurring fundamentally involves the question of the becoming unmotivated of three conditions: the becoming unmotivated of presence, of the sign, and of the subject. The key concept in the process of blurring is *becoming*. For example, there can never be a total lack of motivation in presence. Presence itself is a motivated condition. The *becoming* unmotivated is a movement from the fullness of motivation to something less motivated – a between condition.

Blurring is one strategy for unmotivating not desire itself but the specific desires for such things as presence, ground, and meaning. Blurring is a conceptual activity. This is because it is literally impossible to blur an architectural element such as a column or a wall. A blurring action begins to displace categories such as the visible and the articulate by detaching form from a one-to-one relationship with function and meaning. Blurring seeks to undermine the conceptual as well as the physical clarity of elements such as figure and ground.

In Woody Allen's film *Deconstructing Harry,* a character who has little psychological awareness of himself often appears visibly out of focus. This initially has a disturbing visual effect on the audience, but over the time of the film it becomes a one-liner because nothing more is made of it; very little relates this blurring to the psychological condition of the character. In a sense, it is an effect without substance, and therefore with very little affect.

When we go to the movies, we not only want to be entertained, we also desire to understand what the movie is about. The most popular movies are those that are easiest to understand because they satisfy our desire to know. The difference between a movie and what one calls "film" is that a film attempts to unmotivate the viewer's desire to know and to be entertained in order to present the being of film itself – its rhetoric and its tropes.

Architecture, unlike film, is more often than not an everyday occurrence. While it is not meant to entertain, it is equally not meant to call attention to its own rhetoric, which is seen as a response to a desire for a place, a desire for ground, for containment, representation, and so forth. Whether conscious or not, one of the basic desires of humankind is to make things real, tangible, secure, and comfortable. Architecture is a major locus of such desires, as they involve not only presence, an actual enclosure, but also the metaphysical idea of comfort and security. In post-1968 France, the question of presence became a central philosophical issue. In architecture, presence is both active and fundamental; architecture cannot be thought without presence. The presence of walls, floors, and ceilings is a real materiality. Today, however, the idea of a virtual space foregrounds the question of presence. Since one cannot get rid of actual presence, what is the blurring that occurs? Unmotivating does not do away with issues of comfort and security. Rather it attempts to problematize their use as legitimating factors in architecture.

The idea of a conceptual blurring raises the issue of contemporary media. Does architecture still function symbolically the way it did before print and broadcast media became so dominant? Do we look to architecture for narratives or the kinds of information that are now being provided by other media? It would seem that the public today no longer looks to architecture to provide information in the way it once did. Blurring in architecture is not to suggest a movement from a symbolic environment to one in which there is no meaning. Rather it is to suggest a condition where architecture is neither dependent on its former narratives nor devoid of meaning but resides between the two, where other forms of meaning, and meaningful situations, can occur.

These situations lead to the becoming unmotivated of the sign. The becoming unmotivated is a process of blurring between the clarity of meaning and no meaning. Architecture can never become totally unmotivated, that is, have no meaning. For example, signs like the ground, the enclosure, and the facade, which have dominated architectural discourse since the 16th century, are what might be called "motivated conditions." Because these motivated conditions have been taken for granted, over time they have taken on qualities of the natural, when in fact they are only conventions. Take, for example, the term *facade,* which is used as a catchall term for elevation, vertical plane, etc. Facade is an example of a loaded, or motivated, term that is assumed to be natural and thus aesthetically neutral. But facade literally means face, to have a face; most exterior vertical planes are legitimated as facades by having a face. A face is composed; it has an aesthetic and, from that aesthetic, both an iconic and symbolic meaning. A facade creates difference and hierarchy between in and out; public and private; sacred and profane. Blurring attempts to erase that hierarchy and the conditions that previously legitimated such concerns, but without losing the enclosing condition of the vertical plane. Rather than legitimating enclosure (while being enclosure), blurring allows the vertical plane to be something else.

If it is possible to blur and displace traditional presence – to conceptually dislocate the stability of place – and if the sign can become less motivated and move toward an indexical condition, this then leaves the condition of the subject. This concerns the attempt to move from a motivated, desiring subject to one who is less motivated, that is, to a situation of more pure desire. The human subject will always be a desiring one. This cannot be changed. But in architecture that desire can be expanded beyond the usual motivations of shelter, enclosure, stability, ground, etc., by opening up the realm of the unconscious, where desire operates. This suggests that architecture can move from the conscious world of presence and motivated signs toward a world that opens up to unconscious phenomena. In this way, architecture can think of space and time as motivated by concerns other than the traditional ones of a desiring and motivated subject.

How does one change the motivation of the subject-user or the subject-architect who inhabits or makes architecture? In other words, if architecture is viewed as something that is known and understood, can one change architecture to something that can present the unexpected within the expected? Throughout the history of architecture, when a break with or displacement of the known has occurred, architecture has taken the new and incorporated it into a new normal, or typical, condition. Architecture has traditionally moved forward by transforming itself into something related to its time, transforming the present and thereby upsetting the normative situation. Blurring, on the other hand, displaces the idea of one's time, rather than conforming to time in the present, in order to open up the past to another future. If one assumes that the past as known will always lead to the present, nothing will change. If the present is displaced by looking to the past in order to blur the present to suggest a previously unknown future, it is possible to change the desires and expectations of the subjects.

Blurring takes many different definitions – the between, the interstitial – and many different forms in the work that is presented here. Basically, the process of blurring introduces a third phase into the process of design. The first phase of any design process considers site, program, and function, which are the reality of what is required. Each of these can be seen as textual material constituting the most immediate information on which any specific design is based. The second kind of textual material comes from the interiority and anteriority of architecture. The interiority of architecture defines the discipline, what it is that makes architecture singular; anteriority is the sedimented history of architecture, which has defined architecture at any given historical moment.

The texts of function, site, and program and the texts of the interiority and anteriority of architecture together define a traditional practice. Architects always define what they do in relation to these texts because it is impossible to do architecture without recalling its anteriority, its interiority, or its singular condition of sign and signified as functioning things.

The attempts to create a blurring require the introduction of other, third texts. These texts initially appear to be unmotivated by the traditional concepts of program, site, context, interiority, or anteriority. In one sense, these texts are both arbitrary and contingent, in that they both relate to and have the ability to alter the conditions of the traditional texts. While there is no such thing as the purely arbitrary, the introduction of an arbitrary condition into the relationship with the other two texts begins to blur the previous one-to-one relationship between the forms one produces and their functions or meanings. Thus these supposedly arbitrary texts in many cases are contingent on their capacity to blur. In a sense they are selected to produce architectural effects that will displace traditional ones. When one looks at the resultant forms, they no longer appear to be motivated by site, function, program, interiority, or anteriority. Rather, they appear to be "out of focus," blurred by the superposition of the texts of function and site with these other texts. It is difficult to tell if the resultant forms come about through functional requirements or from a desire to produce meaning; neither seems to explain them. This produces what will be called a diagram, a blurred condition between form and content, between site and program, where signs no longer read as fully motivated. The interference pattern of the diagram prevents a recourse to the former relationship of form and function, form and content.

The projects presented in *Blurred Zones* in one way or another represent a movement toward the becoming unmotivated of the former texts of architecture, which together constituted a hegemony and acceptance of the metaphysics of presence. This project of the becoming unmotivated requires one important caveat: it requires that I also unmotivate myself toward the things that I like and desire, even toward my own theories and designs. Because I have likes and desires, it is sometimes difficult when someone says that a project does or does not conform to the theory of displacement. I often say, damn the theory, the thing looks terrible; we cannot have anything like this. And sometimes the reply is that I am going against my own theory. But I do not care about going against the theory because theory can only take one so far. In the end, I have to trust my own intuition, no matter how flawed it may be, because intuition comes from the unconscious fire of one's own history, and may open up what was previously repressed both in oneself and, for me, in architecture.

Peter Eisenman is an architect and teacher in New York City. This and the other Eisenman writings presented here were developed during the 1990s.

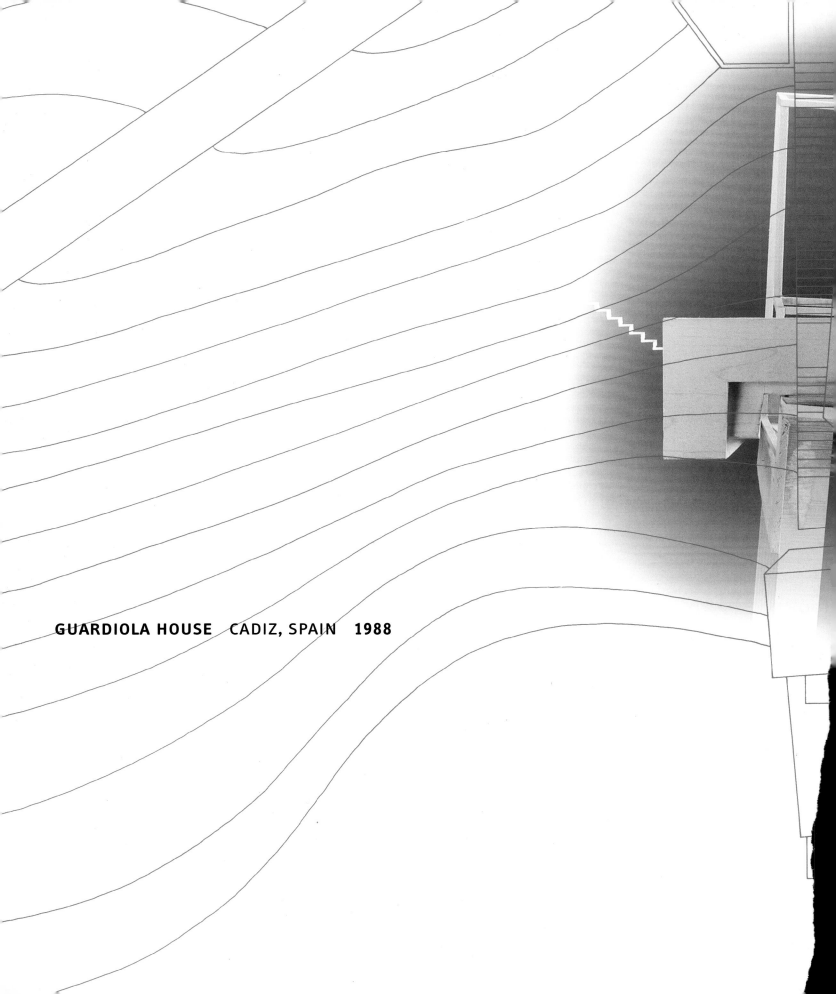

GUARDIOLA HOUSE   CADIZ, SPAIN   1988

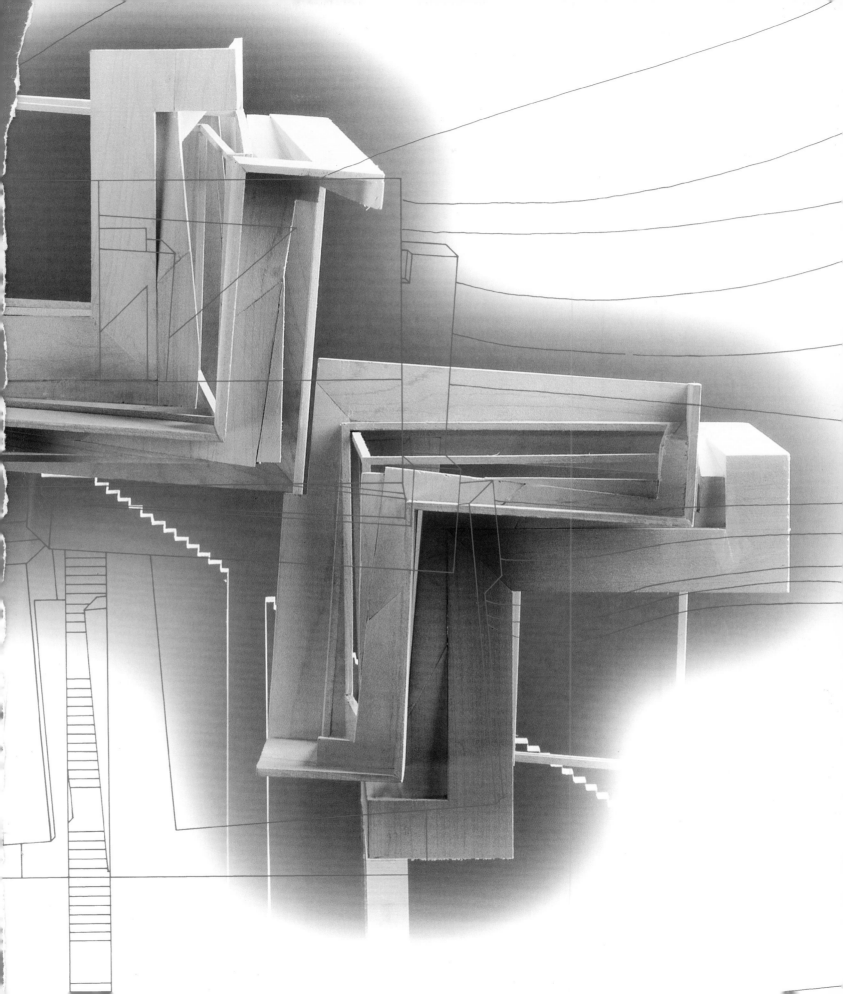

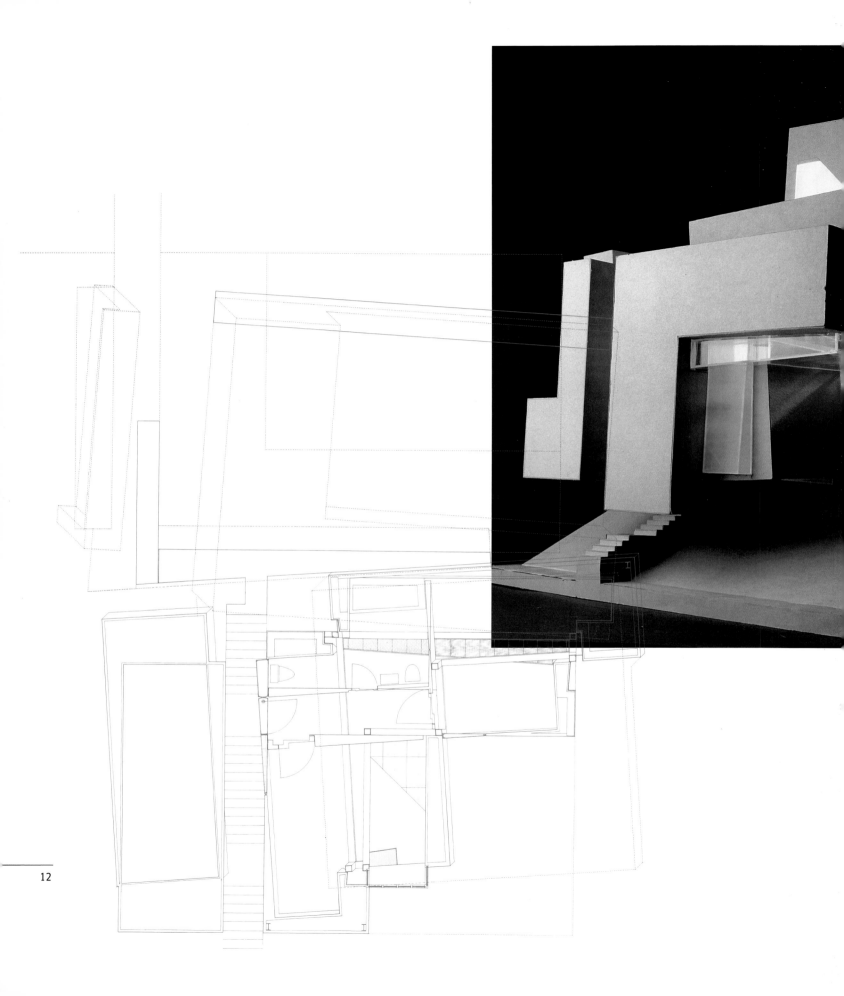

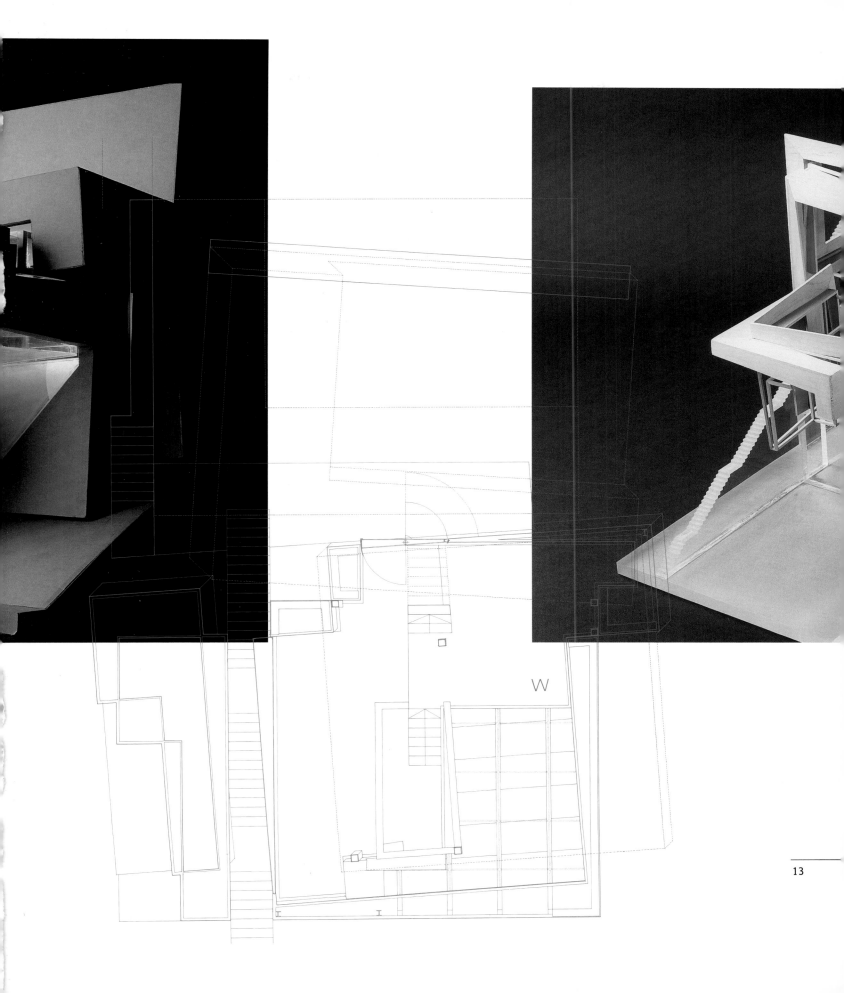

W

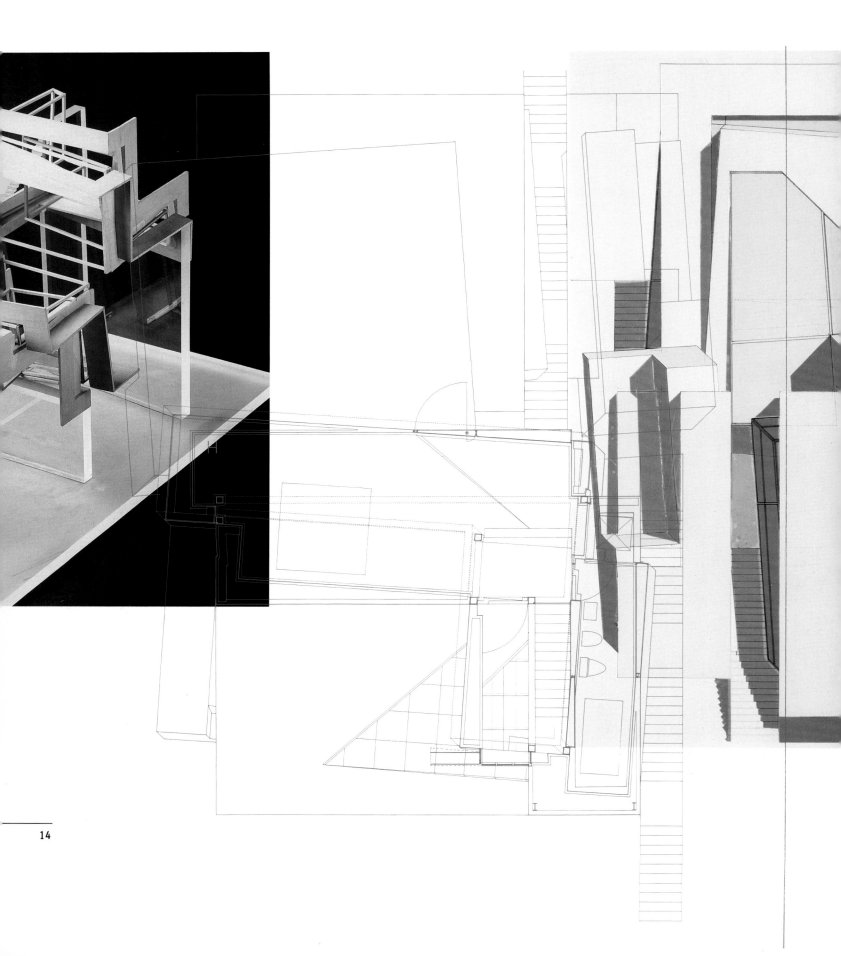

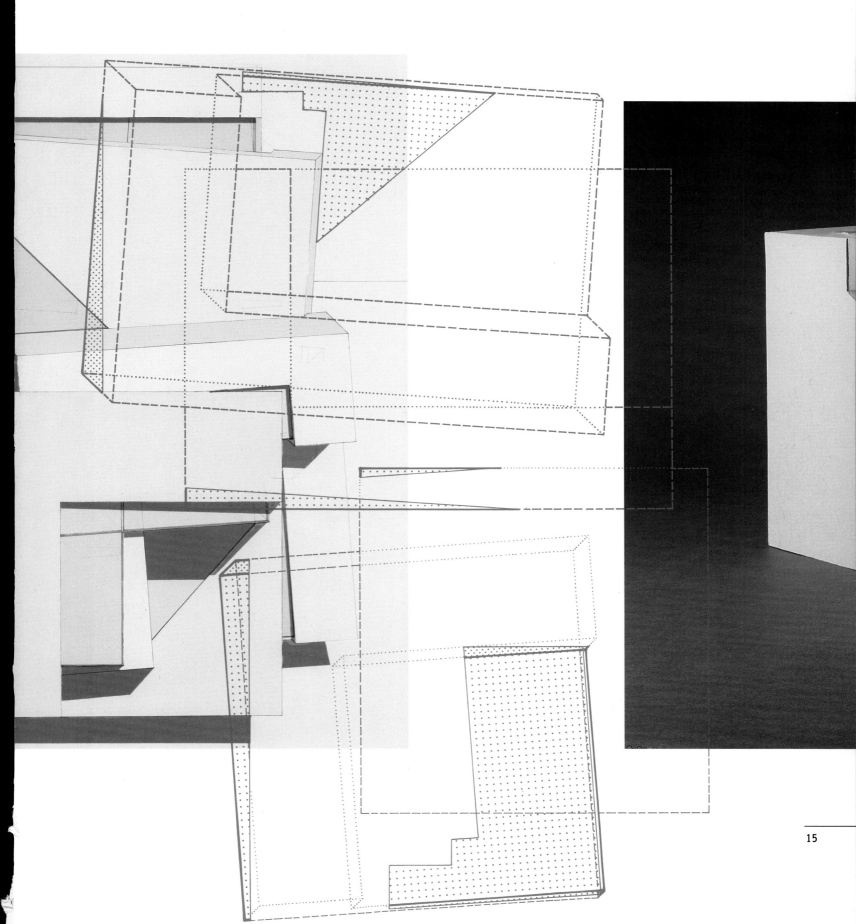

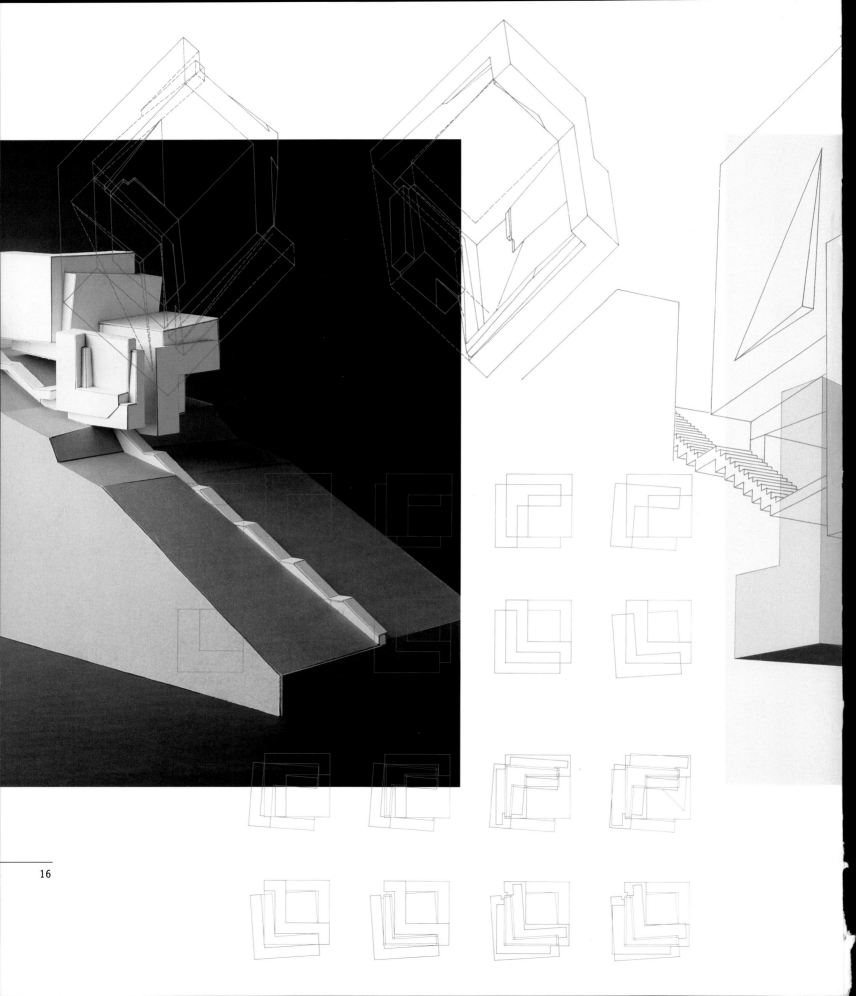

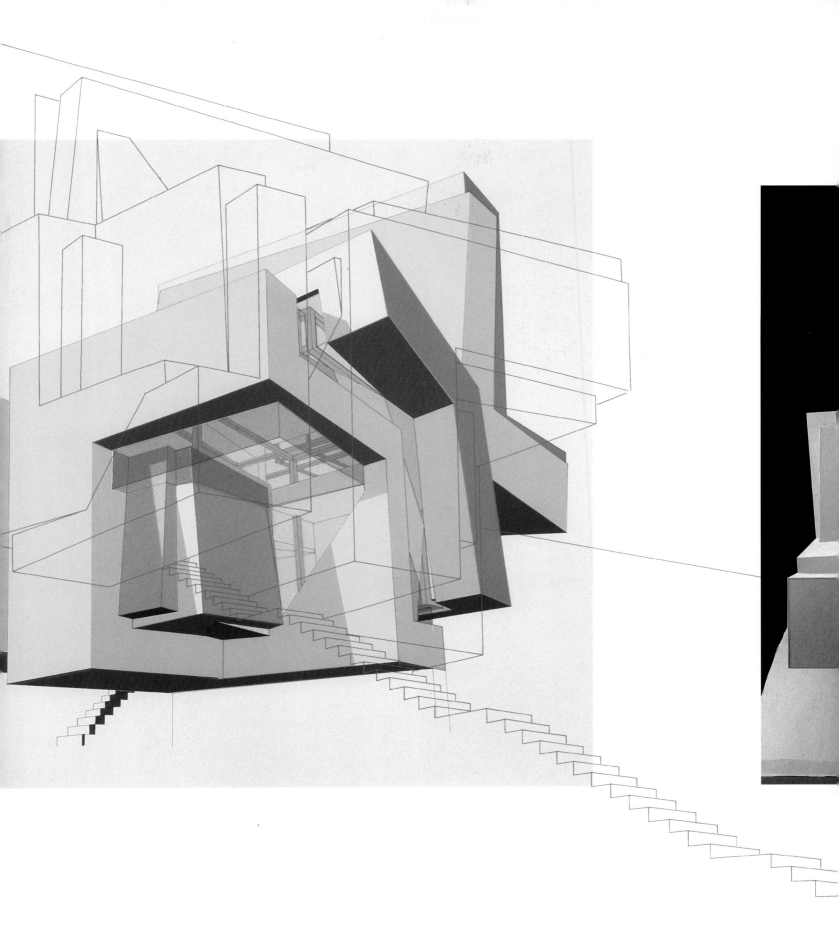

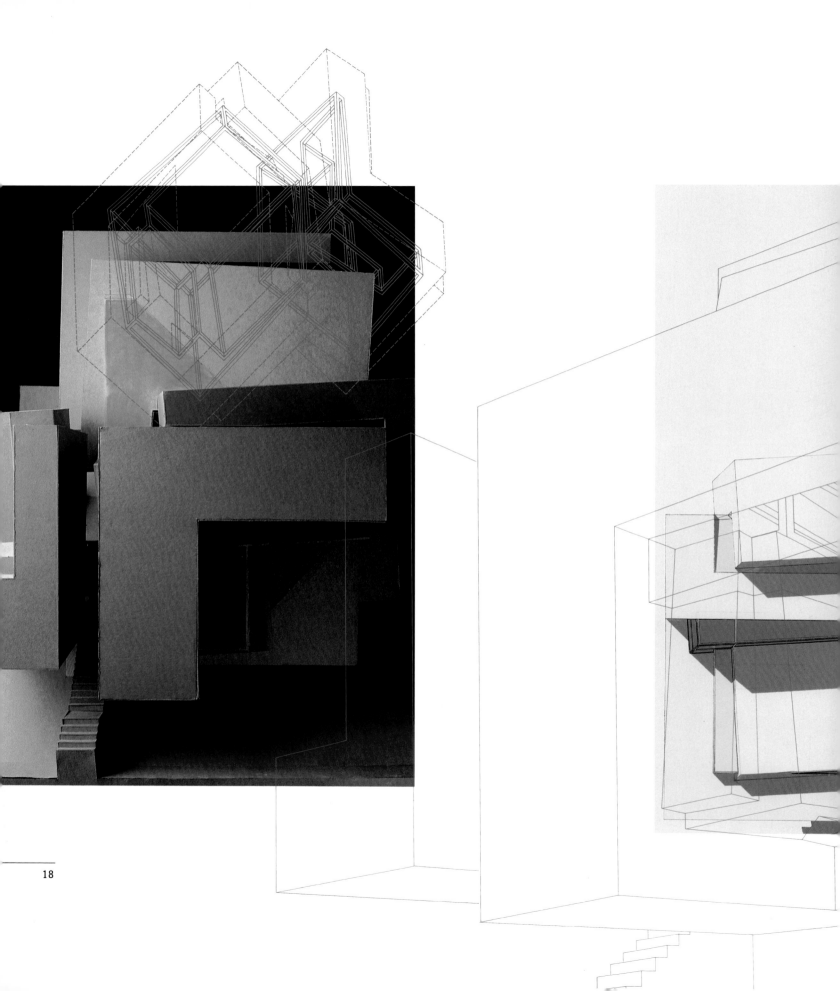

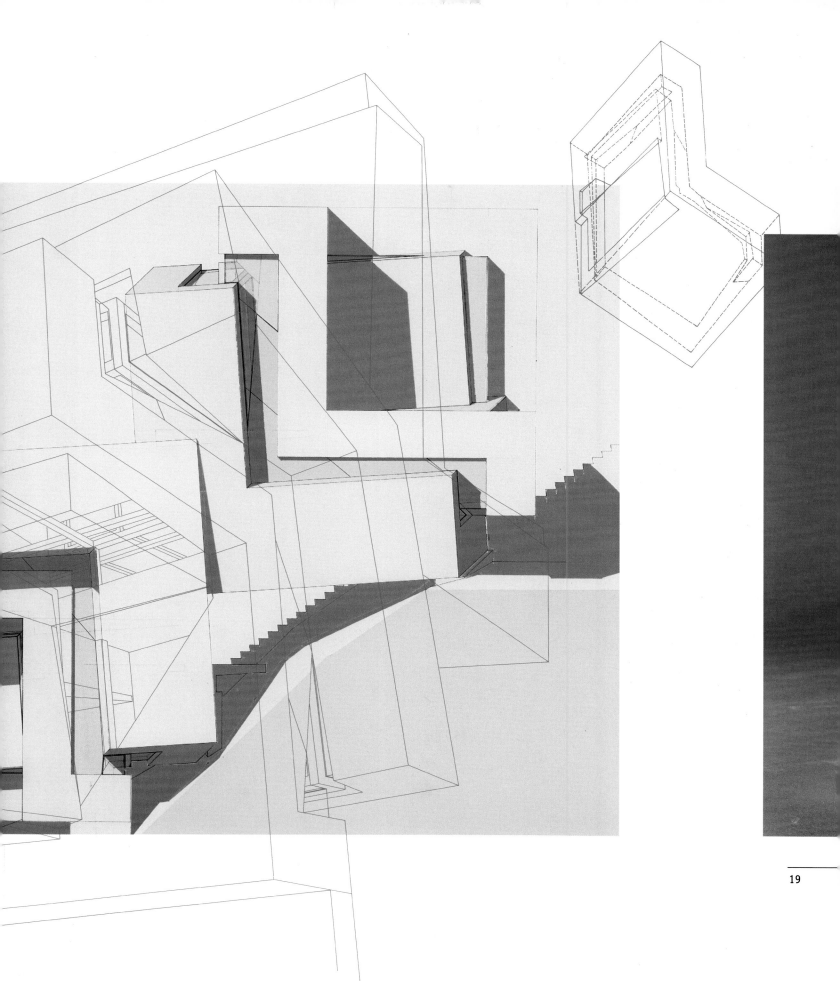

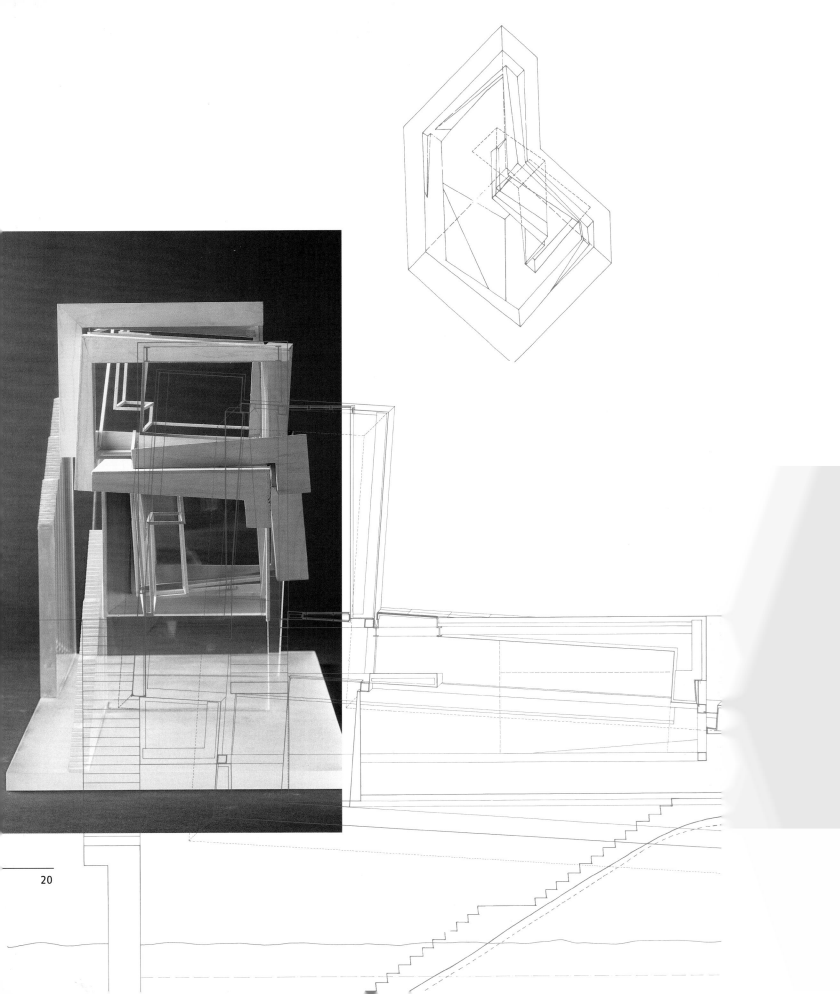

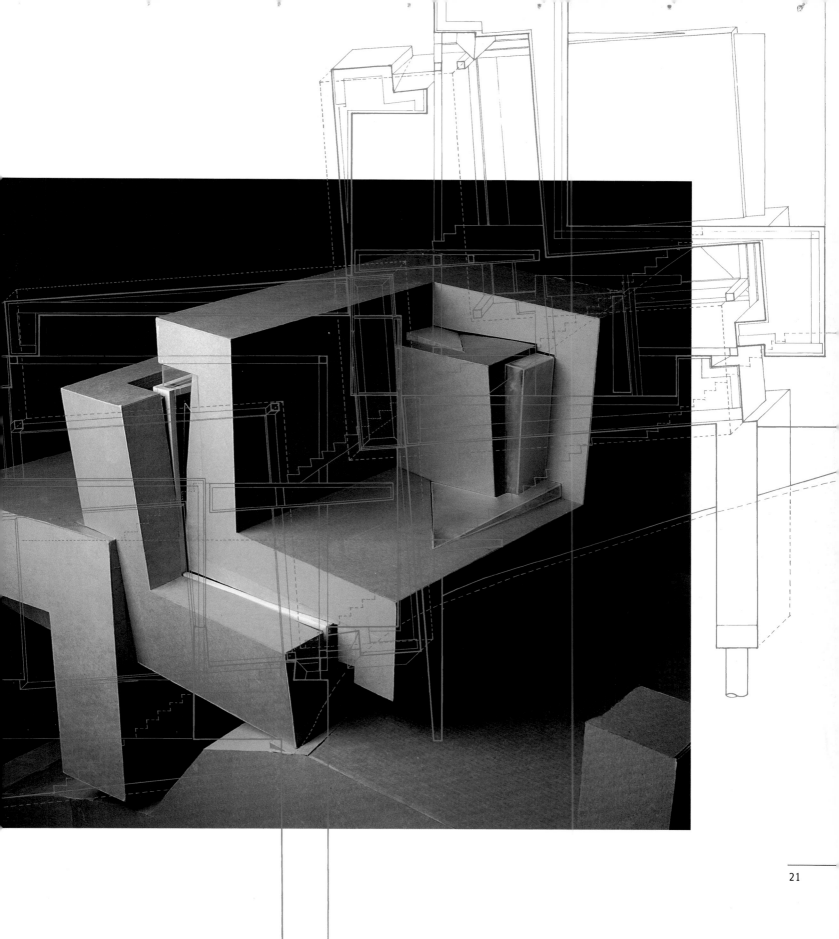

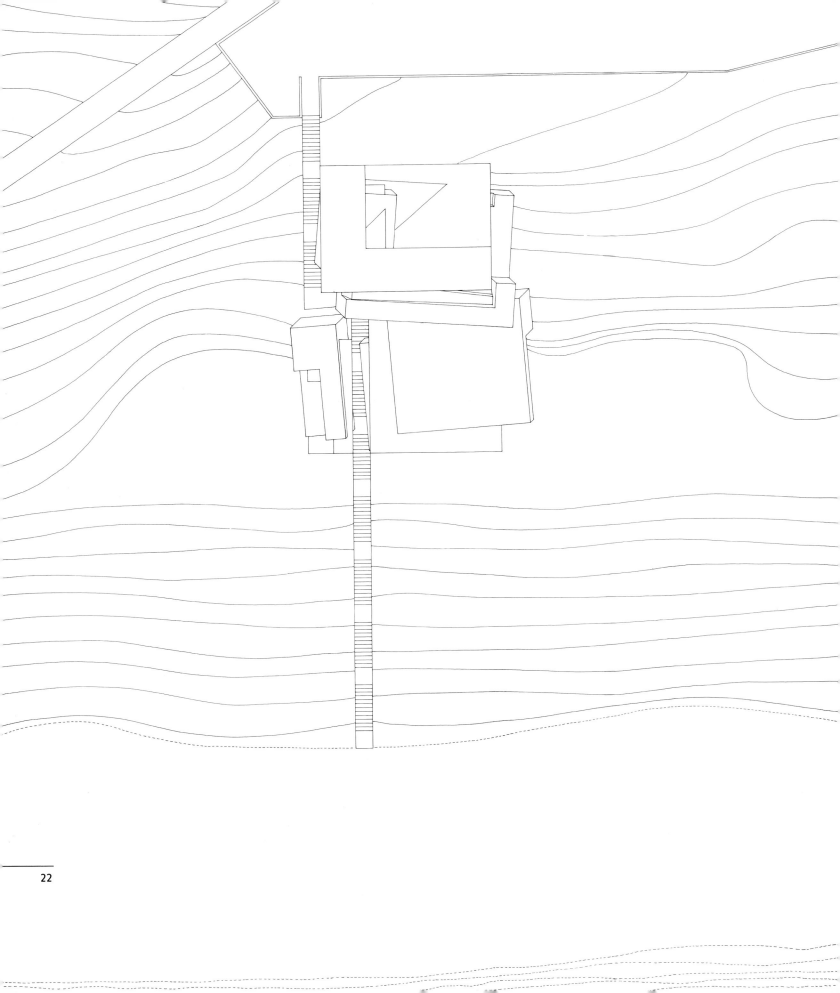

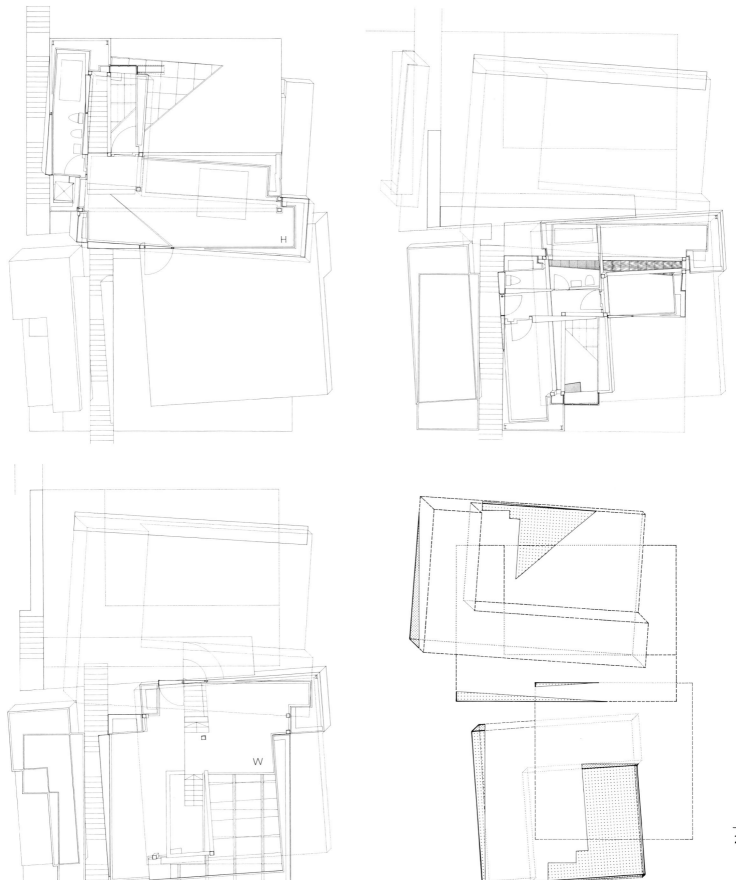

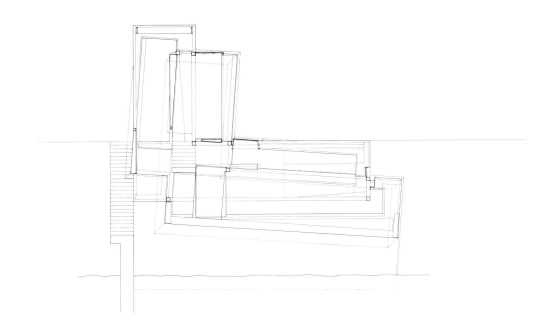

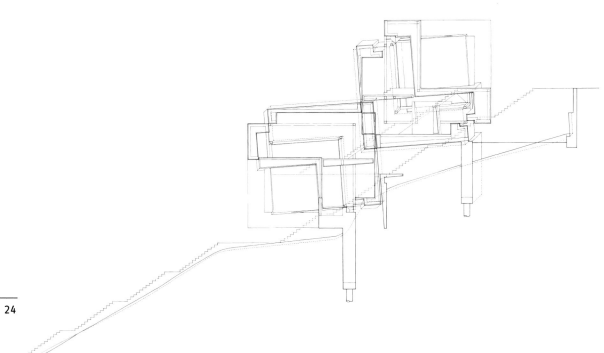

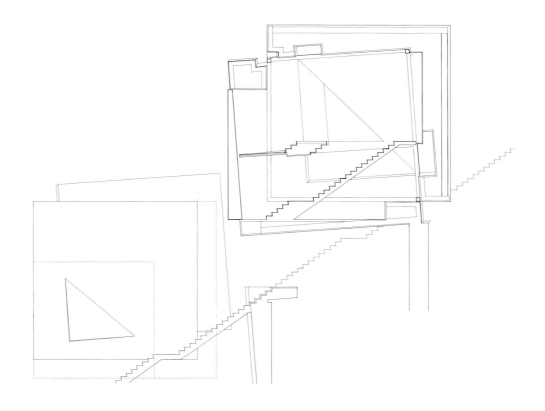

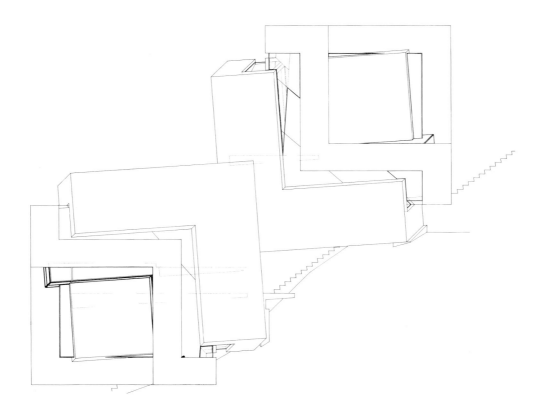

25

Classicism Lost
Franco Purini

The principal effect of the speed and pervasiveness with which information on architectural research moves around the world today has been the destruction of what could be understood only a few years ago as critical distance, which is based on the value of the difference between something that is contemporary and something that is not. Things happen before happening. There is no time to prepare oneself for new events or to elaborate on them from a real point of view. The architecture of instantaneity that dominates the panorama of architectural discourse necessarily transforms the architect into a critic and the critic into a designer.

The rapid succession and multiplicity of architectural events today – the copresence of different tendencies suggests a condition similar to the eclecticism that occurred at the end of the 19th century – require the designer to have a sharp, trained analytical ability that will allow him to identify with satellite precision his own position in the system of theoretical orientations and linguistic choices. This system is so uneven and pluralistic that it is almost impossible to draw a map of it. Hence the architect must become a critic. At the same time, the critic cannot circumscribe and decode any ambit in contemporary research if he does not identify himself with the figure of the artist.

Western society is no longer simply an aesthetic one; it is properly an artistic one in the sense that the artistic practice is no longer exclusively the artist's, for it reaches more and larger classes of people. If it is true that the Beaux-Arts system gave precedence to the art system, it is also true that the artist today is in competition with a mass-artist, represented by the expert and more assiduous visitor to art exhibitions and museums.

As the historian Franco Rella writes, art, or what he calls the new metaphysics, is the pure competition at the end of the millennium. The speed of information obliges the designer to act almost by instinct, but at the same time (and this seems to be contradictory) it constrains him to be rigorous and inflexible. The punishment for not doing this is the loss of recognizability within the panorama of tendencies that has taken the place of identity. But this is not enough.

The possibility for theory also seems to be precluded; only the chronicling of ideas can build the basis for a practice that could be defined as the exercise of the consciousness of the everyday, understood as the registration and daily control of the flux of communication. This provisional mode of operation necessarily merges with the elements of fashion, which is the only place where a seemingly frictionless metamorphosis can occur in this era of invisible networks of conditioning and censures.

Furthermore, that very same speed provokes a neurotic anticipation – we live events but we do not understand them – and precludes the possibility of thinking the local social meaning of the architectural object. The architectural object is no longer an apparatus of forms and functions bound to a specific context but rather a building system that at its very best is generically appropriate to a specific context, as if there is no time anymore to think of the architectural object as being in an unambiguous relationship with its own coming into being in the world.

The cultural condition that we are now in is the result of total deterritorialization – the principal corollary of globalization – which has nullified any idea of place as well as every attempt to forge an urban theory. This deterritorialization has a profound meaning, because it produces a conceptual vertigo in a society now reduced to living in an expanse of virtual equivalencies, which can be decoded and centralized only through a neo-imperialistic approach. Due to its vastness and its fundamental character, this scenario is not limited to the discipline of architecture; it also reveals an eminently political condition that demands a political response. To these profound mutations, one must add the growing spectacularization of events; what does not find space in media does not exist. The duality of high and low culture can no longer present a viable scheme. A high culture operates silently, separately, and in substantial anonymity to build the authentic values of an era, while a low culture, often so close to an idea of trash that it becomes a trash tendency and devoted to the ephemeral, celebrates through the glamour and lights of mass media the exploits of a consumer society attempting its hypothetical sublimation and, at the same time, dedicates itself to the vulgarization of the most thoughtful and challenging themes. The distance between these two polarities has almost completely been nullified in favor of a mediated culture of hyperbole, a culture in which the selected fragment coexists with the gesture exaggerated to the level of caricature. What is subtle or deep is no longer appreciated. A thing is considered of value (which today has become the only cultural reference) only when it has achieved mass success.

The architecture of Peter Eisenman is one of the most convincing interpretations of the conditions described above. It is mainly an eminently political response interwoven with precise ideologies at a time when everyone is singing a final funeral song for the fall of ideologies. These ideologies have been replaced by the media's often opportunistic appreciation of principles gone adrift, of incongruous materials combined in an improbable syncretism suited to a pluralism without perspective.

Placing himself as a countertendency in relation to this situation, Eisenman has claimed in absolute terms the primacy of theory. But there is a limit; the dependence of his projects on ideological options and their expression is so closed to architecture that the projects themselves are finally evaluated more as deductions deriving from an advanced level of philosophical discourse than they are considered for their autonomous expressive values. The result leads to a certain instrumentality of those aspects specific to architecture. It is as if his goal consisted only in verifying the precision of a theory, or in having the possibility to translate directly a philosophical thought in form and space.

Critical writing on Peter Eisenman is too "Eisenmanian." It limits itself to verifying whether the intentions expressed in his theoretical texts have been accurately translated into his projects and searches for a mythical, personal coherency of the author. These critiques are expressed in a strongly biographical atmosphere that often leads to an unquestioned empathetic participation in Eisenman's world. Such a "Vasarian model" does not attempt a reading of the works per se and rarely questions their real architectural value. One effect of this subjection is that critics have focused their attention on what they regard as the novelty of Eisenman's architectural intentions. Rarely have they pointed to the deep antiquity in his projects and the recurrence of permanent iconographic diagrams. From these readings, there follows an unfocused and distorted image of Eisenman as an architect with no roots, completely projected into the future, having a voluntary, ruthless amnesia of the past (the word *amnesia,* as is well known, is an almost perfect anagram of his name).

The relationship of Eisenman with other architects and architectures is one of radical antagonism. Within this, he places himself completely under discussion at the moment that he incorporates the elements of the writings he follows within his own poetic. His by now mythical relationship with the work of Giuseppe Terragni is also antagonistic. But suddenly, and perhaps unpredictably, in the early 1980s, the work of such people as the young Daniel Libeskind made him understand how much his aristocratic and Jamesian alienation in the cold regions of European rationalism in the 1930s – the decade of his birth – rendered him insensible to the new ferments that were maturing in the most advanced research of his own country. Add this to his more open and playful relationship with the formalistic extremism of Frank O. Gehry, with whom he has begun a competition on the basis of a florid and anarchic plastic invention.

In addition to the rich thematic defined by iconological and literary matrices in Eisenman's work, there resides not only the antique but also the world of nature. The antique is present in the metaphor of strata, represented by the layers of variously superimposed grids, a stratification directly related to a celebration of temporality and chosen as an added value of building. The antique is paradoxically evoked at the grammatological root of Eisenman's basic language, from which every trace of narration is so erased as to suggest, in contrast, its overriding necessity. Though at one level it is removed, this necessity is nonetheless still present and pervasive. Another clearly recognizable element in Eisenman's formal universe is the inspiration of the natural, evident in the processes of scaling, a self-similar and artificial device inherent in classical language. The natural is made apparent in the way his volumes are cut, revealing references to the structures of crystals and minerals as formed by stratified planes. This naturalism is also visible in various compositions that evoke vertebrate structures frozen in torsion. Waves and clouds, vortexes and streams, add themselves to these references and introduce in Eisenman's imagery a scientific component in which we find multicolored, changing fractal configurations presented as seductive neodecorative icons. Some of the most recent projects, like the stadiums, for example, look like animal skulls, suggesting images charged by an antiquarian taste for sacrificial skulls. From

the perspective of iconic traces, we find the same complexities in three Piranesian tropes: the bas-relief, the drapery, and the trophy. These are an index of ruins with the same spectral celebratory tone as the multitude of casually juxtaposed fragments that consistently dominate Eisenman's imaginary world. The trope of bas-relief is filtered by its representation in 18th-century engraving, where it gains an analytic virtuality; the conflicting relationship of the drapery with the human figure, for which the drapery is an abstract representation, refuses a dense and uninterrupted spatial fluidity; the anthropomorphic reference to the trophy opens a problematic consideration of the body, which is the outcome of a historical project, the aim of which is the destruction of the body itself exhibited as a spectral simulacrum.

Eisenman's architecture is perhaps today the only work that gives the impression of a spatio-temporal copenetration of forms, which suggests infinity, simultaneity, and restless transmutation in a sort of figural metamorphosis expressed, phase by phase, in its unpredictable phenomenology. The exchange between space and time is realized in a particular parsing of continuity that eliminates the differences between past, present, and future. In so doing, it brings to light a circularity of architectural events in which the fundamental elements of construction present themselves as transitive and mutant entities, hybrid and complex, ordered and chaotic, necessary and indifferent, unique and interchangeable. In this way, the Eisenmanian world configures itself as a chronotopic interlacing that, like many recent American movies, combines different temporalities in a game of interlocking alternatives. These alternatives create a mosaic of opposite eventualities from which it is necessary to choose. The simultaneous ambiguity itself connects interior and exterior, top and bottom, in topological concepts. The result is a cosmological image, where everything is blurred in the other and the elsewhere.

In Eisenman's language, or better, in his many languages, one of the high and essential goals of modernity is always operating: the negation of the representative character of architecture. His language renounces any narrative engagement, and consequently any emotional intentionality, to instead exhibit its logico-syntactical purposes in a kind of premeditated autism. The result is an architecture that poses as its own context, and within a logic that denies place in such a radical way that it does not even anticipate it as a simple topological fact internal to its artifact. Another significant denial consists in refusing the concept of the work as something complete. Instead, the intention is to assert the fragmentary nature of the architectural object that extends to the exterior, so to speak, presenting itself simultaneously as plan, section, sequence of planes, and single perspectival view. Like the dynamic dog in futurist Giacomo Balla's painting, Eisenman's buildings leave behind a visible vibration in space.

Of course, the presence of these complexities is not enough to free Eisenman's work from limits or defects. His projects and built works have a virtuosity that sometimes lessens their effectiveness. They are pervaded by a pedagogic will that often becomes a propagandistic and slightly neurotic rhetoric. Sometimes the natural evolution of his experimental approach seems to be artificially accelerated by unexpected references, which can produce a palpable loss in a project's coherence. The dominance of fashion dictates less time for thinking at the same time that it requires continuous updating and revisions, as if the work of the architect were actually that of a fashion designer; it is as if his horizon is no longer that of culture but that of the world of advertising.

Beyond appearances, what makes Eisenman's work unique is the historical project concerning the body that his architecture proposes. In this context, there is a close relationship with the work of Frank Gehry. The architect of the Guggenheim Bilbao has performed a real autopsy on the body of modern architectural languages, building a biological spatiality that makes one think of the cavities of a living organism. At the approach of the new millennium, the California architect presents a comforting, neo-humanistic parallelism, as if returning architecture to the motherly bosom of the human figure. The intention of this reconciliation seems to be the exile of the machine world. Eisenman, however, does not look at the body in such positive terms, nor does he consider modern technology as negative. For him, the body becomes an analogic translation from the organic to a Kleistian machinic that must

consider, as its principle, a differentiation in relation to the direct image of the body itself. If for Gehry the body is real, for Eisenman it is mediated; that is, a body on which it is possible to operate only after it is transported or displaced into an other conceptual order. This shift allows Eisenman to derive more convincing results at the level of the parabolic transition of corporeality that marks the new millennium. For Eisenman, only the artificial and the superficial can evoke the real substance of a body, whereas its direct mimesis claims only a nostalgia. While Gehry somehow wants to recover an idea of classical sculpture explored in its hidden entrails as an emblem of ideal beauty, his work consciously inverts the path traced by the archaeologist and art historian Johann Winckelmann. Eisenman, however, considers the inorganic as the new substance of any body. In the same way, he does not consider the sum of the languages of modernity a body but rather, in their superposition – in the same way that a superposition of colors generates white – a desert of signs. In contrast to Gehry's autopsy, Eisenman performs the subtraction of a body – a conceptual pyre, an apotheosis – in a ritual of substitution through which he exposes the abstract and the simulacrum.

The same indirect method inspires Eisenman in the use of light. It is neither a dramatized nor a scenographic light, but cold and cruel, according to Antonin Artaud's definition; it is a scientific light, an illumination for a laboratory. In modern architecture there are different lights: the analytic light of De Stijl; the primordial light of Frank Lloyd Wright; the ontological and mystic light of Mies van der Rohe. Eisenman's light represents itself, in a kind of first derivative equation, as a light that enlightens, frames, and surfaces, transforming into value the process through which these fragments constitute themselves as a whole. This is not, however, a Cartesian light. It does not constitute or limit; instead it signals and prescribes. It is a light that imposes a behavior rather than suggests it; a light self-generated by the buildings, coming from the same nucleus that empties them, sucking out the space and provoking their implosion. A contracted light is the place of pulsation – equivalent to a breath of form that in every epoch has signaled a shift in attention, a diversion of the compositional energy.

Eisenman's buildings are constituted by two extreme visual registers. The first is produced by a close reading, an X-ray vision that penetrates the fibers of drawings, especially plans, and by investigating materials according to their ability to produce a tectonic and decorative work. This work does not imply the direct presence of materials; rather, they represent themselves, as in a derivative equation that transforms them into conceptual emblems, where the sensory effect is deferred and distorted, the way a sound emission is marked by interferences. By nature, such a miniaturized glance is as fixed and concentrated as a laser beam, but at the same time it is able to catch the labyrinthine and erratic connections that are the physical constitution of things, just as David Lynch does in his movies.

The second visual register directs us to an infinite distance to project ideally the artifacts on the generic topology of the planet surface, as if it were the building, a fragment of the territory itself, which is simultaneously total and alternative, fantastic and realistic. But these two registers cannot coexist. Once they are superimposed, they produce a blurring effect, as if the figure contours were shading toward an astonished indistinctness, and the space, an atmospheric volume, were taking the place of built form, generating a dramatic inversion of their reciprocal densities. This incompatibility of the immediate and the infinite also inspired Caspar David Friedrich's painting and the rarefied world of Mark Rothko. Among those who have explored this incompatibility, Eisenman and these artists substantially claimed that there is no future horizon in the action that is expressed by the intermediate scale, which is a characteristic of the exploration of the architectural object. Only by looking at the object from a fixed position just a few centimeters away, when it is no longer possible to see it in its entirety, or, alternatively, by looking at the object from such a great distance that it becomes a spot of color in the city or in the landscape, is it possible to think of it as alienated by pragmatic experience, as an indifferent entity. That Eisenman's works stop on the threshold of the empirical and comforting intermediate scale gives them the character of acid pietàs that seems to be missing, for example, in the joyful and sunny work of Frank Gehry. It

speaks of an endemic exclusion. Eisenman puts the very idea of project in suspension; the project accomplishes itself in the present, and becomes the space of an interdicted action.

In the past thirty years Eisenman's architecture has moved over the same course that European architecture traversed for two hundred years: from the classicism of the 16th century to baroque and rococo formalistic *capriccio*. From the sophisticated theorem of a modernist classicism Eisenman moved to a mannerist cult of textual stratification, veined by esoteric shadows. From here, his most recent projects have arrived at a neobaroque conception of space, where Newtonian linearity gives precedence to Leibnizian folds and flexes. But this is a kind of northern baroque, which emerges with a strong memory of the Gothic, in almost the same way that the Gothic came to the surface in Borromini's language of curvatures and dilations. The distance from baroque excitement to expressionist violence is very short. Similarly, it is a short distance between this un-formal architectural writing, apparently free from conventional design constructs in the abstract sense, and its dissolving into landscaping, as Bruno Zevi wrote in his Modenese manifesto. Entering the domain of landscape, architecture can no longer conceive of itself as the construction of buildings, or built contexts. Architecture becomes instead a real re-creation of the earth's surface, a new surface that requires a new beginning. In this way, the Corbusian idea of an artificial ground finds its planetary fulfillment.

Due to its constitutional inertia, architecture has always accepted a certain secondary status with regard to the other arts and disciplines. Eisenman, however, has been successful in bringing architecture back in step with philosophy, science, and art, realigning it with a full contemporaneity. His thought is utopian, but not a social utopia. It is a utopia of form where art, that is, the new metaphysics of today, is posed as a paradigm of human existence. From this point of view, Eisenman is both a prophet and a man of politics. These roles present the risk that his architecture exhausts itself in pure demonstration. Beyond this, however, it is true that theoretical preoccupations often take away the space for the thematic understanding of the building in the sense of its relationships with its inhabitants. This relationship of contiguity and belonging must be found in an existential fullness. As a result, Eisenman's buildings cannot help but become manifestos. His works are architectures that demand to be recognized as architecture. They demand from the observer a process of decoding and restitution, which consists in rebuilding a sense of the compositional operation from its origin. In this way the architectural project is paralleled by an interpretative project that is delegated to anyone who comes in contact with his buildings. His true deconstructivist intent has to be recognized more in this doubling of registers than in a stylistic field. The need to see architecture in an architecture that denies its conventional status could be considered an imposition that borders on violence if the process did not involve the freedom of the interpreter, who is free at any moment to refuse a complex conceptual procedure that culminates in a new project.

As an expression of an imperial culture, Eisenman's architecture is neither influenced by nor obligated to the "outside." It can cease to be, or even to anticipate, a spatial answer to social transformations in order to pose itself as an event. Eisenman works in the wealthiest country in the world, which for some time has resolved the primary problems to which architecture responds. Therefore, the present condition of architecture is superfluous. For this reason architecture identifies itself directly with art, since art has no apparent utilitarian ends. This superfluous condition is physiologically extreme, and it can easily become radical, pushing the architect, by now an artist in the fullest sense of the word (a condition that Eisenman's friend John Hejduk intuited many years ago), toward a practice that is institutionally destabilizing and de facto fully political. From this follows an important consequence: architecture totally loses its own projectuality, becoming instead an experimentalism that can only have the unpredictable and irregular rhythm of art. Crash and implosion, contraction and torsion, fragment and flux, chronotopia and planar enfolding (suggested in the projects with faceted geometries, like those of the "invisible" stealth bomber), come from Eisenman's world as urgent warnings. At the end of the second millennium, the formal utopia strips itself of any metaphorical misunderstanding and appears as one of the most poetic readings of classicism lost, but certainly not ended; a classicism that transforms the future in its own precedent, in its own beginning.

Franco Purini is an architect in Rome. This essay was written in December 1998 and translated from the Italian by Francesco Mancini and Guido Zuliani.

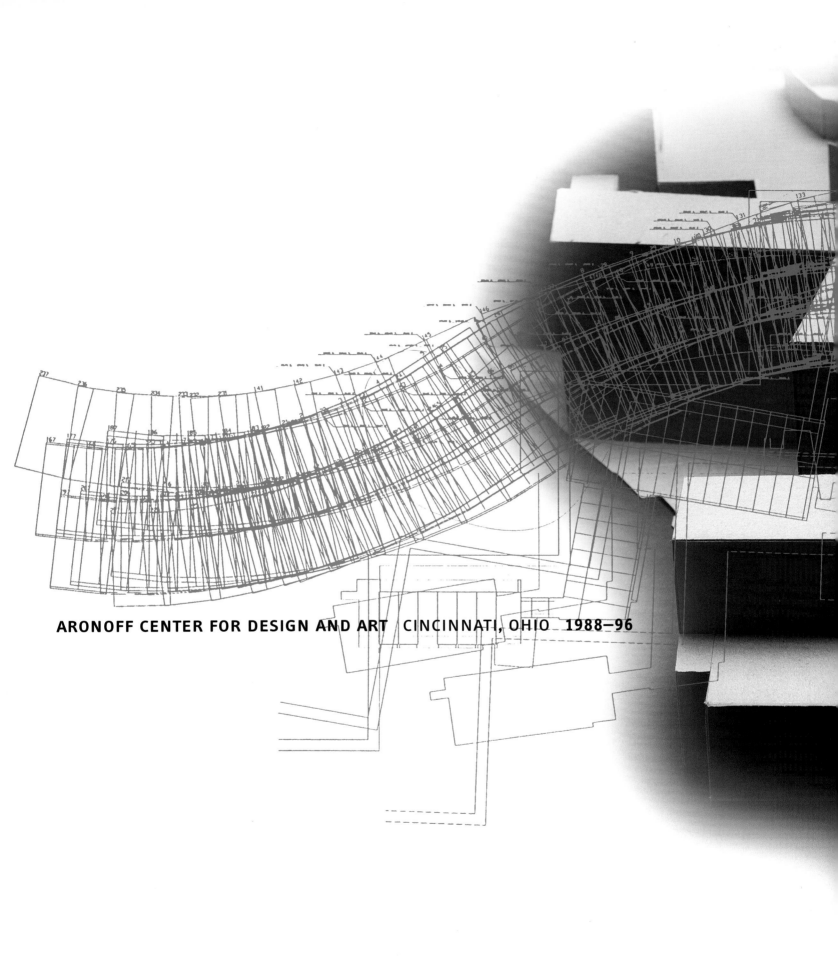

ARONOFF CENTER FOR DESIGN AND ART   CINCINNATI, OHIO   1988–96

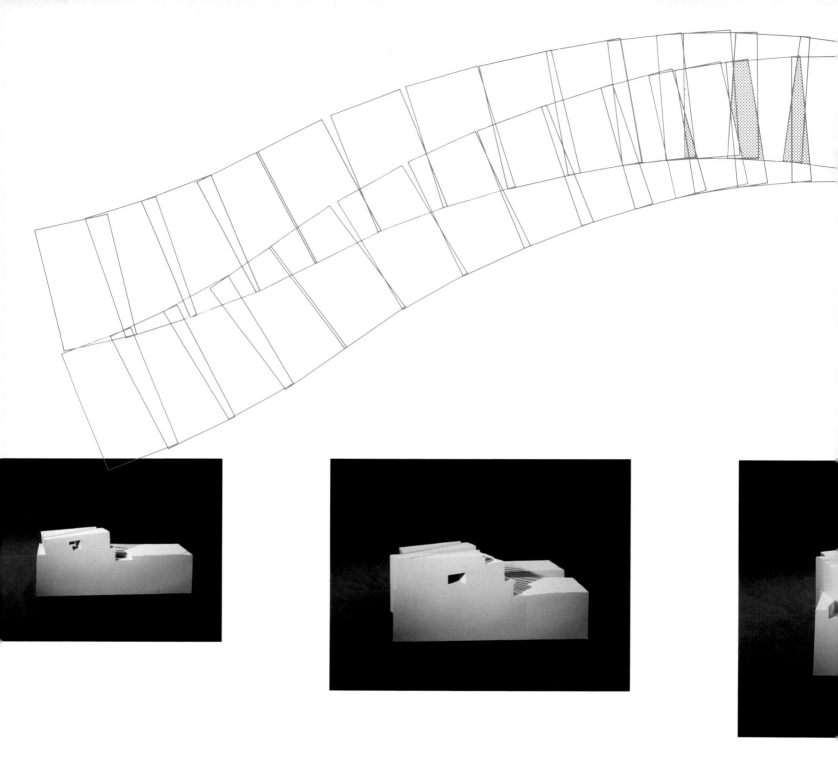

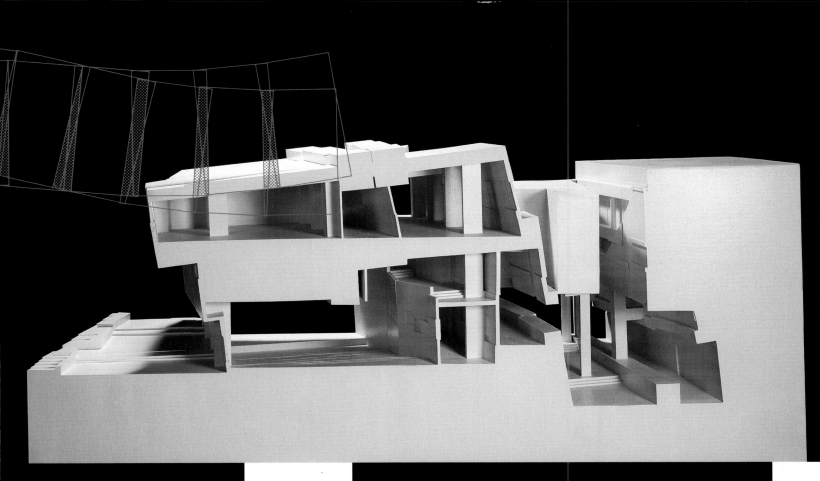

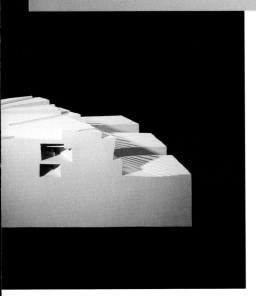

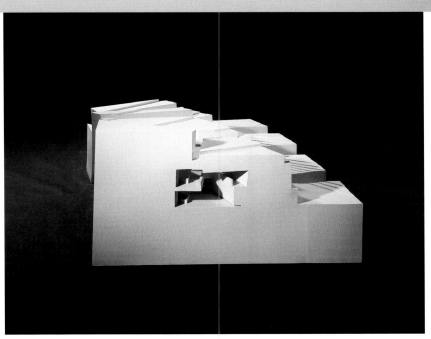

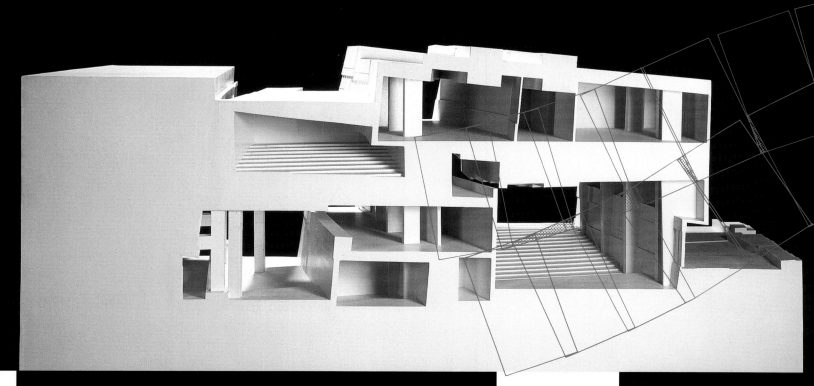

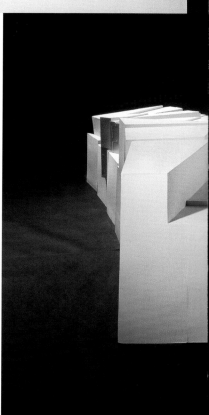

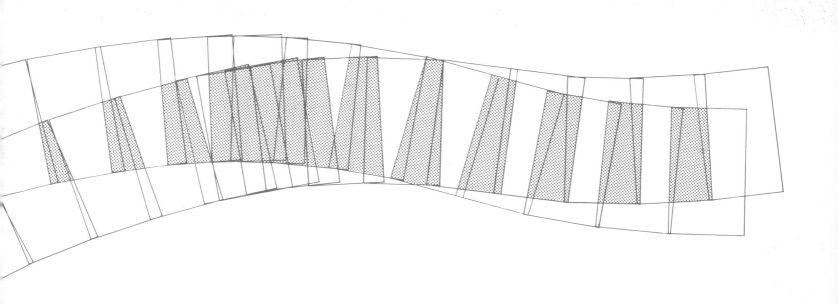

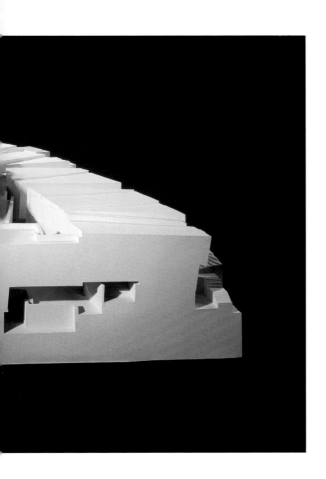

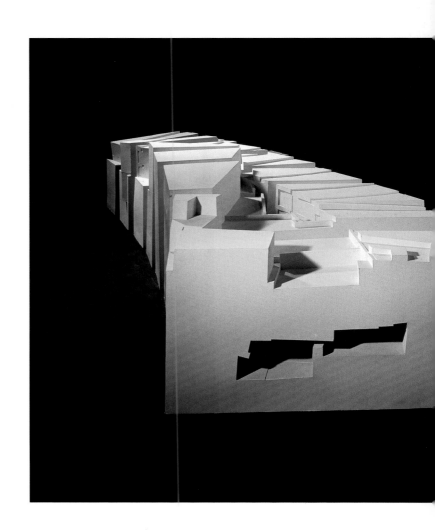

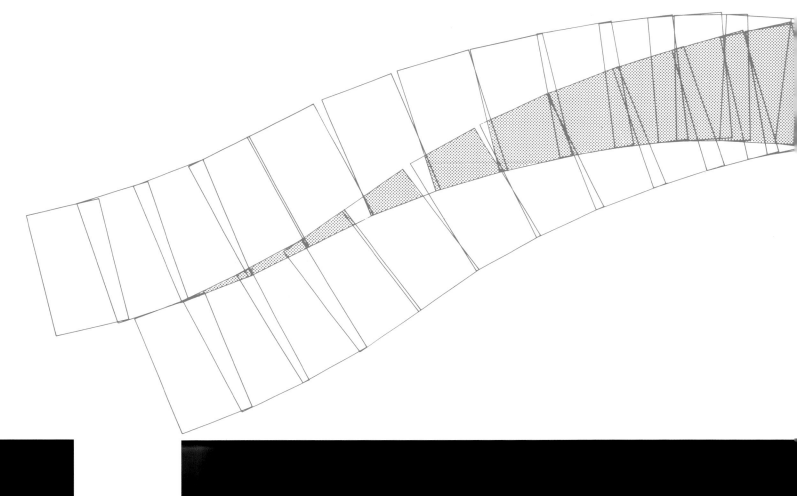

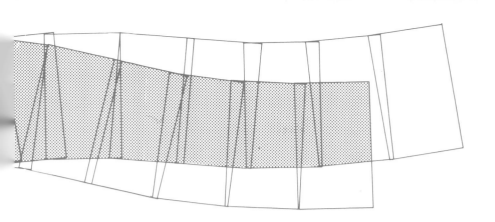

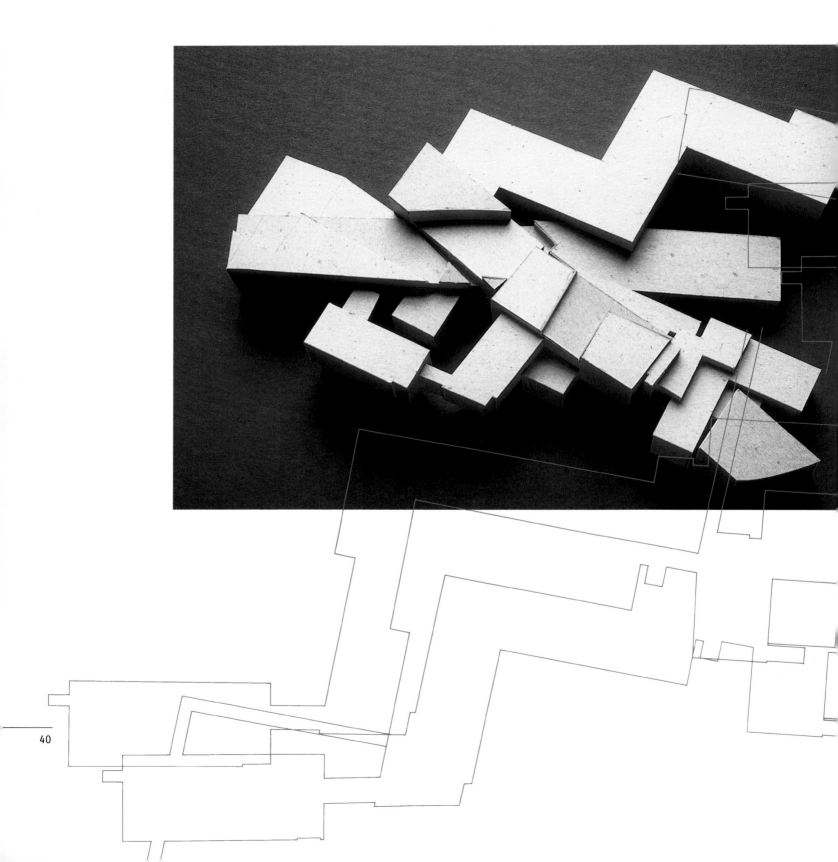

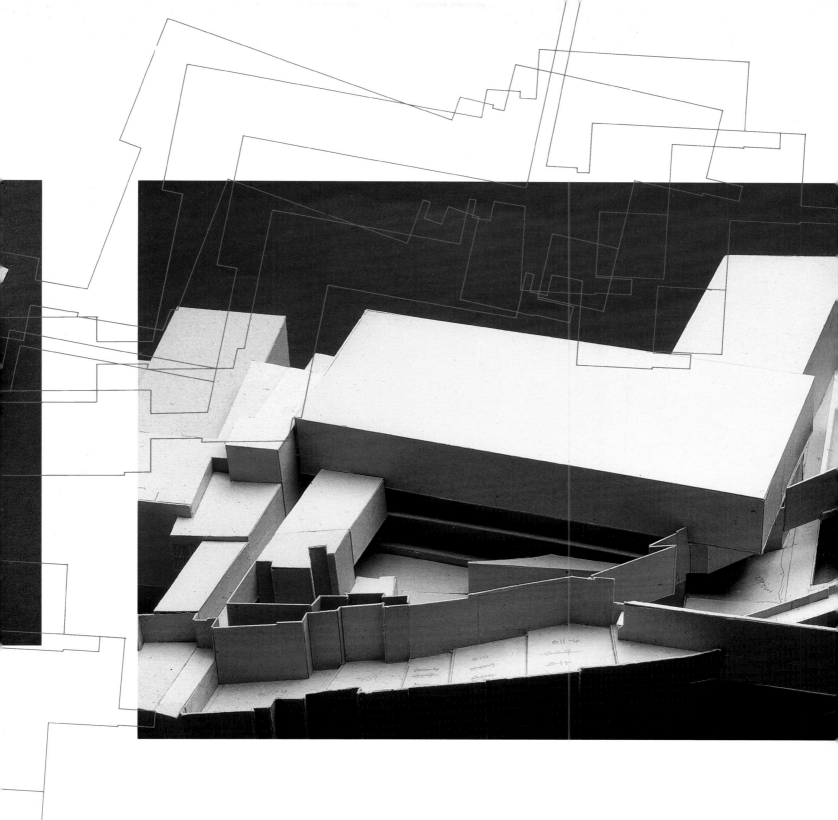

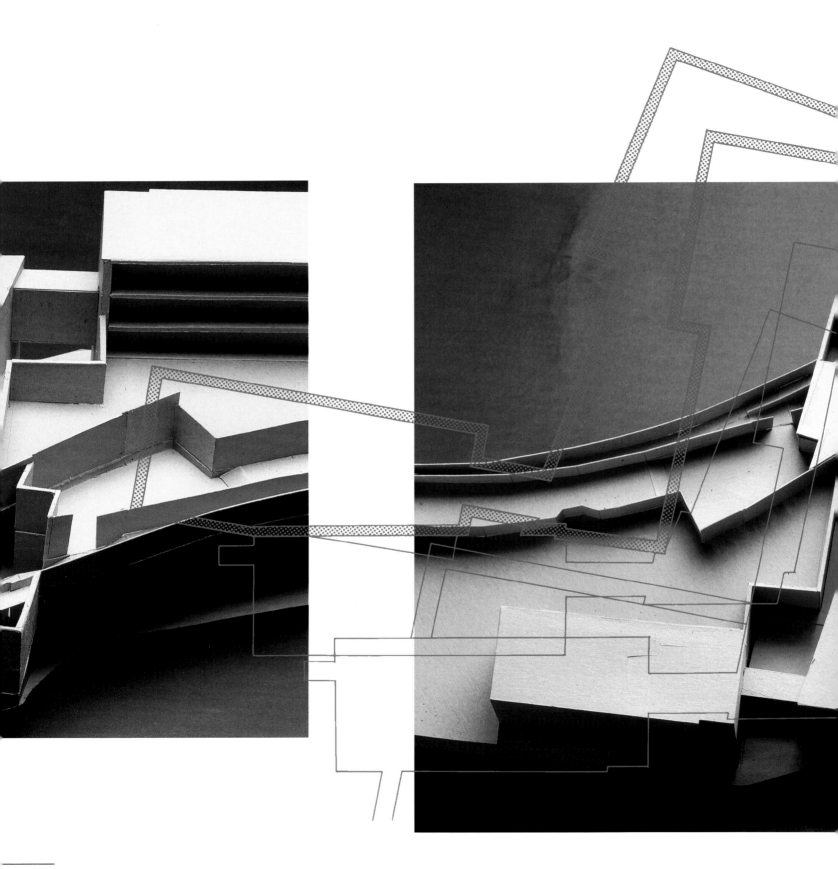

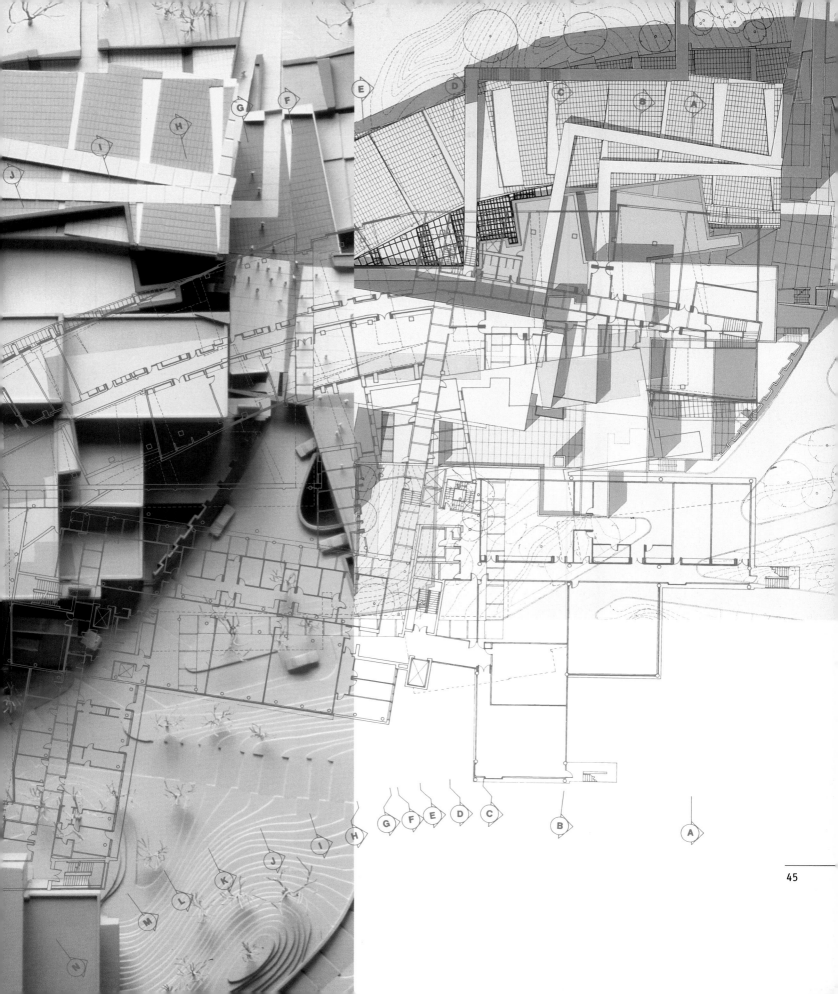

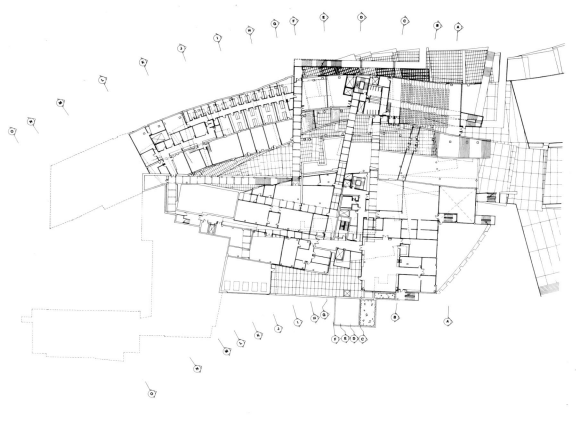

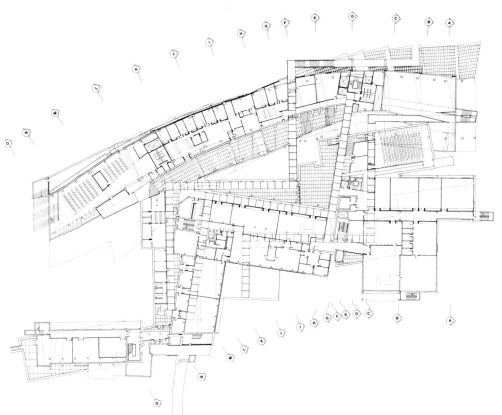

57

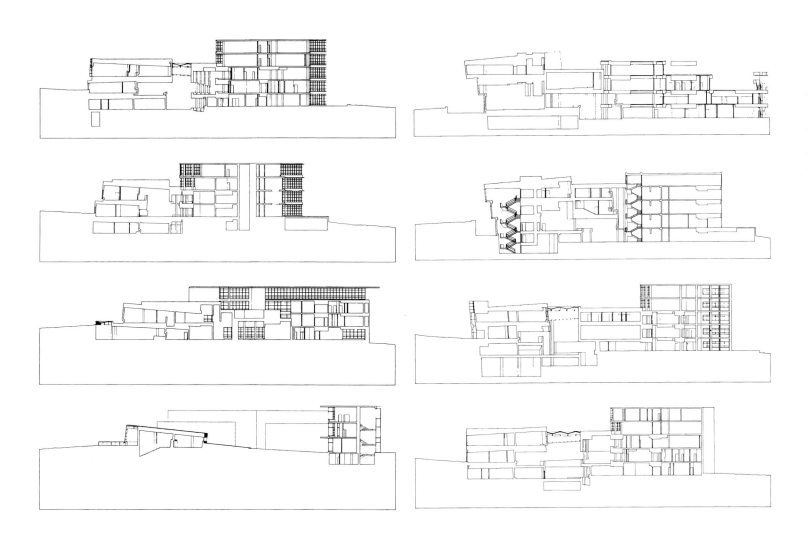

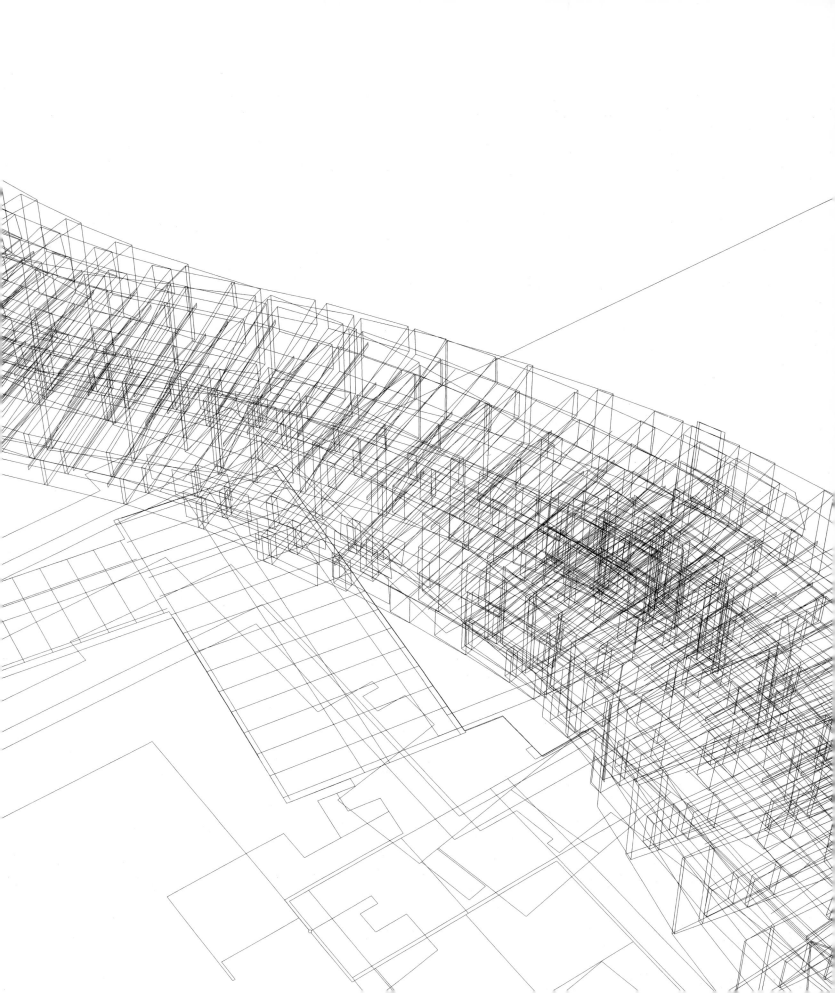

Aronoff and Ideology
Fredric Jameson

The recommendation that we transcend the opposition between inside and outside does not date from yesterday (Jacques Derrida), but at least from the day before yesterday (Le Corbusier), and perhaps even from before that. We are thought to be somehow imprisoned in the binary opposition in question, which we feel as an antinomy – that beyond which we cannot imagine, which locks our categories irredeemably in place – rather than as a contradiction, which we (perhaps irresponsibly or flippantly) imagine it is in our power to modify, however slightly or imperceptibly. Yet in either case, would not the possibility of transcending this particular opposition involve leaving it behind? Not producing a new combination, a new synthesis that satisfied both parties in the dispute, the inside claiming this or that cherished feature, and letting the rest of them go, while the outside agrees to be satisfied with what we otherwise imagined to be a relatively minor item on its wish list – some inner outside, perhaps, or an outer kind of inside – but rather letting both terms go, watching them swirl down the river of time into Nietzschean oblivion, such that nothing takes its place at all, and we cannot even with the tip of our tongue remember the terms that once marked the telltale spot, the vanished gate, the place of the barrier, strolling over its grave with some new and

insouciant innocence. Only the most laden elders are perhaps still in a position to know – ancient and mystical, esoteric formulations – that there is in fact a question of the inside without the outside, if not indeed the outside without the inside: unimaginable bounds of a finite universe this last, or else an interiority without discernible limits, which nonetheless curves back upon itself like a Möbius strip. So many possibilities then, so many alternate formulations for the new space that front-runners want to construct or, better still, want to imagine.

A city within a city perhaps? So I wanted to characterize everything symptomatic about the Westin Bonaventure Hotel: an air pocket or vacuum in which the privileged instinctively take refuge, in flight from intolerable disorders that cannot be faced in the outer city itself, something like a blister, which conjures the outside world by a kind of mimesis of it.[1] (Out of the anthropology of their day, Theodor Adorno and Max Horkheimer constructed a kind of mimetic instinct, cyclically triggered throughout human history by extreme danger and anxiety, counted on – often in vain – to conjure the threats, either homeopathically or by way of camouflage.)[2]

What would it take to make this impulse self-conscious, and do we still attach some value to that once prestigious

1 See my **Postmodernism, or, The Cultural Logic of Late Capitalism** (Durham, N.C.: Duke University Press, 1991), 38–45.
2 See the discussions on this concept in my **Late Marxism: Adorno, or, The Persistence of the Dialectic** (London: Verso, 1990).

condition of heightened reflexivity (now sometimes called self-reference or autodesignation) associated (by modernists) with Hegel and his outcomes and syntheses, his characteristic modes of transcending oppositions? We here approach an internment camp of suspicious concepts, which the new regime of postmodernity has rounded up preparatory to rendering this or that definitive verdict (not to be pronounced again for another fifty years, when not irrecuperable altogether – the death sentence). Here reflexivity and self-consciousness rejoin their activist cousins, the negative and the critical, the "underminers" and the "transgressors." The former might be thought to represent some right-wing deviation – the philosophy of consciousness or of the subject; while the latter, more attractively, still distantly, puts an infantile left through its paces, for that very reason, perhaps, constituting a more serious danger to the new postmodern orthodoxy, for which critique itself is a more tenacious illusion than revolution itself, let alone the old-fashioned reflexivities of the hopelessly outmoded class of intellectuals as such.

In any case, it is hard to say whether "reflexivity" means much more than a seal of approval when we discuss architecture: that John Portman's Westin Bonaventure is not that, but that Rem Koolhaas's Lille Center or even his hypothetical Zeebrugge Sea Trade Terminal richly qualify – these are perhaps judgments it is easier to make than to justify. Is it because Koolhaas not only welcomes congestion but does his best to increase it, while Portman would rather not know (all the while presumably assuring his clients that he has it under control)?[3] And how do we know even this? We know what Koolhaas thinks and says; but how do his buildings tell us, if at all?

Peter Eisenman's Aronoff Center for Design and Art poses the problem even more acutely, since Koolhaas's aesthetic after all enlists the movement of history itself for its programmatic force – the Pearl River Delta forecast, the predictability of the unpredictable – while few bodies of contemporary theory espouse the values of subversion, of undermining the transgression, more enthusiastically or develop it more extensively than the writings of Peter Eisenman. I will not, however, in what follows, attempt a frontal engagement with Eisenman's theoretical writings, which demand a whole monograph in their own right, and a canceled monograph at that, since any study of these writings must include the distance from the actual building itself, along with the experience of the building. ("I no longer believe that knowing is more important than experiencing. I do not think that you need to be able to decode the Aronoff Center in Cincinnati . . . I would say that the only way to make that assessment [a 'meta-assessment' on the formal-cum-politico-ethical value of the new building] would be to experience the building, once it is built.")[4]

Let's make a start on that experience, and also on the properties a description of that experience ought to have in order to enable a theoretical statement. I assume that among these last, some account ought to be provided of the way in which a given building block occludes your imagination of its exterior, your perceptual access to an outside you cannot see. I assume that the mall-like structure does this generally by interposing second-degree interiors – a whole wall of them – between your strolling "I" and what might otherwise be some outer wall that has an outside on the other side of it. I also assume that the Koolhaas structure plans to distract us from its putative exterior by staging perpetual and self-generating eventfulness, a kind of temporal "congestion" in the present, so to speak; "filled time" as opposed to the older "filled space," the "space-abhors-a-vacuum" of the churrigueresque or the Mayan, of Rubens or Gaudí.

Neither of these features can particularly characterize Eisenman's Aronoff Center, which, like his earlier Wexner Center for the Fine Arts, is still plotted along a winding trajectory, still seemingly squeezed in between two mobile pincers, two coordinated external limits that dilate and contract in a rhythm that adds time into this trajectory. In the Wexner, to be sure, these limits are the already existing buildings between which the Wexner has had to affirm its being: the mind brings this knowledge inside with it from the overbuilt campus outside the doors. The subliminal concept of "squeezing" is tactile on an enormous and collective scale, turning static walls into the fingers of giants: it lends the necessarily inert buildings the temporality of subliminal muscular resistance and effort – the Samson-spectator holding off the walls, pressing them open again.

3 Rem Koolhaas, **Delirious New York** (Oxford: Oxford University Press, 1978; New York: The Monacelli Press, 1994), 149.
4 Alejandro Zaera-Polo, "A Conversation with Peter Eisenman," **El Croquis** 83 (1997): 19, 13.

Such subliminal activity is of course a source of enormous aesthetic satisfaction (it plays its part in most conceptions of the sublime, for example), but it is not the only source of temporality immanent in the form. In fact, it constitutes a kind of symbolic praxis in time, which is added on top of, or combines with, the temporality already inherent in our forced trajectory from one end of the winding pathway (unmarked upstairs) to the other, which to be sure has marked entrance-and-exit doorways – which are, however, slung beneath, on a service driveway, which drains them of all monumentality. The trajectory thus aesthetically lacks a beginning and an ending.

Meanwhile, of course, the Aronoff, unlike the Wexner, is not squeezed between two already existing buildings, but rather incorporates the remains of one, and offers its exterior to the outside world on the other side, where like a battlement it follows the contours of a hill inaccessible to the automotive intersection beneath it. Landscaping has been summoned to disguise its presence as much as possible. (You certainly notice the hill from your car; the nature of the walls on top of it remains rather more conjectural.) And as well as I can remember, something happens to the windows inside and the view they ought to offer, which also interferes with our inveterate inclination to imagine and remodel that external surface that used to be the very essence of an architectural work in the first place: facade, monumental statement, the two pillars like two immense chords in front of St. Johannes (Vienna), or even Robert Venturi's decorated shed, which does still project an exterior and a characteristic shape.[5] Meanwhile, the immense cubes of this or that Koolhaas building took on an external density when the voids and inner organs shone through the surface (at least in the drawings and models).

In any case – however surprising it may be to identify a building without any perceivable or articulated exterior – the question turned rather on the way in which the "inside" of such a building could structurally evade its condition as an inside and offer some self-generating, self-perpetuating space without an exterior, in its own right. The Aronoff is clearly a labyrinth rather than a sphere: yet unlike most of the imagery we have inherited from science fiction – underground cities, shopping tunnels, windowless sleeping cubicles, and the like, with radiation poisoning the atmosphere and desolation spread above – it has no dystopian features or affects, and its exploration is – and is meant to be – an "infinite task," the perpetual encounter with unpredictable and unforeseeable spaces. But how one could plan this in advance is indeed one of the most interesting paradoxes of the center, and cannot only be attributed to the superiority of computers over the lumbering pace of the human brain.

The older aesthetics – Kant's for example – wished to assimilate the unpredictability of the work of art to nature itself.[6] The crucial issue was intention, and where classical traditions of rhetoric and eloquence, and also of handicraft, were inclined to celebrate human achievement and to welcome continuities between the intention of the artist and the work itself, the Romantic period (or the modern, or the bourgeois) identified the traces of the artist's intention as a mark of inferiority, as an interference between nature (or the unconscious) and the final product, a hiccup in that transmission process they sometimes called "genius." That the intensified "humanization" of the world inaugurated by the modern machine should have been accompanied by this decisive attempt to open up an enclave in the aesthetic that could continue to count as nature rather than as human praxis is one of those historical paradoxes we probably do not want to solve too rapidly, by pronouncing this new aesthetic "nature" to be a form of resistance to alienated machinery (although it has often been said). At any rate, the paradox seems to have developed to a higher power in our own situation, where we appeal to the computer to reinstate the formerly "natural," or to restore the unpredictable and unforeseeable to an otherwise only too stale and evident human intentionality. Perhaps it is no secret that the architect himself delights in the surprises the Aronoff still holds for him: it is thus to be presumed that he takes some credit for the effacement of artistic subjectivity, which might also be thought in terms of an embrace of strict forms (Racine's Alexandrians) or even mathematical constraints (as in Oulipo). But these constraints in their turn know their own inner paradoxes: in particular, where they are successfully and "effortlessly" overcome, the public ceases to be aware of their presence

5 See Robert Venturi, Denise Scott Brown, and Steven Izenour, **Learning from Las Vegas** (Cambridge, Mass.: MIT Press, 1972).

6 Immanuel Kant, **Critique of Judgment**, trans. W. S. Pluhar (Indianapolis: Hackett, 1987), sections 46–50.

as a central obstacle within the situation of production, and thereby fails to acknowledge the skill of the artist in the first place, or the ingenuity of the solution. Can a building continue to maintain this tension that the literary work effaces?

Not only in the strangeness and novelty of the space, perhaps, but also in its comprehensiveness: a whole underground city is here unfolded in the form of a totality, sufficient unto itself and autonomous, a space that, despite its segmented linearity, cut off at both ends in the mode of Gide's *pourrait être continué*, nonetheless still simulates somehow the infinite self-engenderment of the Möbius strip.[7] Size and scale are clearly fundamental here, for a totality effect requires multiple episodes and extreme structural variety. Roland Barthes observed, during the structuralist period, that the contemporary equivalent to older notions of organic completeness had to be posited on the principle of the combination scheme, and of structural variation – the systematic exhaustion of all the structural possibilities, rather than the Aristotelian "complete action" or the romantic "world." But this no longer seems quite right for a production based on "metric overlapping" and "asymptotic tilt," on "vertical stepping" and "exponential torquing," all of which suggest a more radical attempt to introduce temporality into the building than was the case with the spatial variations and combinational grids, the "diagrams," of the period of high structuralism.[8] Indeed, if we have to do here with a simulation of the city itself, the ideal of putting a city in motion is a curious one indeed, which raises new questions about time and movement fully as much as about the city itself.

As far as this last is concerned, I take it that its relationship to architecture has been profoundly modified in recent years (not to speak of some "postmodern period"). The Modern Movement held the city and the building together in the unity of a single thought, its most ambitious practitioners scarcely doubting their capacity to powerfully modify city form, or else to generate a new collective space to replace it. It is a confidence that has been everywhere sapped and vanquished by contemporary urban developments and complexities. Nor does the spiritual act of envisioning Utopian bedroom communities out of whole cloth seem much of an achievement by comparison. Failing the city itself as a totality, modernist architects have also laid claim to another strategy: imposing a single building that stands at a distance from the surrounding city fabric and setting it ostentatiously in perspective and in question. The building then becomes a "critical" statement on its urban context: thus, for Manfredo Tafuri, the early skyscraper constituted a "unique event," an "anarchic individual" that soared over and against the city and challenged it spatially and ideologically.[9] Yet, as is so often the case, success is also failure, and the proliferation of skyscrapers – now called "high-rises" – renders this particular symbolic act ineffective.

At that point, then, one has the feeling that great architecture became an endangered species, an ethnic minority offered shelter in the reservation space of the noncommercial, noncompetitive enclave. In particular, the university campus offered a haven to the grandest variety of ambitious new structures, which thereby no longer had to solve the dilemma of housing, or that of the standard office. This is of course still the case, and Aronoff is but a particularly splendid jewel in what will be, on the University of Cincinnati campus, one of the great collections of contemporary architecture.[10] Yet museums, classroom buildings, stadiums, or concert halls – these are still genres, so to speak: they have their interest and stimulation in an age of generic pastiche, no doubt, but probably do not absorb the very greatest ambitions.

I think that what happened next was the symbolic appropriation, by the individual structure, of city space itself, as the very model of "untotalizable totality." The greatest new buildings, whatever their formal identification and classification – ferry terminal or multipurpose art center – all carried in their heart the secret ambition to become everything, that is to say, to reincarnate the impossible city itself on a smaller and potentially self-enclosed scale. But as with the city – or at least the city today – this closure had to seal itself off from an outside whose very existence it denied, turning back on itself like that very closed universe whose theory and image were themselves a reflex and a spin-off of the city proper (a proposition based on the

7 See the last lines of André Gide's **Les faux-monnayeurs** (Paris: Hatier, 1926).

8 Alejandro Zaera-Polo, "The Making of the Machine: Powerless Control as a Critical Strategy," in **Eleven Authors in Search of a Building**, ed. Cynthia C. Davidson (New York: The Monacelli Press, 1996), 33.

9 Manfredo Tafuri, "The Disenchanted Mountain," in Francesco Dal Co et al., **The American City** (Cambridge, Mass.: MIT Press, 1979), 389.

10 We must give particular credit for this project to the imagination and creativity of Jay Chatterjee, dean of the University of Cincinnati's College of Design, Architecture, Art, and Planning.

assumption that scientific concepts are extrapolations of social ones, and limited by the limits of social conceptuality and form).

But *reflex* is perhaps the word to be underscored here, since I am tempted to believe that architecture's mimesis of the urban (or at least the urban of postmodernity) is not necessarily a conscious or intentional process (although it might also be, or become, that). Rather, like tropisms in biology, or auto-referentiality in modernism, the process strikes me as a relatively instinctual or evolutionary one, related, at least as far as culture is concerned, to the gradual withdrawal of the latter's content. It is therefore problematic enough to evaluate such a development: one can imagine a negative judgment, a critical ideological analysis, in which the symbolic replacement of the city by some glittering postmodern space is very precisely tantamount to a class defense mechanism, in which privileged enclaves are sealed off against a city whose possibilities have been written off in advance. One can equally well evoke the driving force of the new, and the attempt to pioneer a new space that would be equal to the postmodern demands made upon it, and which might well offer revolutionary possibilities for both a culture and a social order to come. In fact, in the abstract, and from a purely formal standpoint, either of these interpretations is true, or both at once, since only collective use and appropriation can offer any reliable index of social value. In this particular instance, the academic setting continues to render the social question moot, or at least to tilt its center of gravity toward the matter of formal innovation as such.

But even leaving the question of class aside, people are very much a part of this building; and on reflection about the work of Koolhaas, as well as about the Aronoff, one begins to come to the conclusion that the question of building temporality into a building, or of producing a Deleuze-Guattari "machinic" building (after all the qualifications, one is tempted to conclude that this means little more than "process-oriented," or even "self-producing" or "auto-poetic," to use another slogan of the current age), is wrongly posed when it is thought of exclusively in terms of "inert" space.[11] When framed in this way, the temptation is clearly to imagine that space powerfully taken in hand and twisted,

torqued, spun, projected into its own future like a wormhole, spinning on its axis like the wobbling spiral of some gigantic history, and punched full of holes, intervals, "spacings," like a Henry Moore sculpture. But what intervenes here is "defamiliarization" or "estrangement": perception, as the Russian formalists taught us in one way and Brecht in another, has the habit of lapsing and becoming numb. The "familiar" seals the novum over us and leaves us in a state of perceptual indifference. We are then, to use a now charged Benjaminian word, "distracted," which is to say, focused exclusively on our own concerns and registering built space out of the corner of our eye.[12] But I suspect that Benjamin's concept included that of Proust, who posited the lateral, and the indifferent neglect of our experience, precisely as something that could then, in a second incarnation (that of writing), be revived and relived freshly and directly, "as though for the first time." The hardening over of unusual and subversive space into the indifferently "familiar" does not, I think, generally allow for this second moment of Proustian resurrection. And in that, like all works of art of whatever medium, the work can never be so structured as to enforce its own reception; it cannot, on its own, resist this "fading" (probably characteristic of all named human experience).

We must therefore imagine that it is people who endow a building with its relationship to stasis or to change; and we must imagine the streams of people moving through such a building as the very source of its "becoming" or, on the other hand, its "being." The structure of the building cannot be said to cause this specific collective "dwelling-in-motion"; but it can block off or exclude the undesirable kinds of movement. I would like, for example, to explain to myself how Koolhaas's collective buildings, with their planned congestion and heightened traffic velocities, are designed to omit and separate off the aimless milling around, the confused crowd behavior that I have described in the instance of Portman's Westin Bonaventure Hotel.[13] The people bring their becoming to the building in question, which then shapes it into specific forms of multiple movement, like a sculptor removing the inessential from his raw material, and organizes precise congestions, articulated confusion, masses infused by specific vectors and multiplici-

11 Zaera-Polo's characterization in "Making of the Machine," **Eleven Authors**, 29. See also Peter Eisenman's reply, "Processes of the Interstitial," **El Croquis** 83 (1997): 21–35.

12 See Walter Benjamin, **Illuminations** (Chicago: University of Chicago Press, 1974).

13 My explanation differs from John Portman's critique in that he sees an inherent ideology present in the forms of the Westin Bonaventure. See his **The Westin Bonaventure and Criticism** (Minneapolis: University of Minnesota Press, 1994).

ties that carry their movement – images within themselves. It should at least, however, be clear that this way of drawing one's movement from its inner population has nothing to do with use or function or program: those continue, as Eisenman has insisted, on some lower level.[14] They are presupposed, and a genuine architectural work of art seizes on that already existing set of pragmatic operations and indications in order to achieve something supplementary, to opportunistically exploit it to the higher power, much as the art of cuisine transforms our ingestive necessities into something socially, semiotically, and aesthetically more complicated. We may approach the Aronoff Center's way of molding the raw material of its users into just such heightened or second-degree constructions less through the nature of its crowds – even though hundreds of students may be assumed to stream through the building every day – than through the omnipresent relationship of the Sartrean look that governs the proximities and the distances of all these people from each other and from the spatial envelope in which and through which they move. In other words, something in the way they see each other may be expected to be transferred to the building itself, and to generate the architectural specificities we are seeking to describe. I like Cynthia Davidson's incisive account of this whole dimension:

> On the 500 level, the chevron bridge that overlooks the cafe leads to an art gallery that overlooks an area that abuts a former DAAP building exterior wall, the windows of which now look into the Center. Everything is looking, watching, but discreetly, perhaps even unknowingly. Views unfold and then dissolve one into another as quickly as I move my eye. Through the cuts in the building I see fragments of bodies – legs without torsos, torsos without heads, and find myself watching, waiting for the building to reveal more. To watch, the building forces me to move, pushing me through the space in search of a better view, another perspective from which I can enhance my role not just as the viewing subject, but as a voyeur. Here the idea of montage suddenly collapses into the idea of the subject as voyeur, simultaneously watching and watched.[15]

She has thus registered the internal heterogeneities of the center – the persistence of the older building's traces within this new one (to which we will return in a moment), the pedestrian bridges and misplaced monumental staircases, the unexpected piazzas (or better still, since it is a kind of interior and underground dry-land Venice one wants to convey here, the miniature *campos* that surge unexpectedly out of this particular artificial and brightly lit alleyway), the office windows whose landscape view is turned back in on the stairwells and the corridors – which make for a multiplication of possible views, and thereby for an abstraction of the view or the look from its normal bodily conduit, just as the body is itself shattered and fragmented here into a jumble of viewed organs. Yet the Sartrean reference usefully corrects this account by reminding us that, in the realm of the look, we are voyeurs but we are also objects seen, ourselves fragmented, and even our looks are looked at. It is a generalized state of ricocheting ocular projectives, whose spatial frame is made from that, for redirecting this multiplicity of looks in new directions and prolonging and perpetuating the movements – at a distance themselves. In Davidson's interpretation, the Aronoff Center then replaces "the traditional architectural narrative, the *promenade architecturale*" with "a process of montage," in the process fracturing the old-fashioned centered subject.[16] This seems right to me, but I want to lend it further precision by juxtaposing it with a now very old-fashioned modernist conception of "montage," namely that of Sigfried Giedion's "space-time," in which the essential feature was the way in which the architectural or urban object needed to be seen from a variety of perspectives (and speeds) in order to be somehow fully and properly apprehended, for example, the view from above, from a helicopter or airplane; the view from the passenger car; the photographic registration in which a number of perspectives would be superimposed, much like cubism.[17] It will be clear enough that such an aesthetic (whatever its conceptual weaknesses in its own right and on its own basis) has nothing to do with the experience proposed by the Aronoff Center, from which even that fixed, yet multiple and provisional standpoint of the camera eye has been excluded. Giedion's are relations of externality

14 See Eisenman, "Processes of the Interstitial," 14–16.

15 Cynthia C. Davidson, "Introduction," **Eleven Authors**, 16–17.

16 Davidson, "Introduction," **Eleven Authors**, 17.

17 It is clear that the works of Picasso and his contemporaries were very much involved in a deconstruction of the perspectival view prevalent in Western ideology.

and exteriority: if we then conclude that Eisenman's impose new types of interiority, have we said anything useful? Only, perhaps, by way of sealing us more impenetrably within this interior without an exterior, this pyramid without a mummy at its heart.[18] (And without claustrophobia, one would want to add: being inside the Aronoff is as open and joyous as being out of doors.)

Let me also juxtapose something else, by way of marking a future topic: namely, Peter Eisenman on sight and vision itself. The relationship between the various stages of modern architecture and some reification of the visual faculty has been discussed endlessly and theorized (as well as evaluated) in a variety of ways and from a variety of "perspectives" (if you excuse the expression). For some, the innovative struggle of the late, or post-, modern has been to free the building from visibility: you can transform it into glossy color photographs, but you cannot seize it from any privileged perspective. For Kenneth Frampton, the more meretricious contemporary efforts seek to reinvent some central and essentially theatrical perspective that tempts us to expect the emergence, within it, of the event as such: what he calls, in a memorable expression, the scenographic. For theorists of the society of the spectacle or the image, disembodied vision is not only omnipresent but corrupt and productive of infinite alienation in all directions: a conclusion that led Martin Jay, in his compendious survey, to characterize the modern French obsession with sight and looking as "the denigration of vision."[19] Yet Deleuze rereads Bergson as proposing a world of images in which the internal visibility of things – their inherent being – is so much light and luminosity that pours out of them toward us. Eisenman himself seems to confirm the diagnosis that this modern, or postmodern, visibility saps and vitiates the traditional experience of the bodily: "We live in the media world. There has been a detachment of the mind and the eye from the body. You do not need the body to experience media. In the media world, the only thing you need your body for is sex."[20]

He goes on to add that the unsettling of visibility in his own work is meant to restore something of the experience of the body in space; but this does not necessarily follow. In particular, we have just seen how the neutralization of

traditional architectural visibility – a central place to observe the building from, points that allow you to map its spaces in your "mind's eye" – led, as though in compensation and some peculiar "return of the repressed," to an almost pathological intensification of the play of looks within this no longer visualizable building.

But perhaps we need to examine Eisenman's view of vision from a somewhat different angle: he characterizes the relationship of traditional architecture to the individual subject not as looking, but as what the building "looks like." The Vitruvian triad of commodity, firmness, and delight enjoins the building not to be these things but to look like them, to offer an "idea" of such features and qualities:

In this context, the design process, as it has been known, produced something called architecture that always looked like something which was characterized by a genre; either something looked rational or it looked expressionistic. Recently the signature, as another category of representation, another look-like, differentiated individual as opposed to generic representation.[21]

This is also, I think, a subcutaneous periodization scheme (the genres being some largely "realistic" moment, the signatures being the moment of the modernist styles), but what is more significant for us at the moment is the relationship between looking and looking "like." Or are they related? Is it possible that looking is an experience of particularity, before all names; while looking-like involves the flexing of abstract identifications and the classification of the nameless sense-data under so many general ideas? In any case, the large project – the building that, like this one, does not wish simply to be one kind of building among others but rather the building in general, all buildings, building as such – must necessarily eschew and repudiate the generic, just as it wishes to dissociate itself from the individual subject and from individual subjective intention.

I want now to "look" at another feature of movement through this building, which we have come close enough to identifying as the very movement of the building itself, its inherent temporality as a machinic process. Of course, this is the matter of its vectors, whose informing presence

18 See John Portman, "The Failure of the Modern," in **Modern Perspectives** (Minneapolis: University of Minnesota Press, 1989), 12.
19 Martin Jay, **Downcast Eyes: The Denigration of Vision in Twentieth-Century French Thought** (Berkeley: University of California Press, 1993).
20 Peter Eisenman, interview with Alejandro Zaera-Polo, **El Croquis** 83 (1997): 12–33.
21 Eisenman, interview with Alejandro Zaera-Polo, 25.

is clearly owed to the computer, which runs them through the emergent structure like so many laser beams. Descriptions of the Aronoff's production process seem to stage all this in a manner reminiscent of Descartes's invention of the differential equation: keep your straight lines, if that is all you can comprehend with your human limits and imperfections, but multiply them to infinity; and let that very multiplication come close to registering sheer movement and sheer nonlinear velocity in your human, your all-too-human, equations. So also here, I like the idea of Peter Eisenman staring with fascination at the airport conveyor belts on which our luggage is made to arrive, the overlapping scales like some complex mathematical or postmathematical rippling surface of self-production and internal auto-momentum: admiration is after all one of the supreme Cartesian virtues. And I like to reintroduce this "social equivalent" into the Aronoff Center and to sense its "box geometry" as a dynamic process, along with all that superbly bristling nomenclature – exponential torquing and the like – in full deployment all around me.

But I think that something is also gained by the notion of a third "dimension," or this "wireframe provided by the computer."[22] For the experience of two simultaneous vectors running through a given built space and tensing it from their various directions is perhaps not so new, even though it is always exhilarating. This is something like meter and accent, I believe, in which the two series are distinct and yet inseparable from each other all at once: they place our senses at the crossroads, which are however mobile in time – a tension that hands you on to the next present of tension in a kind of relay. If now to this we add a third vector or tensor, we begin to see how movement might take on a kind of autonomy in its own right, through which the body makes its way as a fourth: a pressure we have to maneuver through and against, "a wind blowing at us from paradise," a Tao with which we cannot remain in sync but which has at least been fitfully revealed to us. This three-dimensional movement is somehow separate from the walls and the building itself, or rather, those are just the inert materials that feed its energies. So, just like the people, the human users in our earlier analysis, here the very building

materials become mere starting points for a process that transcends them and pushes them back in time as so many springboards for its forward momentum.

I have little enough time to evoke the "archaeological traces" of the three older buildings enveloped in this new one and incorporated within it, like gravestones in a cathedral, or like ghosts, or like the forgotten place names of now fully urbanized former suburbs. And indeed they are referred to in that way, and if you had to live here forever, like living the rest of your life in a science-fictional underground labyrinth world, you would start to call them that, and the geographical names themselves would dimly subsist in time just as the facades do now, transformed into inner walls: the "Wolfson trace," the "Alms trace," the "DAAP chevron."[23] I have spoken elsewhere of the persistence of Eisenman's work, of this layering of the past, whether in the characteristics of a specific site that leave their traces within the building's configuration, or the coordinates of an older city grid, the incorporation of this virtual or future ruin, this monumental lid half-uncovered by the ground itself. This is evidently Eisenman's way of keeping faith with the past, or rather with the very existence of a past and a historical temporality that has elsewhere in postcontemporary art been effaced without a "trace," to use the crucial word. Yet this temporality, if that is the word for it, seems utterly unrelated to that new kind of temporality within the building itself, which we have tried to characterize above: all movement and self-production, momentum, the snake growing and sloughing its skin. Nor is the difference merely that between the modality of one or various futures and that of the past as such. Yet my sense is that the meaning of the process is here rather different from what we find in the Long Beach, California, University Art Museum project, for example, where it is as though the new construction process irritates a deeper new virtual past and stirs it back into being, veins that gradually begin to show through the built materials of the present. Here it is as though the present itself reached back and powerfully appropriated the past, absorbing it in an expansive gesture, as with the taking of an unusually deep breath: this appropriation is active and joyous, rather than commemorative; it lends the rather nondescript older

22 Eisenman, interview with Alejandro Zaera-Polo, 25.
23 Donna Barry, "Connecting the Dots: The Dimensions of a Wireframe," **Eleven Authors**, 48–59.

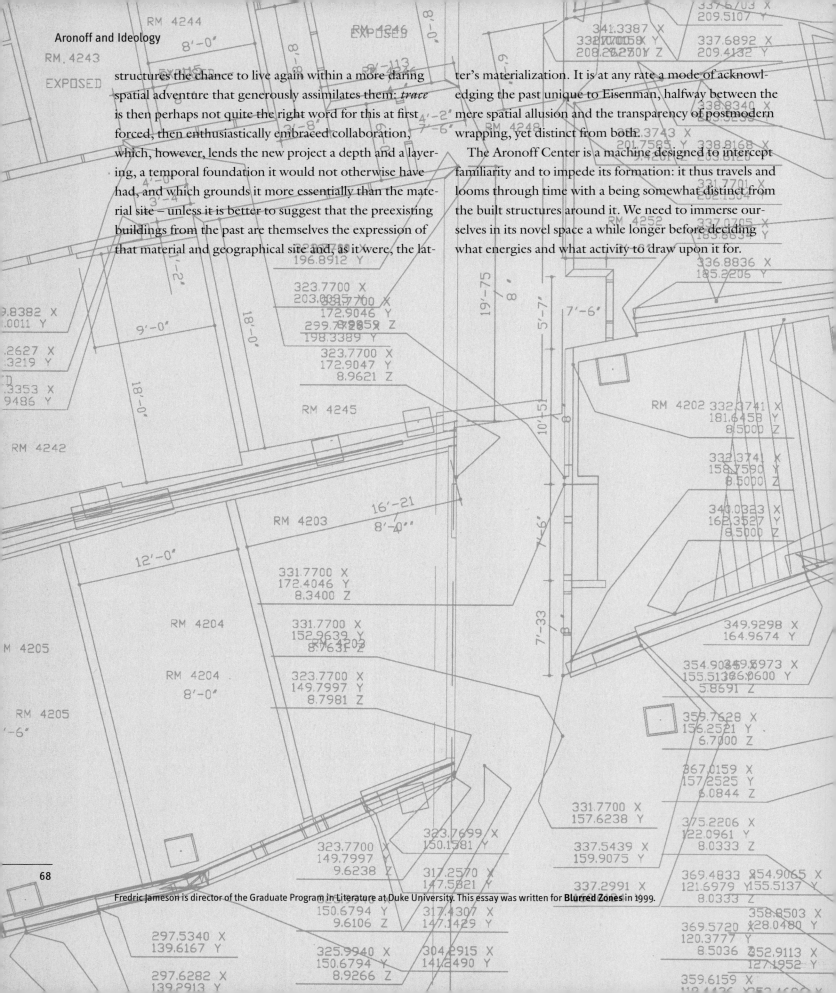

structures the chance to live again within a more daring spatial adventure that generously assimilates them: *trace* is then perhaps not quite the right word for this at first forced, then enthusiastically embraced collaboration, which, however, lends the new project a depth and a layering, a temporal foundation it would not otherwise have had, and which grounds it more essentially than the material site – unless it is better to suggest that the preexisting buildings from the past are themselves the expression of that material and geographical site and, as it were, the lat-

ter's materialization. It is at any rate a mode of acknowledging the past unique to Eisenman, halfway between the mere spatial allusion and the transparency of postmodern wrapping, yet distinct from both.

The Aronoff Center is a machine designed to intercept familiarity and to impede its formation: it thus travels and looms through time with a being somewhat distinct from the built structures around it. We need to immerse ourselves in its novel space a while longer before deciding what energies and what activity to draw upon it for.

Fredric Jameson is director of the Graduate Program in Literature at Duke University. This essay was written for **Blurred Zones** in 1999.

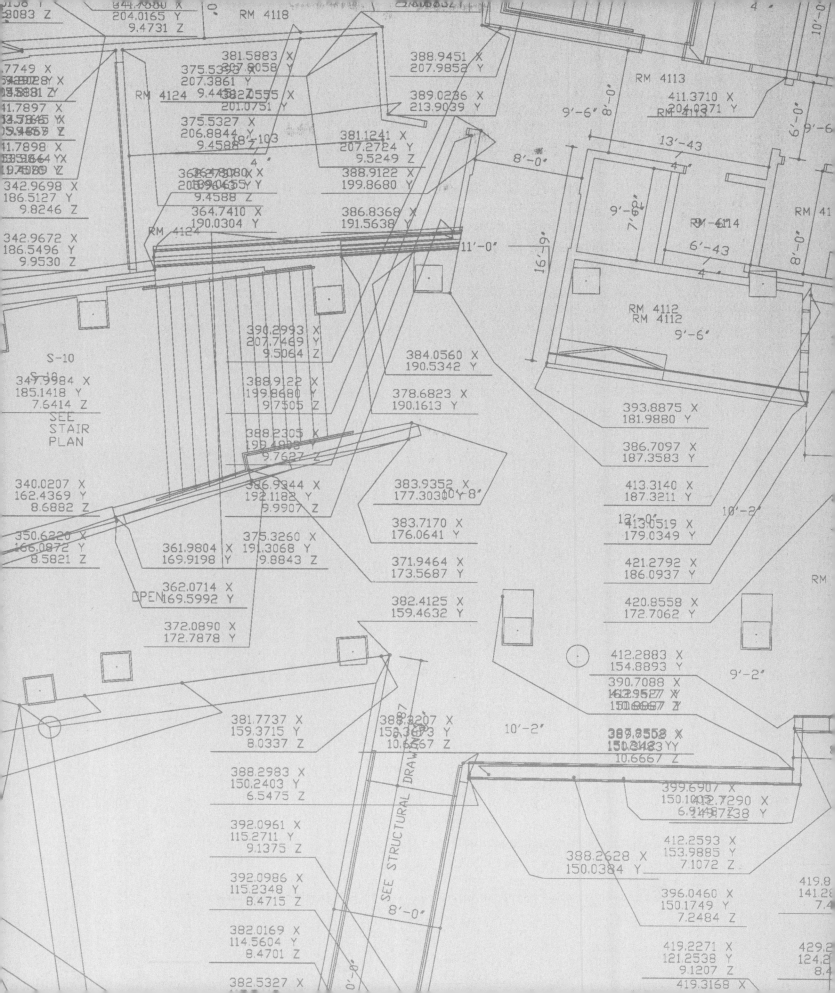

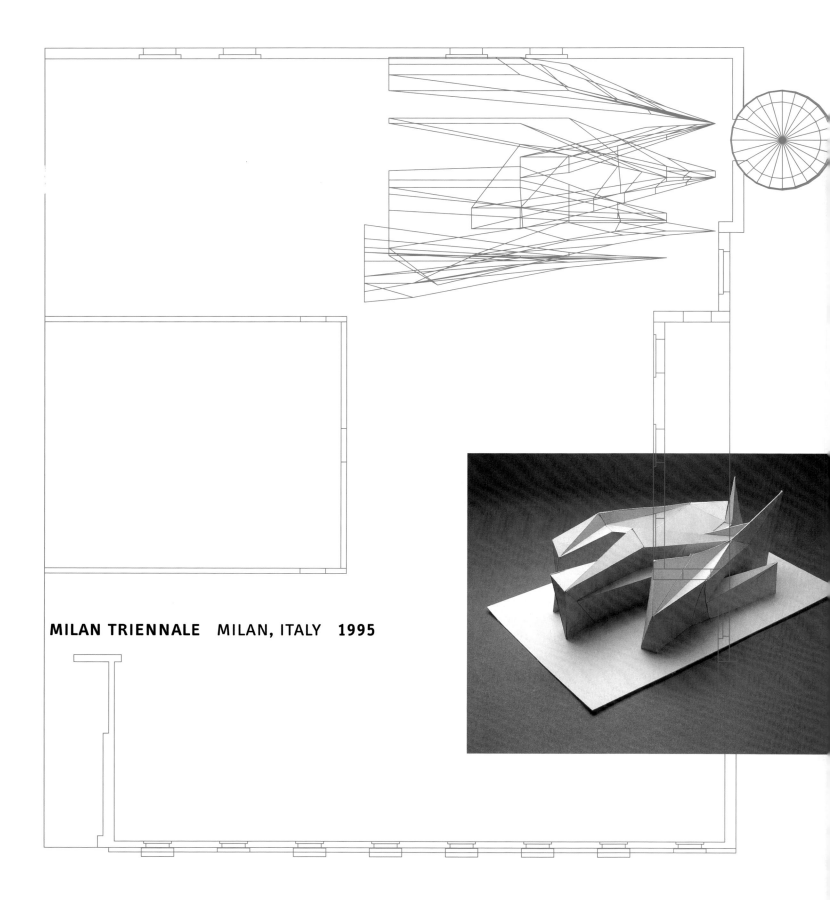

MILAN TRIENNALE MILAN, ITALY **1995**

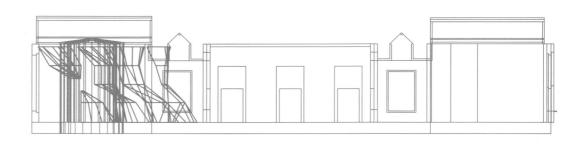

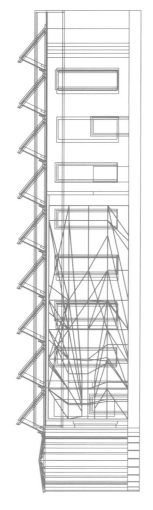

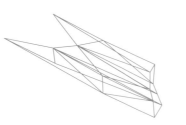

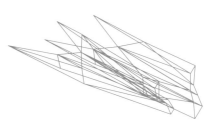

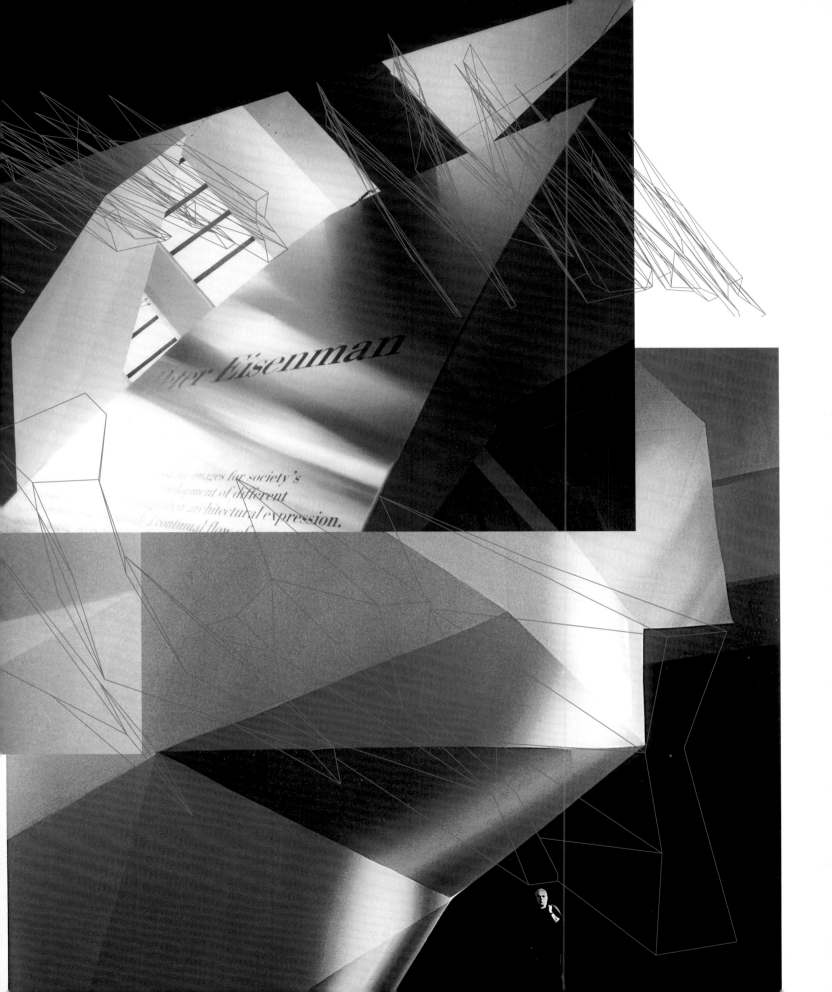

Peter Eisenman

...images for society's
...velopment of different
...their architectural expression.
...a continual flow...

KOIZUMI SANGYO OFFICE BUILDING   TOKYO, JAPAN   **1988–90**

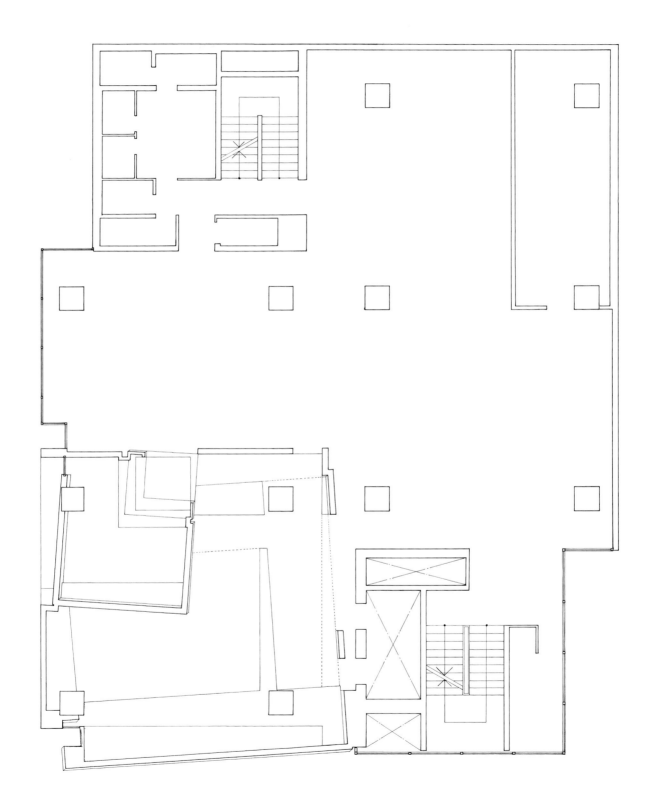

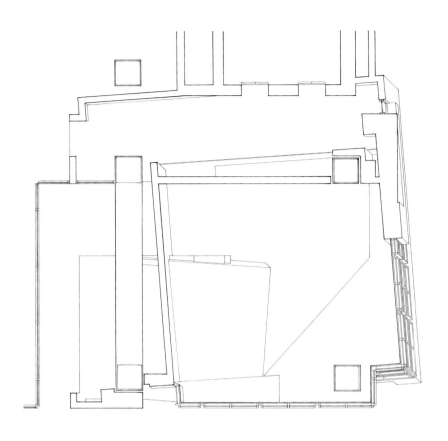

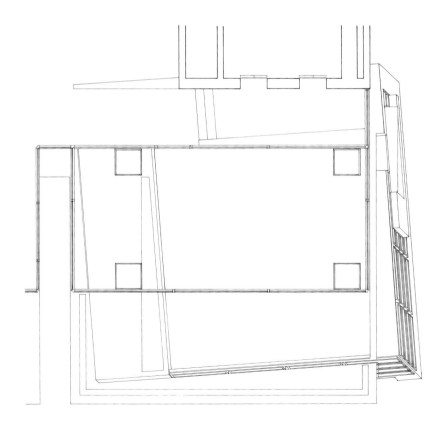

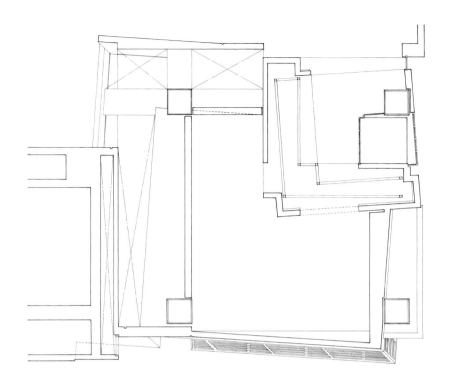

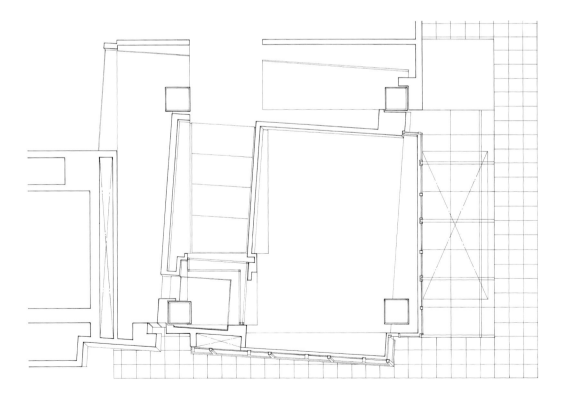

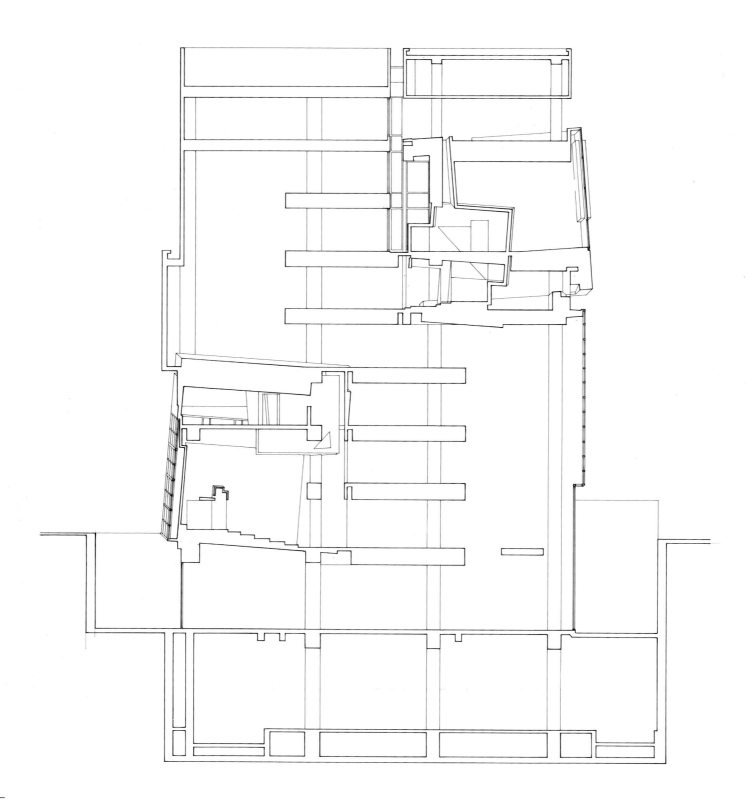

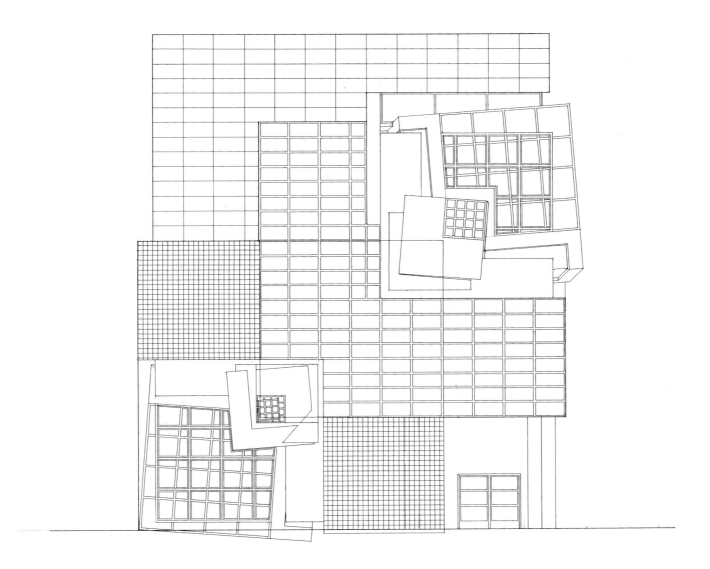

Processes of the Interstitial: Spacing and the Arbitrary Text
Peter Eisenman

My resistance to what has been called "the space of power" is produced in part through the replacement of the subject by what might be best described as an instrumental process. My research into the instrumental has focused on locating the space of the performance of such a process. One such performance is the process of the interstitial, which attempts to resist the traditional terms of design – personal expression, aesthetic preference, taste – that are seen to be compliant with the space of power. While most resistance attacks the compliant forms of the object – how it looks and what it means – my work challenges both the object and its processes and, in so doing, questions the object's basis in what has been a "forming" process. Central to such a questioning is a movement from design as a process of forming presences, or object gestalts, to what can be called "spacing," or the articulation of voids, absences that have the density of presences without their material being. The attempt is to produce an architectural object that is no longer complicit with its previous terms of embodiment or with the form/matter dialectic. While such processes will be seen to deal with the idea of becoming as a state of the object, becoming in itself does not differentiate between forming and spacing; both could be understood as equivalent processes of becoming. Yet it is precisely this shift from forming to spacing that will be seen to be crucial in the context of an architecture in which space, as opposed to form, has often remained untheorized.

Architecture, according to most of its traditional descriptions, embodies meaning and is legitimized by function. This means that architecture, in addition to its being in form, also has to look like its function, that is, it must represent its being in its form. Thus in architecture, the "firmness" of the Vitruvian triad – commodity, firmness, and delight – was not so much about a literal structure or firmness as it was about a structure that had to embody the idea of firmness; it had to look like it stood up. Instead of merely having an object that stood up, the act of standing was also always represented in that standing up. Because of the dominance of material presence, that representation was primarily theorized in the visual. When something looked like structure, its being was legitimized by this "looking like" and not necessarily by the structure itself. This embedded relationship of thing to meaning, of image to icon, has always been thought to be a natural condition of architecture. Thus one aspect of the nature of embodiment in architecture is the a priori, "already given" linkage of iconicity and instrumentality.

In this context, the design process as it has been known and understood produced something called architecture, which always looked like something that was characterized by some architectural genre: it looked rational or expressionistic, classical or modern, or some other typology of representation. Recently, the signature, another category of "look like," differentiated individual from generic representation. In all cases, the architectural object was seen as a result of authorial intervention and expression. The necessary precondition of the process proposed here is the attempted displacement of authorial expression from the production of the object.

Traditionally, the authorial role can only use traditional methods, which in turn can only produce objects legitimized within a traditional discourse. An *other* process, one that is different from and perhaps at odds with these traditional design methods, has three primary concerns. The first is to deny architecture's traditional modes of legitimation by function and meaning without denying their necessary presence in the object. While architecture is not truly legitimated by function, since its being is in function, it is not function that is at issue but its use to legitimate form. The second is to suggest a process that undercuts the legitimation of architecture's modes of functioning, yet can extract an other condition of the object that will still contain function, meaning, and an aesthetic. It is not only the idea of this kind of extraction that is critical to to this process but also the recognition that architecture is different from other disciplines, since cutting architecture from its previous modes of legitimation in function, meaning, and aesthetic does not mean that architecture will not have these functions. The third concern is to define the new context of the object as the differences in affects that such a process necessarily produces in what will be called here the tropic conditions of architectural space. Just as there is no literature without literary tropes such as metaphor and metonymy, and no painting without pictorial tropes such as flatness and edge stress, there can be no architecture without formal tropes such as shear and compression. However, the change from forming to spacing will be seen to have important consequences in figuring architectural tropes and in particular in their traditional basis in formal, figure/ground relationships.

The processes of architectural design have traditionally used what can be called on/off procedures of choosing between two alternatives – solid and void, figure and ground, etc. – rather than operating in a way in which the two conditions are possibly embedded within one another. The traditional ways of deciding which alternative to choose were based upon a condition of architecture as already embodying significance, that is, by a container or enclosure that, by its very naming and function in meaning and use, legitimized the role of the container's presence. Since these presences always looked like architecture, that is, looked like they functioned and stood up, and since architecture uniquely contains an iconicity embedded in its instrumentality, architecture was seen to contain an embodied sign system; it operated within a regimen of signifiers and it conformed to that regimen of signifiers. Further, such an idea of architecture could be said to be legitimized by these signifiers when they represented or looked like certain desired meanings, functions, or aesthetic preferences.

One possible process uses a traditional forming trope, the interstitial, as a condition of spacing. Such a process would begin from the idea that architecture does not a priori either contain or legitimize an already given or embodied sign system; that an architecture could be proposed that does not conform to an already embodied condition, that does not have a preexistent condition of meaning in relation to its function, and that does not have an already given system of signification in the dialectical or metaphysical sense. For such a process to be manifest and active, there must be means for evaluating its effects, that is, what it uses to do this and the nature and number of differentiated affects that could be produced from these effects. How does one know, for example, when one has arrived at an effect that can cut off previous forms of legitimation or an affect that is also cut off from such a formal condition? If such a detached condition does not exist a priori, how does one know that such a cutting represents, in a subjective assessment, the best within a set of circumstances? And of what value is the "best" in a set of circumstances, since it cannot be judged by traditional modes of legitimation – of the best aesthetically, functionally, formally, or significantly – since these are the very traditions that the process is attempting to displace? For example, in this case the best could be identified as the most differentiated, not necessarily in number but in distance from previous modes.

While the value systems for assessing the existing process of forming are already in place – the classical value system of aesthetics, the classical system of signs and signified, and the conditions of use that have traditionally demanded certain conditions of signing – there are few value systems in place for a process called spacing, or the becoming unmotivated of formed object presences. While there is no model of invention for such unknown conditions, the processes of the interstitial propose that in their own internal consistency there are operative processes for such a valuation. For example, in the traditional forming process, presences such as enclosing walls, floors, and roofs are given an initial value because they are designed and theorized first; the functioning spaces are usually seen as resulting from this initial forming of walls, floors, etc. The resultant spaces have traditionally remained untheorized because it is assumed that the forming process exists a priori and thereby gives meaning to the spaces. When these spaces have been theorized, it has been in the rather limited sense of figure/ground gestalts, dialectic oppositions like void/solid, and phenomenological reversals like transparency/opacity. In this context, the forming process also placed a priority on knowing and thus signaling, for example, the location of a front door or the clarity of internal circulation, thereby putting a responsibility on architecture to provide a level of visible information. The process of spacing does not rely on providing a clarity of information, a set of yes/no answers, or a condition of form versus space or presence versus absence. Rather, it involves an idea of spacing that lies within forming, in which a type of conceptual or virtual presence lies within absence. While such a process of spacing may initially seem to be able to extract one of these conditions out of the other, that is, space out of form, and thereby produce necessarily different tropic conditions, it will be seen below that such a process cannot a priori achieve this; to produce a spacing, which in turn will condition what will be proposed as the necessary resultant differences from the traditional conditions of architectural form and space, requires something in addition to a process of extraction.

In the context of architecture, the process of spacing will be seen to function out of its own immanence or interiority, that is, internally, and by contagion rather than by comparison, subordinate neither to the laws of resemblance nor to the laws of utility. Architecture, if it is anything, has always been subordinated and legitimized by laws of resemblance and utility in such dicta as "form follows function." If form follows function, then form already has meaning; and when form follows function, form is already subordinated to the laws of resemblance and utility. While form is subordinated in both of these contexts, it has always had a priority over space. The process of spacing does not subordinate such values but rather is a special type of production. For example, when organic and mechanical processes such as those traditionally found in architectural designs are functioning, they are in a state of so-called equilibrium; they tend to minimize difference. On the other hand, complex living bodies and certain technological apparatuses sometimes are characterized by the production of difference.

For architecture, an idea of *becoming* would mean that it is not subordinated to the laws of resemblance or utility and does not produce conceptually stable forms, but rather gives priority to conditions of space in a perpetual state of becoming. The idea of architecture as a state of becoming defies the traditional ideas of equilibrium, stability, and stasis. But one then must ask, what is an architecture of becoming?

Félix Guattari distinguishes between being and becoming. A becoming, he says, as in the becoming unmotivated of the sign, would have a direction and energy that might deal with forces and flows, which could be multiple, reversible, and deformative rather than linear and transformative. The implicit suggestion in Guattari's idea of becoming is that it is a process that can be repeated infinitely, that in its iteration never produces the same condition of being; that is, in its repetition is always a singular instance of being.

At first glance, any existing architectural design process would seem de facto to be a process of becoming (a transformation of a written program to a physical plan and section). This is not what is meant by an iterative process of becoming. Yet such an iterative process could become part of any attempt to distance both authorial expression and authorial aesthetic from such a process. In a traditional design process, after the specification of a program there is the production of a diagram. Such a template usually contains several factors: one, an organization of functions; two, an organization of the functions by type; and three, an organization of the first two by site considerations. Often the site is defined by several factors, not just its actual physical conditions but also its past and present histories – buildings, roads, contingent contexts – all of which are figured into the site diagram. This site diagram interacts with the diagrams of function and type in a transformative process that produces a melding of all three. Such a melding, in classical terms often called a parti, adds architectural effects to a quantitative diagram. These effects usually manifest latent desires such as the best entrance point and the clearest idea of circulation. These become legitimizing conditions for the resultant architectural scheme. This three-part process of transformation is usually as far as most traditional processes go, in that it provides the form of a two-dimensional plan container. This container is then extruded into a three-dimensional volume with an aesthetic, materiality, and profile. The form of the container is clearly predetermined by its function as shelter and enclosure and, because of this, has an a priori meaning, whether intentional or not.

An iterative process of becoming would begin only after the hypothetical two-dimensional template is produced, and would replace the process of extrusion. Here the process enters what might be called a phase of deforming rather than transforming. At this point it is possible to undercut the traditional modes of legitimation produced in the template described above. This does not mean there will be no function or image; rather, as will be seen, function and image will no longer be used to legitimize the container. Therefore, the process must propose a way to include function and image without seeing the container as a necessary result of their intervention.

At this point, it is important to step back and say what the intention is: to produce architectural effects – tropes or rhetorical devices that have the capacity to produce multiple affects in real space and time, which can be understood as differences from previous affects such as tangibility, tactility, and sensorial responses. The question is, what is the nature of the difference in the effects produced? Is it in materiality, as Jeffrey Kipnis has argued in the theorizing of different material presences to produce material affects? I am arguing here that in spacing a differential series of effects (architectural tropes) is operating.

Formerly, I would have used these effects to produce a reading in the actual form of material presence. For example, the porosity of the long wall surface at the Wexner Center at the Ohio State University can be read as producing a conceptual transparency, an ambiguity between where inside begins and outside ends. This porosity was not intended as a means to produce a particular quality of light in the space (even though this was a desired affect by the client). In many ways, a quality of light will always be present in one form or another, and clearly there will be differences in its affects from one to another. But these are not the kinds of differences being proposed in the experiencing of the interstitial. These are two different things – the effects of the diagrammatic process and the experiencing of differential affects.

In order to produce such a condition of porosity, another deviation from traditional forming processes is necessary. Here is a problematic juncture. It first requires the choice of an outside agent, another diagram, that acts like a deus ex machina. This diagram must contain processes that, when superposed with the original parti or template, will produce a blurring of the form/function and meaning/aesthetic relationships that seem to have produced the first diagram. A second diagram may be immanent in the first diagram, such as in the Frankfurt Biocentrum project, where DNA strands were used to overlay a plan organization. Equally, such a diagram may be immanent to the interiority of architecture. In either case, the second diagram must always contain the intuitive possibility to modify the first diagram at the same time that it can modify the extant conditions of architectural space. Diagrams of soliton waves, neural functioning, DNA structures, liquid crystals, and other formal conditions from outside architecture are other possibilities. While external to architecture, in some cases they may be seen to be immanent to project programs. Equally, geometric processes such as sine waves, fractals, and morphing can also function as a second diagram. These processes seem to derive from possibilities latent or immanent in the interiority of architecture. The nature of the second diagram is crucial. Do the processes of the second diagram need to be immanent in the program, site, or architecture of the first? While at first thought it would seem that there should be some immanence, it is precisely such an immanence that could be said to resituate architecture in the same forms of legitimation from which such a diagram is trying to escape. Perhaps it is the seemingly arbitrary nature of a second diagram that could help to open up and reveal new possibilities that previous modes of legitimation have obscured. However, there is one caveat. The second diagram must be capable of producing architectural effects, effects that do not necessarily come from architecture's interiority or from the specific conditions of site or program, and therefore cannot be predicted or known a priori. So how does one select a supposedly arbitrary diagram that will produce architectural effects without any authorial intervention? Clearly that is not logically or intuitively possible. Rather, it requires a different kind of authorial intervention.

The seemingly arbitrary nature of the second diagram introduces an other process, in this case, spacing, into what was formerly an authorial process of an organic or mechanical nature. A mechanical process would refer to a structural interrelation of discrete parts working harmoniously together, while an organic process would imply a similar organizational model such as a living body. The process of spacing, on the other hand, implies an authorial intervention of a more aleatory, arbitrary, iterative, even chaotic activity. In one sense, this process may no longer be seen as transformative, as in a typical organic or mechanical process, but as deformative.

Here an idea of Gilles Deleuze becomes useful. In writing about the work of Francis Bacon, Deleuze speaks of the *extraction* of the figural from the figurative. He says that the figurative is associated with the illustrative and the narrative character of things. In this context the illustrative is representational and therefore embodied; the figurative embodies an idea of narrative meaning. For Deleuze, the figurative is not a universal condition but a convention derived from the Renaissance system of perspective, a convention that came to be thought of as a natural relationship of subject to object. Modernism's attempted escape in cubism, De Stijl, and constructivism was only a symptom of the problem, not a solution, Deleuze writes. He proposes an alternative to embodied figuration with the idea of the figural, which, he says, was probably suppressed by the abstractionist moderns. Deleuze suggests that the figural may be extracted through a process of *blurring*. In this context, it is important to understand the difference between architecture and painting. A literal blurring occurs in painting in two dimensions; a conceptual one can only occur in three dimensions.

When talking about blurring as a process, Deleuze says that what concerns us here is an absolute proximity, a coprecision, of the field that functions as a background and the figure that functions as a form on a single plane. This is why there needs to be a certain blurriness of the contour between the background and the figure. The blur is obtained in two ways: by destroying a clarity of the figure with another clarity that by its very mechanical precision is opposed to the legibility of one over the other (two clarities equal a blur) and by a wiping, where the distinction between the two becomes blurred.

The process of blurring in painting is of necessity different for architecture. This can be seen in the difference between a contour in painting and a profile in architecture. A contour in painting is merely a membrane, a line between a figure and its ground, while a profile in architecture is a three-dimensional formed container. When architecture is drawn, it is always as a formed profile. For example, Heinrich Wölfflin says that the difference between the Renaissance and the baroque lies in the profile. In the Renaissance it was hard-edged; in the baroque it was softened. Equally, a profile presents different conceptual problems. Contour in painting is on the same plane as both its figure and its ground. In architecture the profile is not on the same plane; it is always elevated and separate from its ground. Therefore, the architectural profile and the contour in painting cannot be blurred in the same way. While different conditions of blurring of contour, such as deep or shallow space, illusionistic space, and stretched space, are possible in painting, in the literal volume of architecture there is no such possibility. Literal profiles cannot be blurred. What is possible is a blurring of the idea in the diagram, where not only the profile but the entire organization is blurred conceptually so that it is no longer seen as merely fulfilling a function, as embodying its functioning form. Rather, the blurring that two superposed diagrams can produce is an extraction of each from their previous functions. This could bring the process to a condition of form, which in many ways approximates Deleuze's idea of the figural.

In modeling a process of blurring in architecture that is capable of first cutting and then extracting the object from its embodied conditions, such a process would contain a condition of an already given *difference*, which might lead to what is being called an *other* condition of architecture, or a spacing. This process might contain new possibilities for the tropic effects, which in turn would lead to potentially displacing affects. But the figural in itself does not necessarily embody displacing tropes within an architecture. There is no a priori guarantee that a superposition and consequent blurring of two diagrams would provide a modification of the traditional tropes of architecture, nor is there any mechanism that can move the process from a forming to a spacing, which is implied in the figural.

A trope is architectural in the sense that it contains a level of conceptualization, acts as a rhetorical device that can only be considered architectural (i.e., three-dimensional, enclosing, meaningful, etc.). In themselves these are necessary but not sufficient conditions to produce a level of criticality. Producing an architecture without its tropes would be similar to producing a painting without any pictorial content, such as flatness, opacity of pigment, etc. Thus a necessary movement toward a more arbitrary and aleatory process would take a blurred two-dimensional diagram of superpositions and project it in some way other than extrusion into the third dimension. This is because the process of projecting cannot be expected a priori to reveal in the third dimension the supposedly inherent figural possibilities of its process. Ultimately there will be changes in any initial diagram, changes that would somehow incorporate spatial figural tropes so that the diagram could become autonomous in an architectural sense. This autonomy, or running-by-itself, would give further small-scale articulations – windows, rooms, corridors that, because of the diagram, are no longer legitimized by function, aesthetics, or meaning – the possibility of being realized in the same way as large-scale elements. It is understood that the operations that modify the diagram in three dimensions may be already latent in it; thus the process is merely one of finding them. This is the most authorial part of the process, since it requires a constant back and forth between processes to articulate architectural tropes no longer legitimized by their traditional functioning.

These changes in the initial diagram must somehow offer the possibility of tropes, which are spatially displacing and can engender in real architectural space and time a displacement of expectations. If these tropes could be considered as figural rather than formal in the sense of figures of

space, and thus as *other* than the tradition of formal figures, then it is possible to introduce an other possibility for them. Any system of representation produces an image whose elementary units are signs. These images produce meaning effects which are beyond function, shelter, etc.; in other words, a trope. Rhetorical transference and analogical relations are basically the tropes for literature. Conceivably, any formal or figurative element with such an excessive component could be considered a trope in architecture. In the past, these tropes were limited to formal conditions such as shear, rotation, compression, and tension. While these may be invisible because there is no literal compression in the space, they are still effects that are affective in the space because they can be sensed by the body. The difference, for example, between a space by Le Corbusier and a space by Adolf Loos is in the different tropes used by each architect.

The processes of the interstitial are an attempt to propose a tropic displacement, which would necessarily produce a different affective space. What is here being called the figural is different from the formal, in that the figural is marked by its processes of becoming. The figural is a matrix of forces, a condition of becoming that uncovers potential effects of space previously repressed by the formal. The figural uncovers these effects in the formal through an act that is here called spacing. Spacing is a process that lies within forming. With the introduction of the figural, spacing can no longer be seen as secondary to forming.

Architecture's being has an internal logic that is the basis for any figural tropes; these are different from formal tropes, which are usually added to a functional container. A figural trope is one that already exists prior to its unfolding in functional coordinates. When articulated, the figural will appear differently in space than the formal; this difference can be seen in the trope of the interstitial.

Traditionally in architecture, the interstitial could be considered as a formal trope, as a solid figuration usually known as poché. Poché is an articulated solid between two void conditions, either between an interior and an exterior space or between two interior spaces. The important condition of poché is twofold: first, it is not merely a containing presence such as a wall, but is also a figured or articulated presence; and second, this articulation is figurative, not figural, since it already embodies its functional contents as a container, which encloses, shelters, and has an aesthetic.

In order to see the interstitial as an affective difference from its condition as an articulated presence between two spaces, its status as an embodied figure must be changed. This change in status could be proposed initially as a presence within an absence – or a double absence. Such a condition of space might require a different design process, one that could begin as spacing rather than forming. Forming is a condition particular to architectural figuration, since a priori there must be a container that encloses and shelters. Thus forming as a process is presumed to be preexistent in the idea of traditional architecture. It is this priority of forming that must be displaced in what is described below. In architecture, the container is always thought of first as an outline of a figure that contains a function and thus a meaning and an aesthetic. Since there will always be a container that exists a priori with a function and a meaning, somehow to cut off its embodiment, while necessarily retaining its function and meaning, would mean to have both forming and a difference from forming as part of the process; in other words, a displacement of forming as a dominant mode of design production. The idea in the process of spacing is to manifest this already given difference to extract a process of something that lies within forming.

Jacques Derrida first suggested the term *spacing* in reference to writing. He attempts to differentiate between the notion of *écriture,* which is writing in itself, and architectural writing. For Derrida, architectural writing implies a condition of inventive reading, that is, the possibility of a reading that has not previously existed. This is a reading by a subject who is no longer simply content to walk about and within architecture, but who would transform these elementary responses into a condition of what Derrida calls a spacing. From this condition of spacing would derive the possibility of the invention of a system of writing from the gestures of the body, or what Derrida calls "the spacing of another kind of writing." The term *espacement* is distinguished from Heidegger's

use of the term as a gathering; for Derrida, it is more of a distancing.

In the context of a process of blurring, spacing will be used in a somewhat different way from Derrida's idea. Spacing, as opposed to forming, begins to suggest a possible figure/figure, as opposed to figure/ground, relationship, which in turn suggests a new possibility for the interstitial. Spacing produces a displaced condition of the interstitial. The interstitial could be a void within a void, an overlapping within space of space, creating a density in space not given by the forming of a container with a profile. Where figure/ground was an abstraction, a figure/figure relationship is a figural condition that is no longer necessarily abstract. It is space conceived of as a matrix of forces. It is affective in that it displaces previous forms conceived *of* the interstitial.

The interstitial in this context implies a certain movement as opposed to its former condition as a static interval. Here the interval assumes a new condition. As Deleuze says, it is no longer the material structure that curls around the contour in order to develop the figure. Rather, the figure (here an interstitial figure) passes through the contour in order to dissipate into the material structure. Thus the contour assumes a new function, since it no longer exists as a transparency between the exterior and the interior but becomes a porous membrane whose primary task is to create a density of space. Such a porous membrane was first proposed in the Wexner Center's long glass facade, which separated an external passageway and an internal ramp.

Here the process for the production of the interstitial becomes crucial. The interstitial can be understood in the same domain as inertia and entropy. It cannot be wholly produced within a system that relies on aesthetic value judgments or functional and representational criteria; neither can it be produced by geometric processes. The idea of the interstitial as spacing requires an alternative idea of a design process. This is because such an other tropic condition in architecture cannot be produced in the same way as in writing or painting. In this sense, such a removal of the interstitial from a process of forming, or from an embodied figuration, does not seem to be possible through an act of authorial expression or individual desire, because all individual design processes, whether using the hand or the computer, result in embodied systems; they are already conditioned by significance. In this sense, the production of the interstitial can be seen as a critique of the operational idea of process.

Deleuze and Guattari would argue that process is not necessarily mechanical or organic, rational or linear. Process does not operate dialectically between organism and mechanism, but between mechanism and organism on the one hand and chaos on the other. Chaos is not the final collapse of a system but rather something already given in a system that is building toward collapse. For example, a sandpile can collapse when one extra grain of sand is added. Most systems of description see the pile of sand as stable – its quantity and density can be measured through traditional measurements. It cannot be known at what moment the next grain of sand is going to cause collapse. However, it is not the last grain of sand that causes the collapse from a steady state to an unstable state, but rather something that begins when the first grains of sand begin to accumulate as a pile.

Normal complexity can be understood through a logical consistency. A cube is a simple form, and a hyperbolic paraboloid is a more complex form that requires a more complex explanation. Hypercomplexity is not explainable through traditional logical equations. Spacing is another such condition. It can be explained, but it requires a level of complexity not found in conventional geometries; it is already another realm of description.

Hypercomplexity, for example, might describe spacing as a condition of self-similar repetition rather than self-same repetition; it is neither mechanical nor organic. Equally, its objects must be seen as different from authorial expression. In authorial expression, the desire is for every result to be unique. In a self-similar repetition, the results are singular rather than unique, because the process contains an already given difference in architecture's interiority. Such a difference cannot be produced by a traditional authorial process of design because an author only produces what is previously known.

The process of spacing can progressively develop different means of expression, ones that are different from the traditional means of architectural representation. In the process of spacing, it would be possible to classify architectural signs in a different way. Indeed, classification may not be an issue if architecture is thought in terms other than the traditional types of representation. Rather, it is possible that other conditions of signification are repressed by these traditional classifications. Equally, if other modes of transfer can be proposed between the sign and the signified, then other means of expression, different conditions of signing, can be developed. Because of the embedded nature of the architectural sign, it is thought that one cannot change the object of architecture, only its means of signification, that is, the language with which one communicates. If the means of communication in traditional language systems were limited by the regimens that were assumed to be in place, then it would seem that changing architecture from forming to spacing could change these systems of expression. While in architecture these conditions have always been more complex because of the icon/instrument relationship, the investigation of this complexity has been repressed in order to maintain the utility and clarity of architectural communication.

Ultimately, systems of clarification and utility create an excess in the space of power. The political system of transnational capital already suggests an organization of space and time, city, building, etc., that demands clarity and utility in order to create this excess. Standardization and technological processes are used to create the possibility of an excess, which presently resides in capital. To suggest the possibility of an excess, an excess that requires a radical change in the existing modes of production and consumption, becomes a political act. To produce a condition of spacing, of interstitiality, of something that cannot be consumed because it is no longer legitimated by utility and significance, is not merely an aesthetic argument, it is a political one; it is speaking of a different kind of excess. Processes that produce such a difference through displacing affect can be seen to be resistant to the existing spaces of power.

GREATER COLUMBUS CONVENTION CENTER   COLUMBUS, OHIO   1989–93

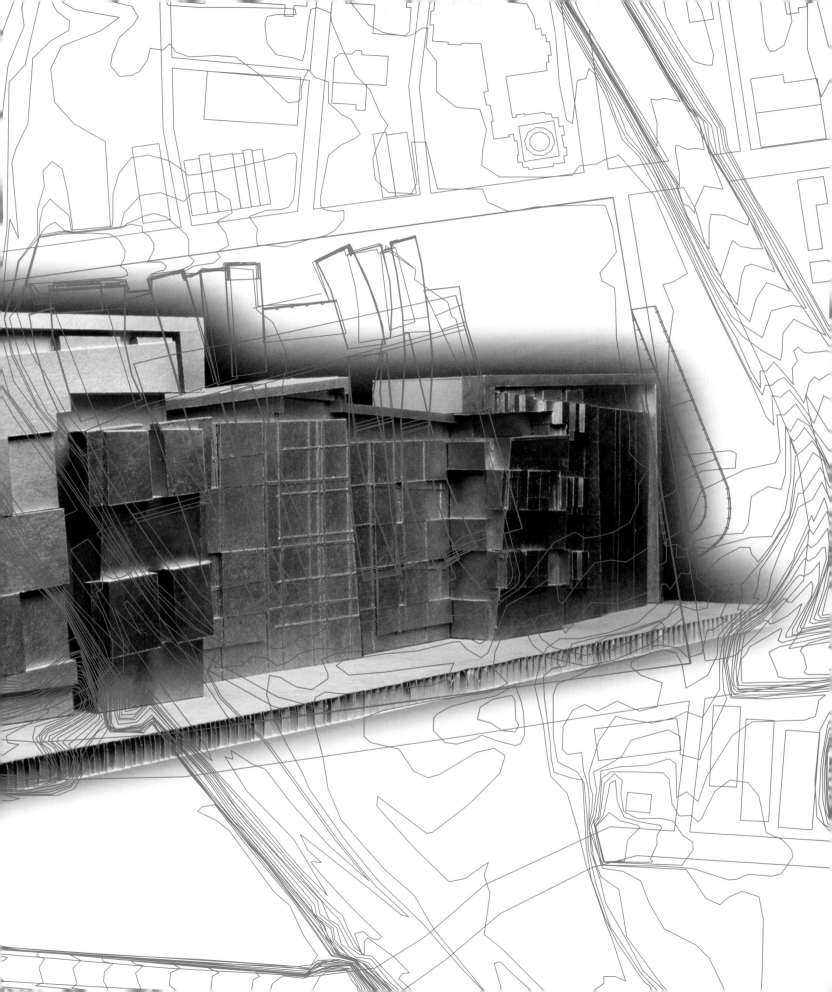

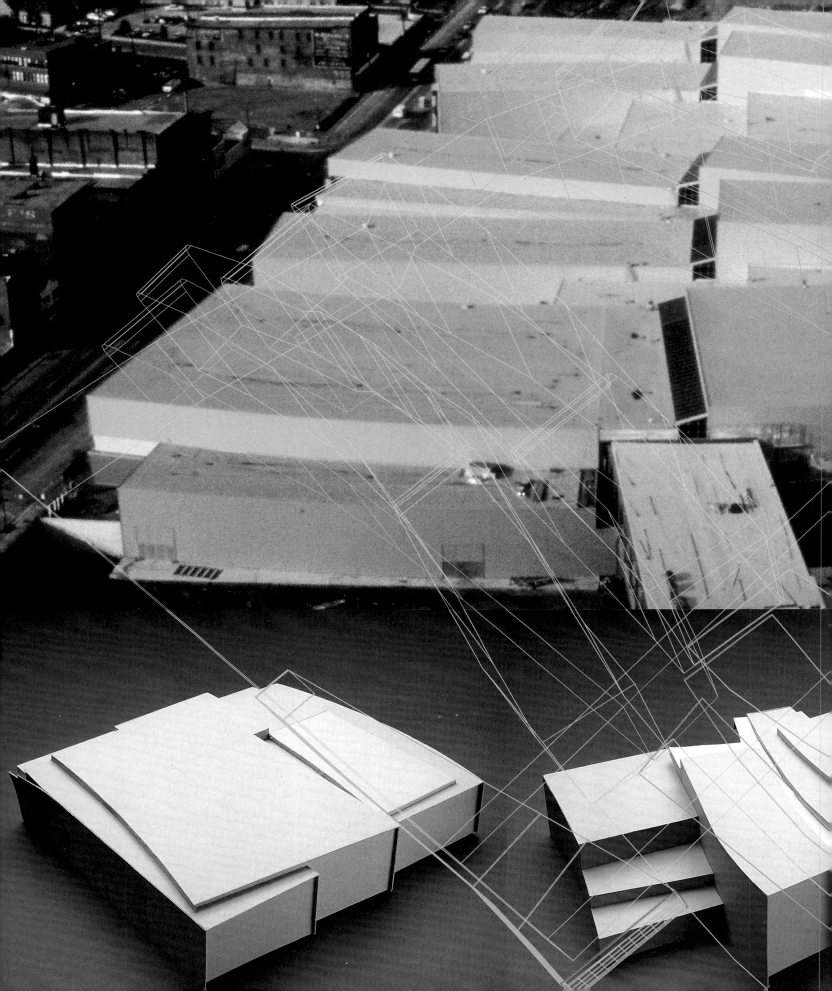

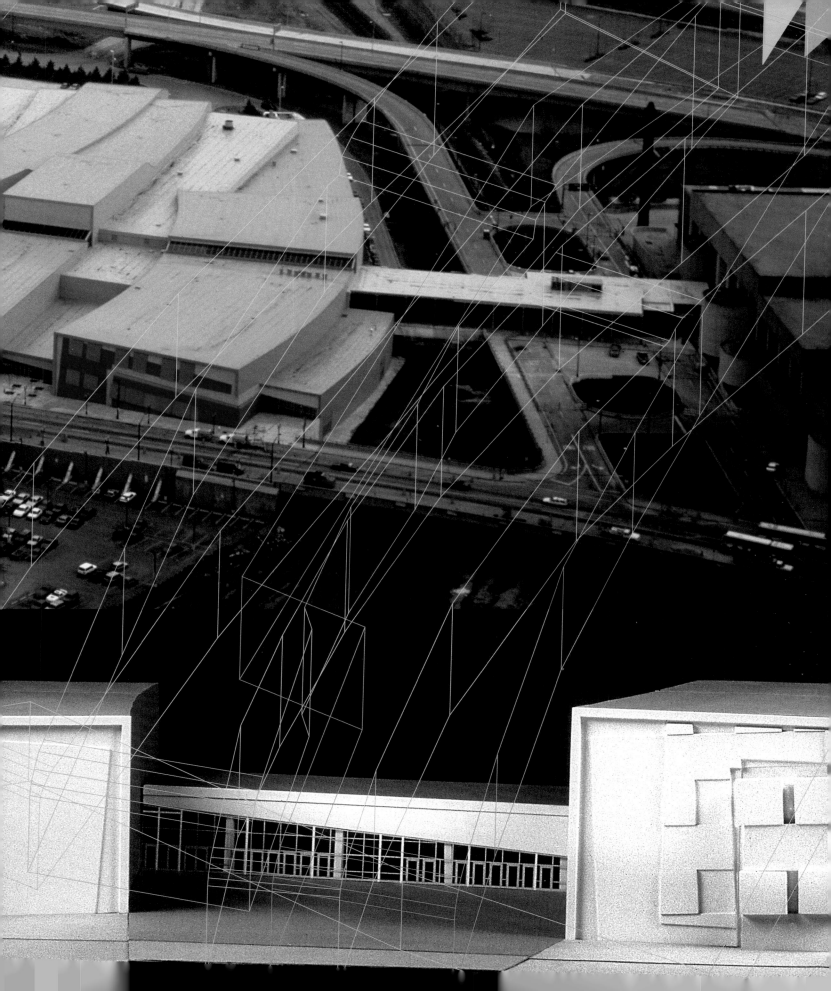

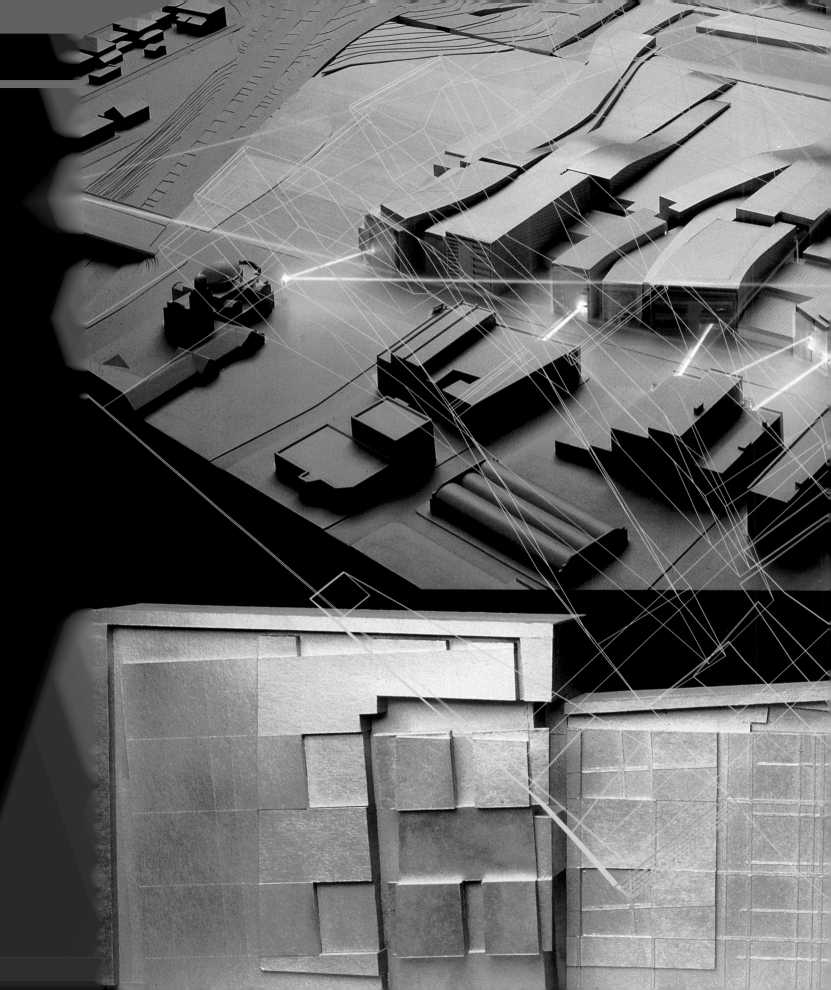

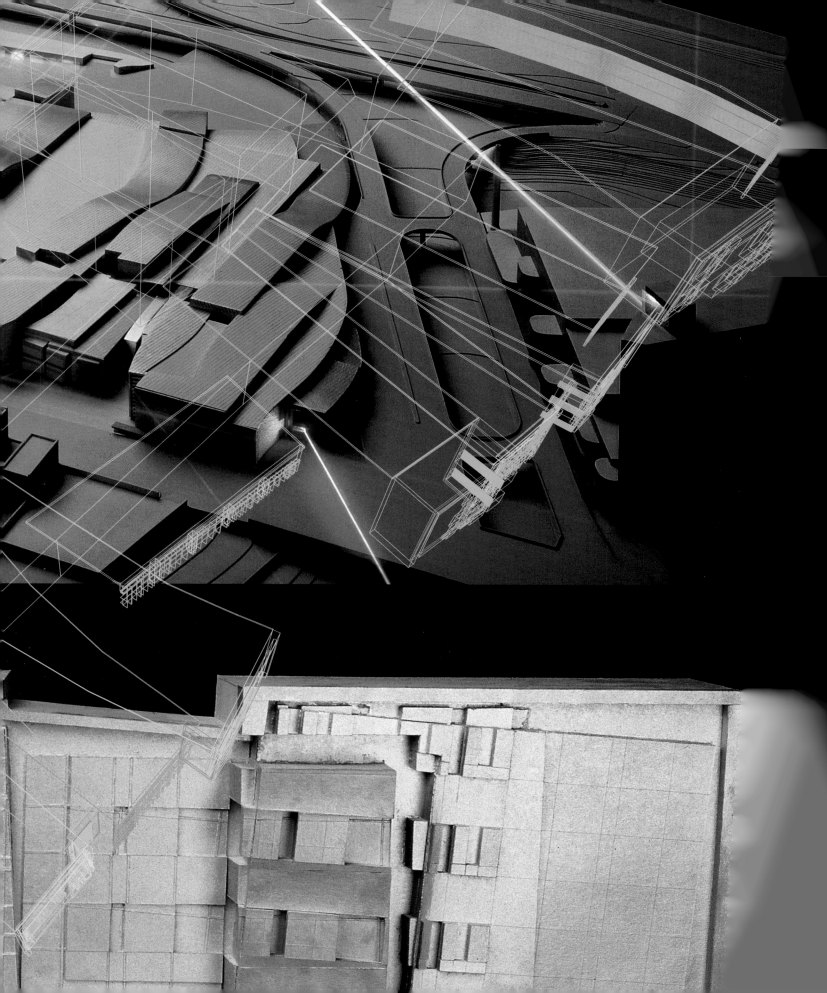

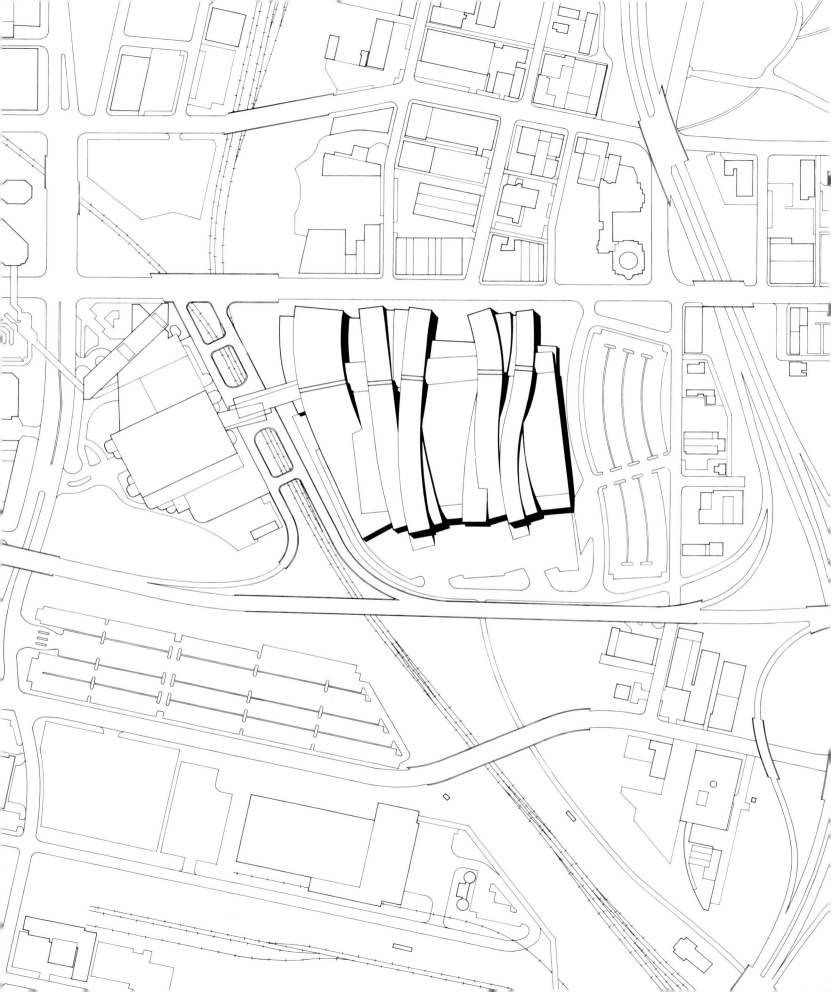

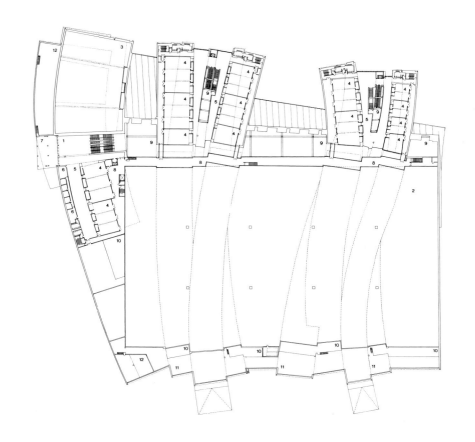

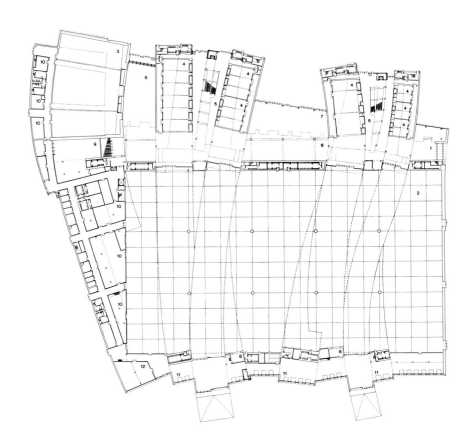

119

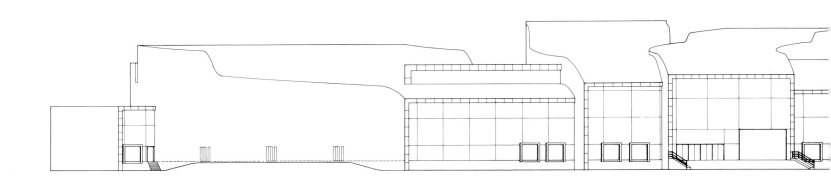

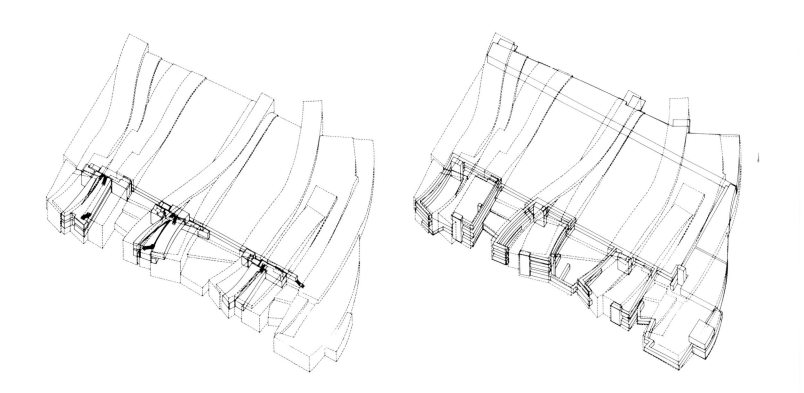

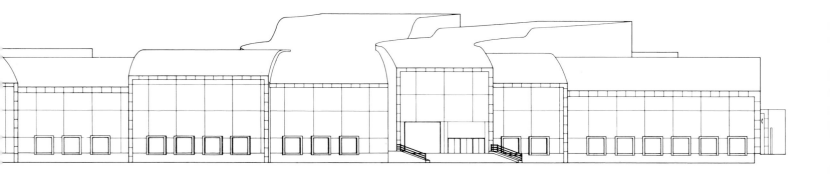

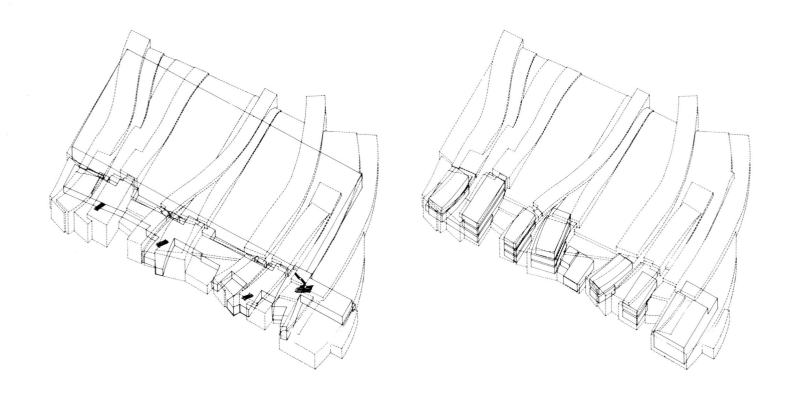

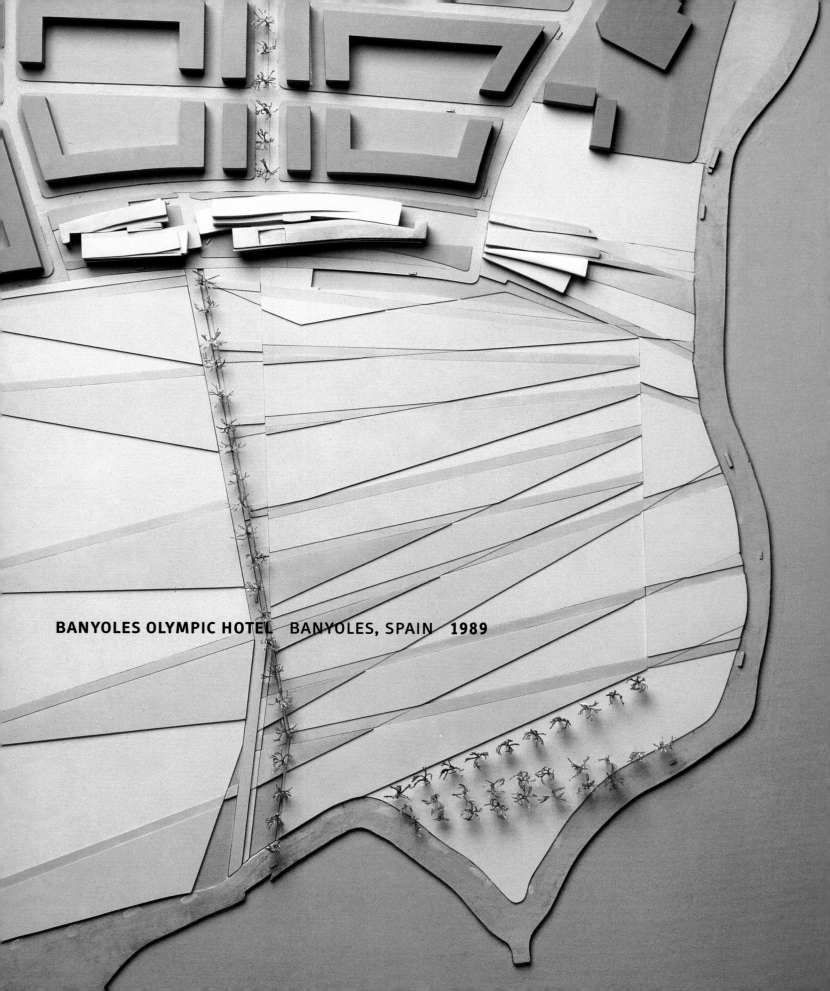

BANYOLES OLYMPIC HOTEL   BANYOLES, SPAIN   1989

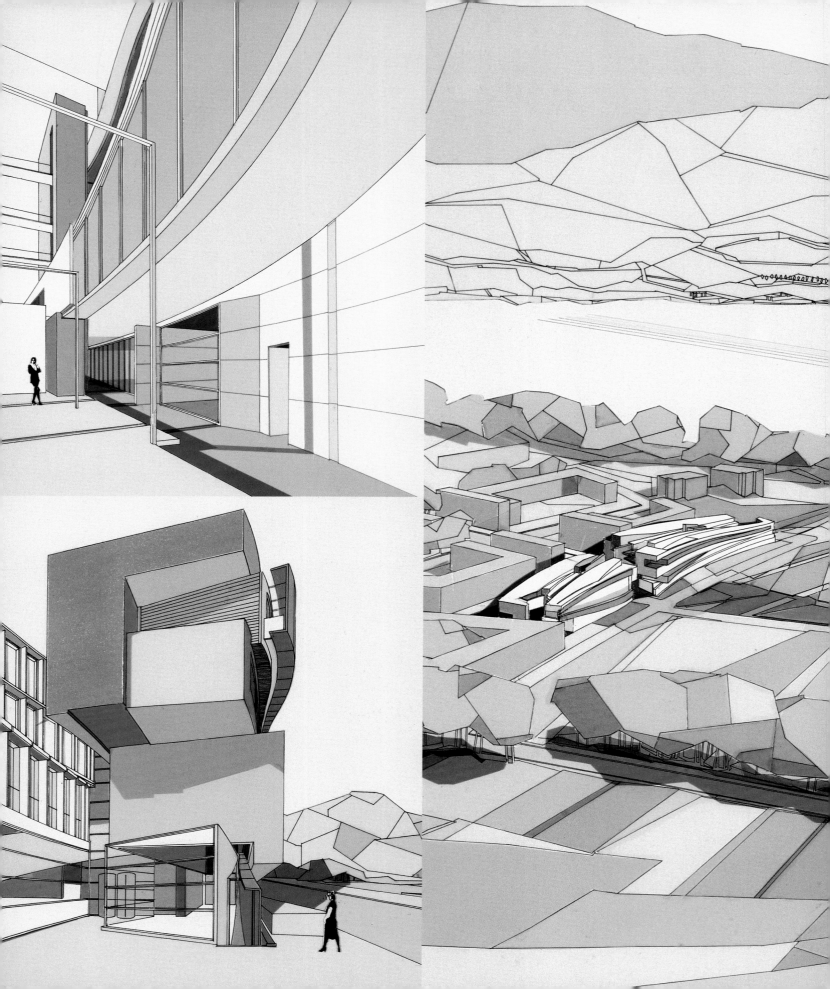

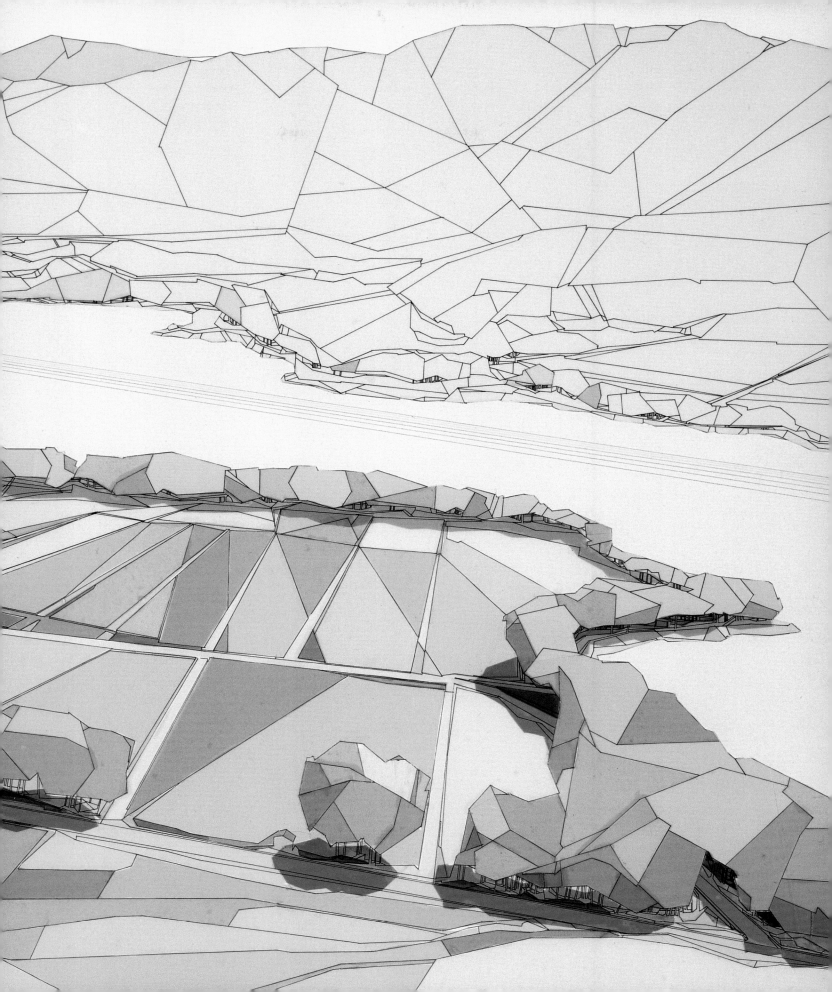

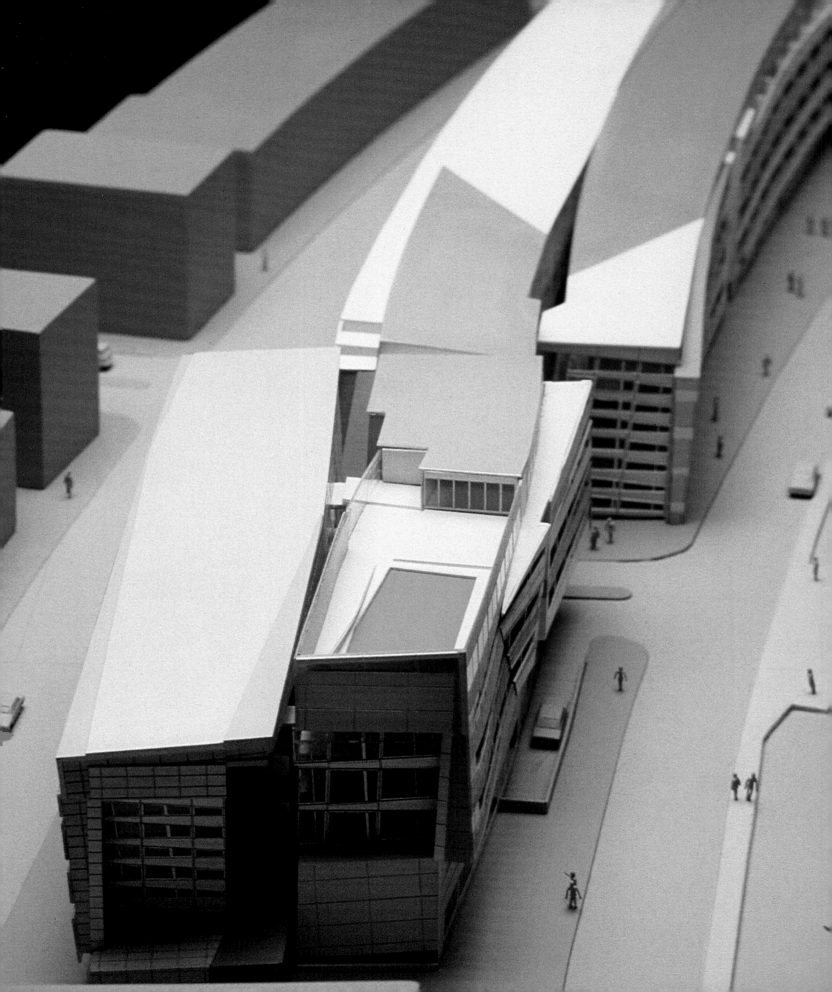

UNIVERSITY OF WINCHESTER
LIBRARY

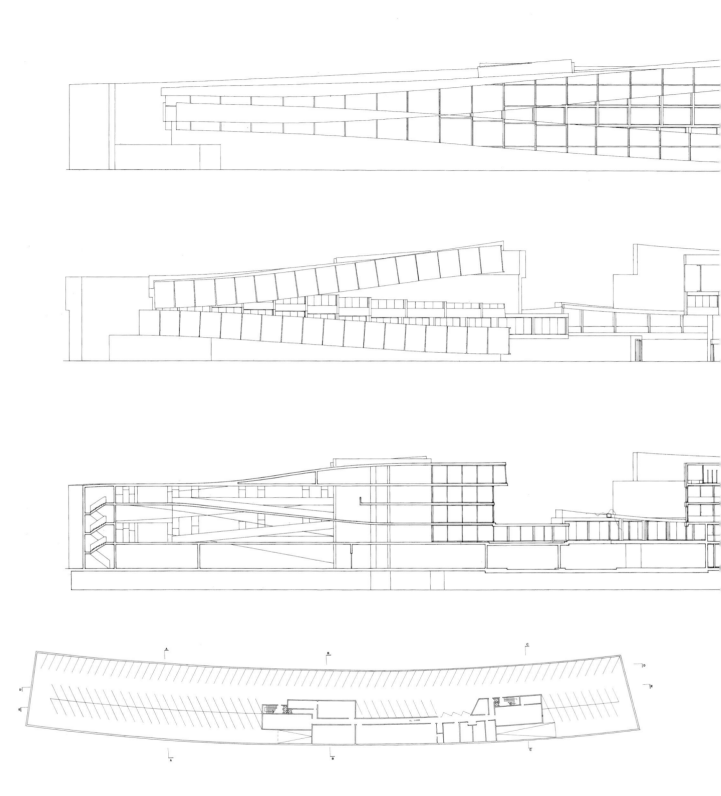

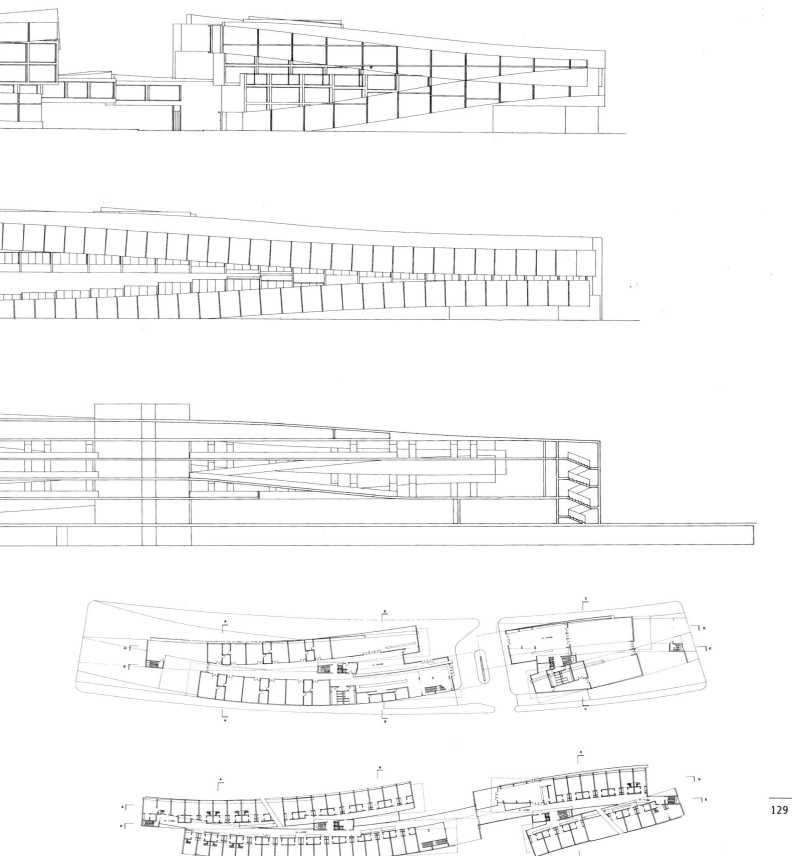

Folding in Time:
The Singularity of Rebstock
Peter Eisenman

In all of the design arts today there is a paradigm shift from the mechanical to the electronic, from an age of interpretation to an age of mediation. This shift has many implications. For example, mechanical reproduction of the photograph is not the same thing as electronic reproduction of the facsimile. The former is the essence of reproduction because change can occur from the original; with the latter, however, there is no change from the original, that is, no interpretation, and hence no essence. While in both cases the value of an original is put into question, mediated reproduction automatically proposes a different value system because it involves no interpretation. Contemporary media undermines the essence and aura of the original, indeed the very nature of reality. Media environments such as advertising, or synthetic realities such as Disney World, have become so potent that they now form a new reality. Previously, architecture served as a baseline for reality; bricks and mortar, house and home, structure and foundation were the metaphors that anchored our reality. What constitutes this reality today is not so clear.

Traditionally, architecture was placebound, linked to a condition of experience. Today, mediated environments challenge the givens of classical time, the time of experience. For example, on a Sunday afternoon anywhere in the world, whether it be at the Prado in Madrid or the Metropolitan Museum of Art in New York, hordes of people are passing in front of artworks, hardly stopping to see. They not only have no time for the original, they have even less time for the experience of the original. Because of electronic media the time of experience has changed; the sound bite – infinitesimal, discontinuous, autonomous – has conditioned our new time.

Hence architecture can no longer be bound by the static conditions of space and place, here and there. In a mediated world, there are no longer places in the sense that we used to know them. Architecture must now deal with the problem of the event. Today, rock concerts might be considered an architectural event. People go to rock concerts not necessarily to listen, because the music cannot really be heard, but in fact to become part of the environment, a new type of environment that comprises light, sound, and movement. This kind of event structure is not architecture standing against media but architecture being consumed by it. Media deals neither with materiality nor with interpretation but rather with the autonomous condition of electronic reproduction. The rock concert with amplified sound and flashing strobe lights attempts to deny physical presence. Architecture cannot do this. It can, however, propose an alternative, some other kind of event, in which a displacement of the static environment is not merely an electronic one-liner but rather one in which the interpretation of the environment is problematized, where the event comes between sign and object.

Traditional architectural theory has largely ignored the idea of the event. Instead, it assumes that there are two static conditions of the object: figure and ground. These in turn give rise to two dialectical modes of building. One mode concerns figure/ground contextualism, which assumes that there is a reversible and interactive relationship between the solid building blocks and the voids between them. A typical example of contextualism suggests that latent structures capable of forming a present-day urbanism exist in any historical context. The other mode concerns the isolated point block or linear slab on a tabula rasa ground. Here there is no relationship between old and new or figure and ground. Rather, the ground is seen as a neutral datum, projecting its autonomy into the future. In each case, the terms *figure* and *ground* are both determinant and all-encompassing; they are thought to explain the totality of urbanism. But as in most disciplines, such all-encompassing totalities have come into question; they are no longer thought to explain the true complexity of phenomena. This is certainly true of urbanism.

Germany, specifically the city of Frankfurt, always seems to clearly trace the changes in Western urbanism. In the late 18th and early 19th centuries, the typical perimeter housing and commercial block in German cities defined both the space of the street and the space of the interior court as positive. These spaces seemed literally to have been carved out of a solid block of the urban condition. In the mid-19th century, with the development of the grand boulevards and allées, a new kind of spatial structure appeared. The streets were still positive spaces but were now lined with ribbon buildings, whose rear yards became leftover space. This idea led to the development of the German *Siedlung,* where, without adjacent streets, the backs and fronts of the buildings became the same. Here the open space was in a sense left over; the "ground" became a wasteland. The object buildings seemed detached, floating on a ground that was no longer active. Nowhere was this *Siedlung* urbanism more prevalent than in the developing ring around the urban center of Frankfurt. While Ernst May's prewar housing was revolutionary, its corrosive effect on the urban fabric is now seen everywhere.

In the postwar era, with the expansion of the autobahn and air travel, a new, more complex task faced urban development. The simple *Siedlung* and the figure/ground perimeter block were no longer adequate to contain the new complex urban realities; the city no longer totally defined the possible context of an urbanism. The form of the perimeter block in the historic urban centers became the basic unit of an urban theory known as contextualism, the vogue of postmodern urbanism, but its nostalgia and kitsch sentimentalism never took into account the manifold realities of contemporary life.

What is needed today is the possibility of reading figure/ground from another frame of reference. This new reading might reveal other conditions that may always have been immanent or repressed in the urban fabric. Reframing would perhaps allow for the possibility of new urban structures and for existing structures to be seen in such a way that they too become redefined. In such a displacement, the new, rather than being understood as fundamentally different from the old, is seen as being merely slightly out of focus in relation to what exists. This out-of-focus condition has the possibility of blurring or displacing the whole, that is, both old and new. One such possibility for displacement can be found in the form of the fold.

The mathematician Leibniz first conceived of matter as explosive. Turning his back on Cartesian rationalism, he argued that the smallest element in the labyrinth of the continuous is not the point but the fold. From Leibniz, one can turn to two contemporary thinkers whose work concerns the fold: one is Gilles Deleuze and the other, René Thom. In the idea of the fold, form is seen not only as continuous but also as articulating a possible new relationship between vertical and horizontal, or between figure and ground, thereby breaking up the existing Cartesian order of space.

According to Deleuze, the first condition for Leibniz's event is the idea of extension. Extension is the philosophical movement outward along a plane rather than downward in depth. Deleuze argues that in mathematical studies of variation, the notion of the object is changed; it is no longer defined by an essential form. He calls this idea of the new object an object/event, or *objectile* – a modern conception of a technological object. This new object is no longer concerned with the framing of space but rather with a temporal modulation, which implies a continual variation of matter. The continual variation is characterized through the agency of the fold. For Deleuze, the idea of the fold was first defined culturally in the baroque. He differentiates between the Gothic, which privileges the elements of construction, frame, and enclosure, and the baroque, which emphasizes matter, and where mass overflows its boundaries because it cannot be contained by the frame, which eventually disappears. Deleuze says that the fold/unfold are the constants today in the idea of an object/event.

The linking of fold and event also influences work in other disciplines, specifically the mathematics of René Thom. In his catastrophe theory, Thom lays out seven elementary events or transformations. These transformations do not allow any classical symmetry, and thus the possibility of a static object, because there is no privileged plan of projection. Instead of such a plan, there is a neutral surface formed from a variable curvature or a fold. This variable curvature is the inflection of a pure event. For Thom, the structure of the event of change is already in the object; it simply cannot be seen, only modeled (by the neutral surface of the catastrophe fold). Thus, while a tiny grain of sand may appear to trigger a landslide, the conditions leading up to the moment of movement are already in place in the structure. Thom's seven catastrophes were proposed to explain precisely this phenomenon.

In one sense, catastrophe theory can also explain abrupt changes in the state or form of figure to ground, urban to rural, commercial to residential, by means of a complex fold that remains unseen. This type of folding is more complex than origami, which is linear, sequential, and ultimately involves a frame. This quality of the unseen in the folding structures of the Rebstock project site in Frankfurt deals with the fact that the folded object neither stands out from the old nor looks like the old, but is somewhere in between the old and something new. Such an in-between or third figure may be likened to the *passe-partout*, which is the mat between the frame and the figure in a painting. The idea of a *passe-partout* is always another framing, however, a kind of reframing that can never be neutral; it will always be more or less than what is there. In this sense the fold is neither figure nor ground but aspects of both. Architecture can then

interpret the fold, which is essentially planar, in three-dimensional volumes. This fold is not merely an extrusion from a plan, as in traditional architecture, but rather something that affects both plan and section. The neutral surface of the catastrophe fold is already between figure and ground, between plan and section, yet it is homogeneous; it is not simply the appearance of a third, but a third in its own being.

By introducing the concept of the fold as a nondialectical third condition, one which is between figure and ground yet reconstitutes the nature of both, it is possible to refocus or reframe what already exists in any site. This was the strategy for the conditions latent in Rebstockpark. The reframing changes what exists from what was repressed by former systems of authority (such as figure and ground) to a potential for new interpretations of existing organizations. Through the concept of the fold, it is possible to refocus what already exists in Frankfurt.

The fold, then, becomes the site of all the repressed immanent conditions of existing urbanism, which, at a certain point, like the grain of sand that sets off the landslide, has the potential not to destroy but to reframe existing urbanism, to set it off in a new direction. The idea of the fold gives the traditional idea of edge a dimension. Rather than being seen as an abrupt line, it now has a volumetric dimension that provides both mediation and a reframing of conditions such as old and new, transport and arrival, commerce and housing. The fold can then be used both as a formal device and as a way of projecting new social organizations into an existing urban environment.

As we near the end of one era and are about to enter a new one, the idea of the fold presents an opportunity to reassess the entire idea of a static urbanism that deals with objects rather than events. In a media age, static objects are no longer as meaningful as time events; now the temporal dimension of the present becomes an important aspect of the past and the future.

This essay was originally published in **Unfolding Frankfurt** (Berlin: Ernst & Sohn, 1991).

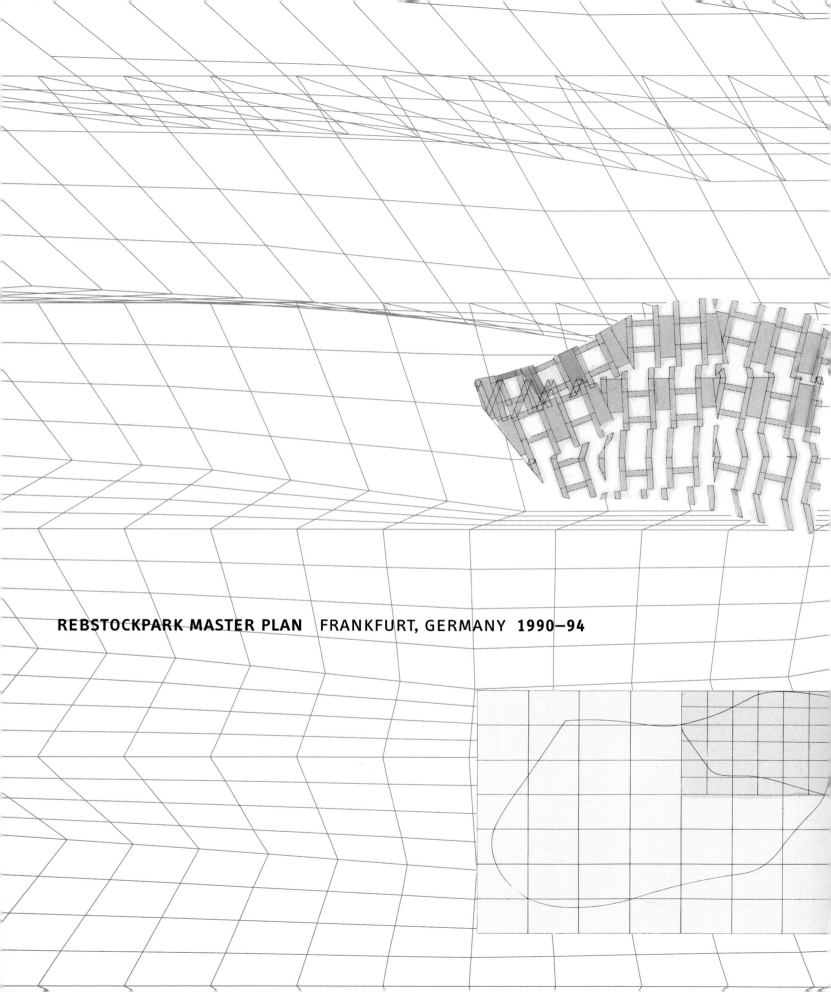

REBSTOCKPARK MASTER PLAN FRANKFURT, GERMANY 1990–94

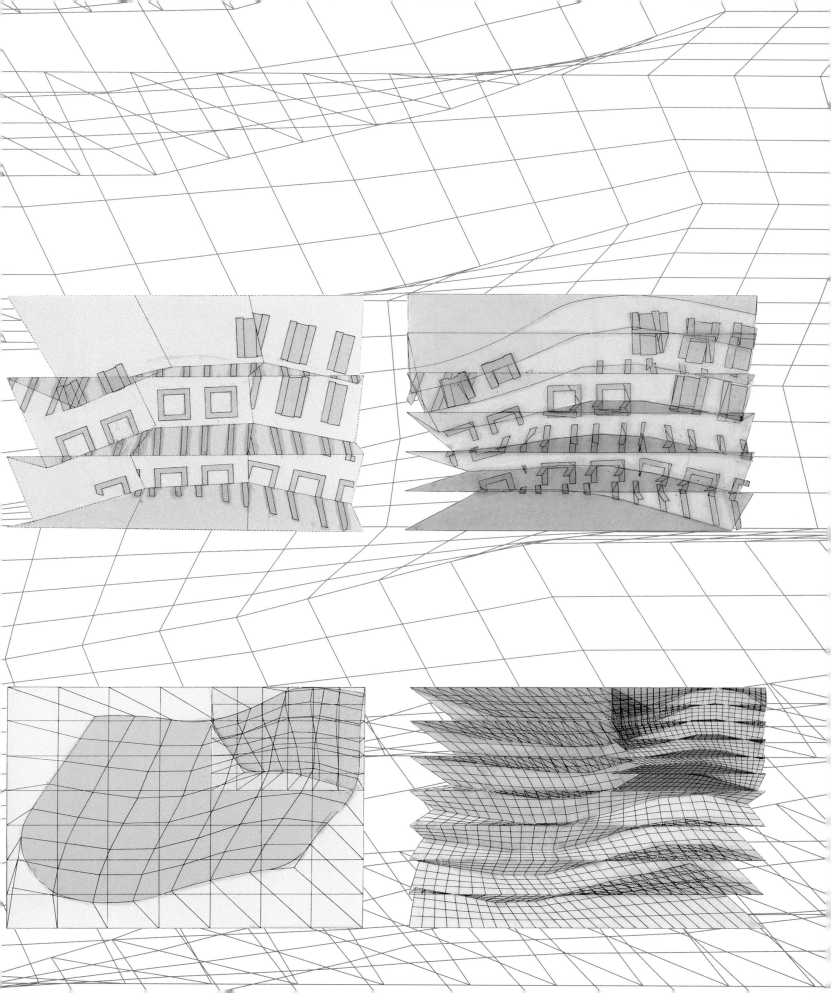

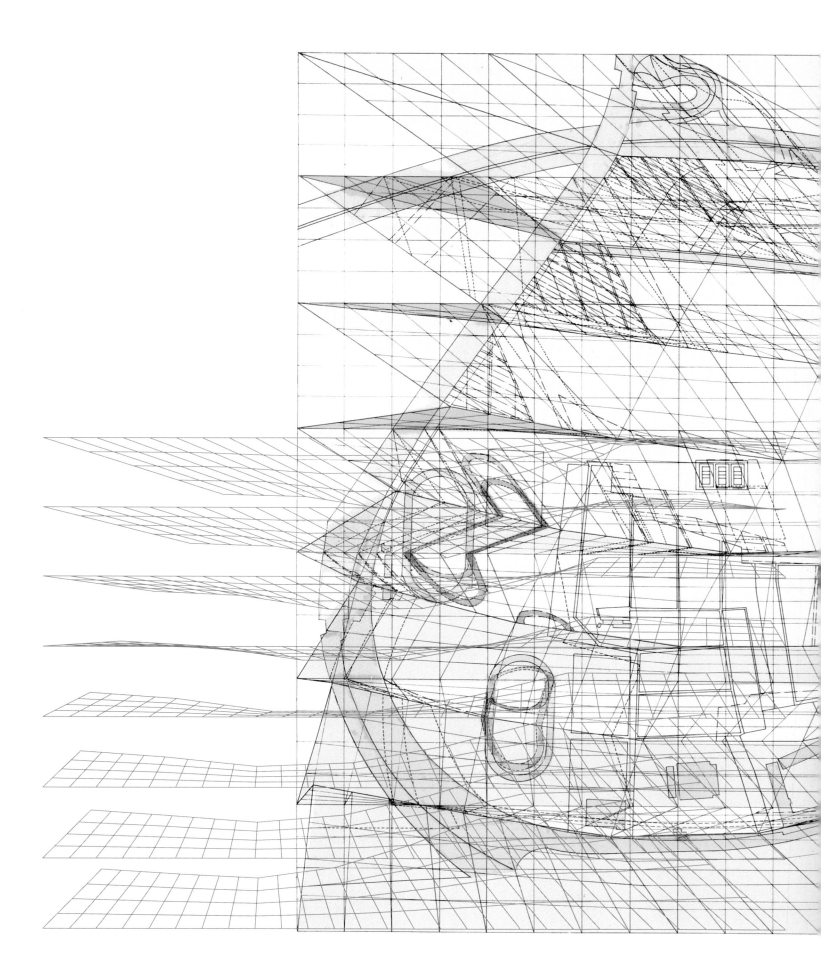

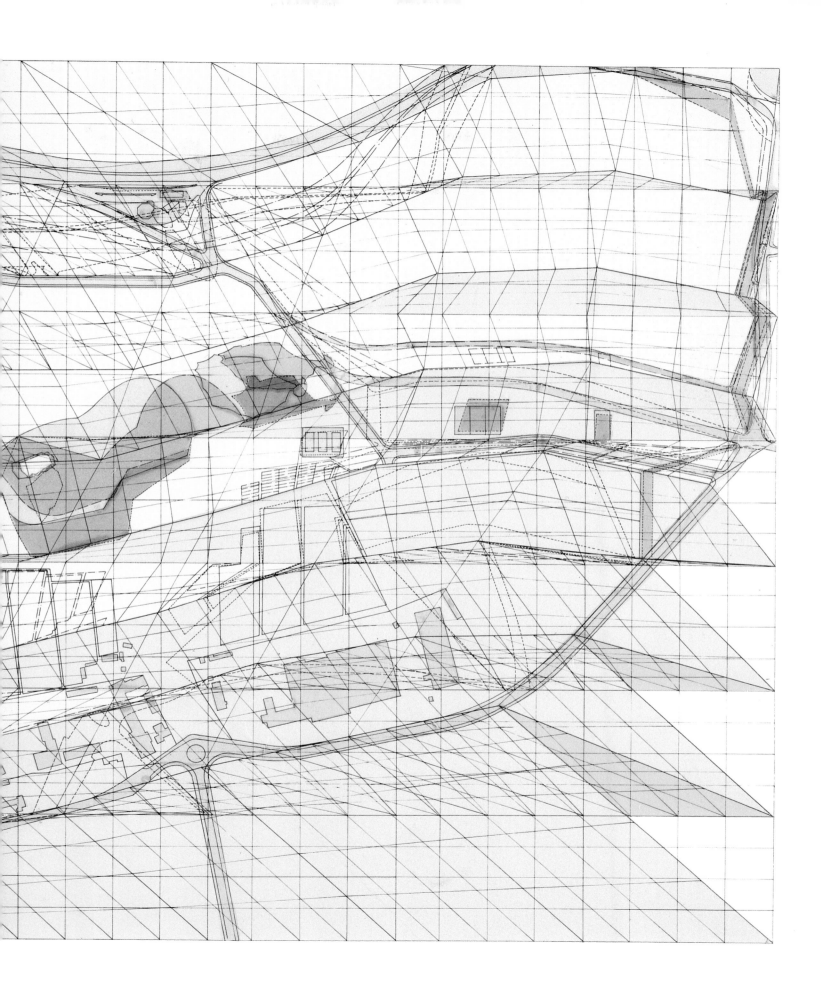

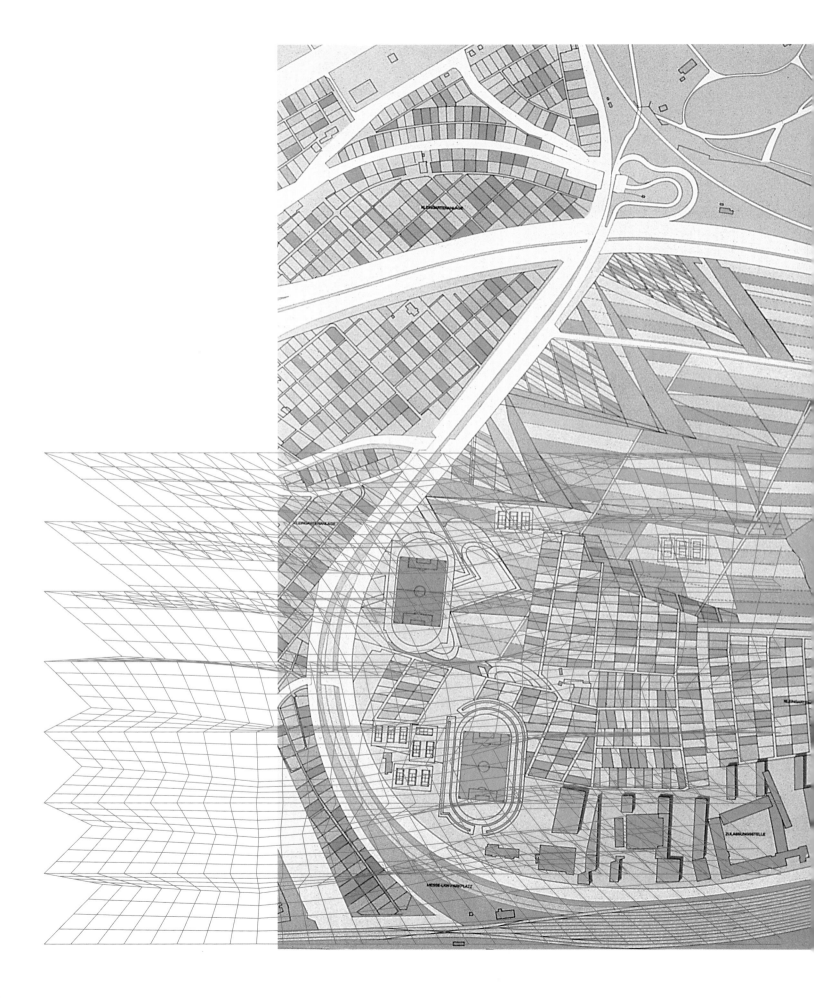

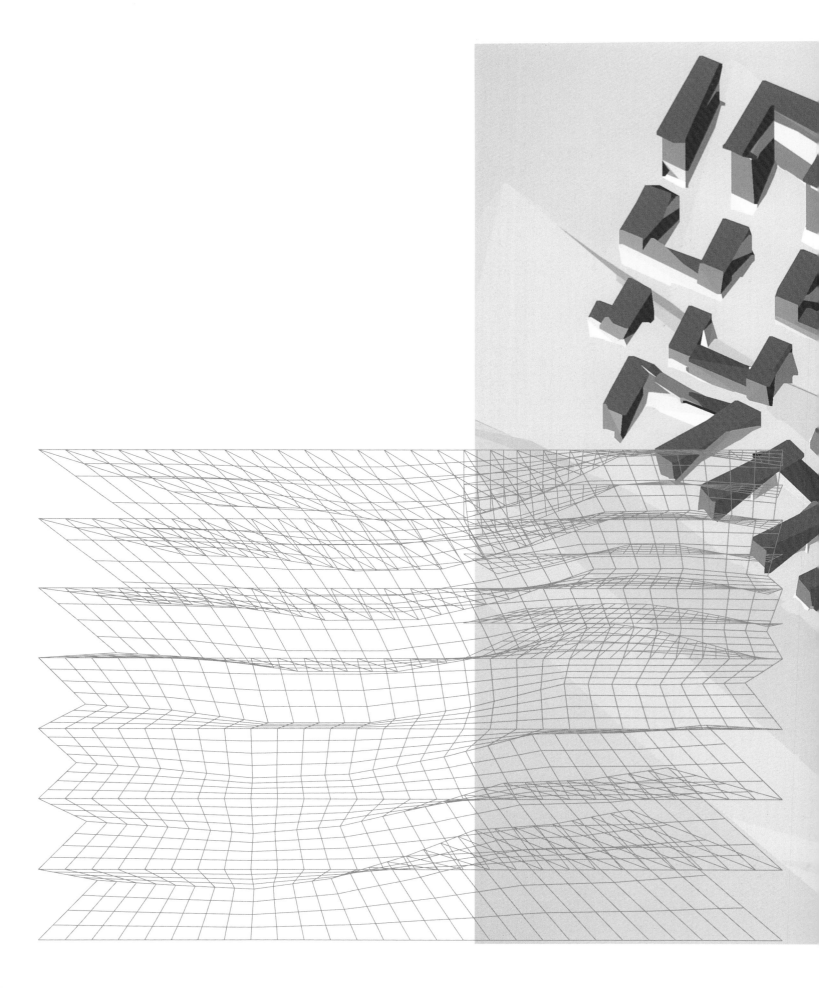

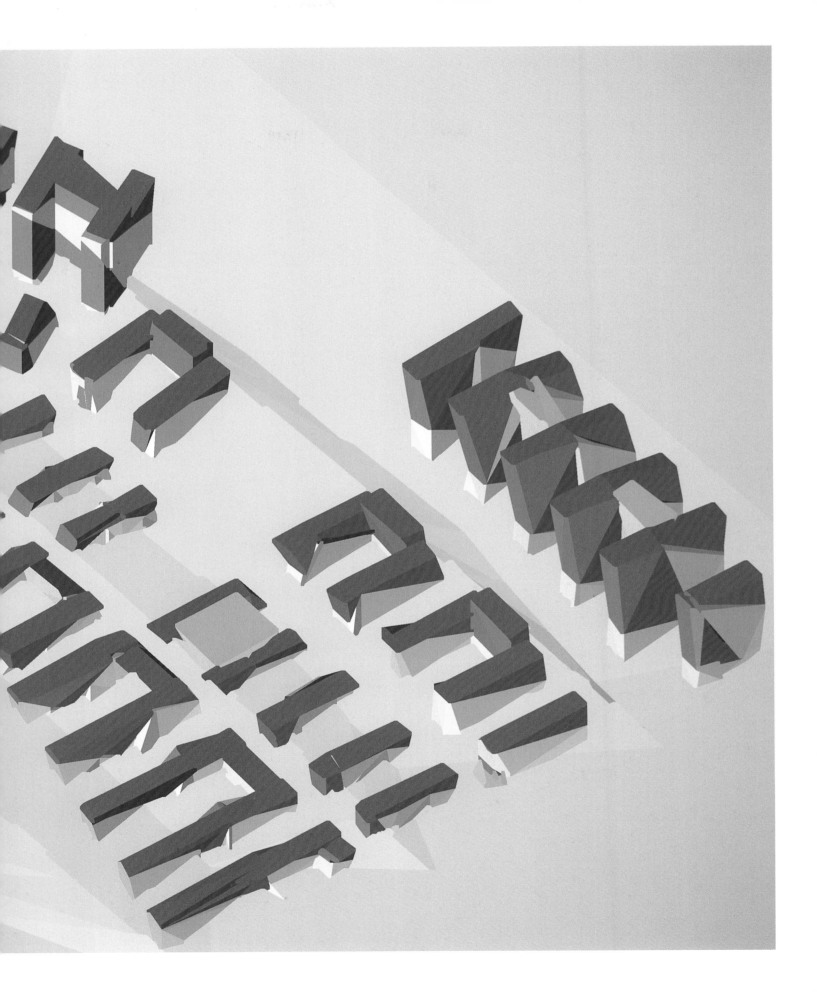

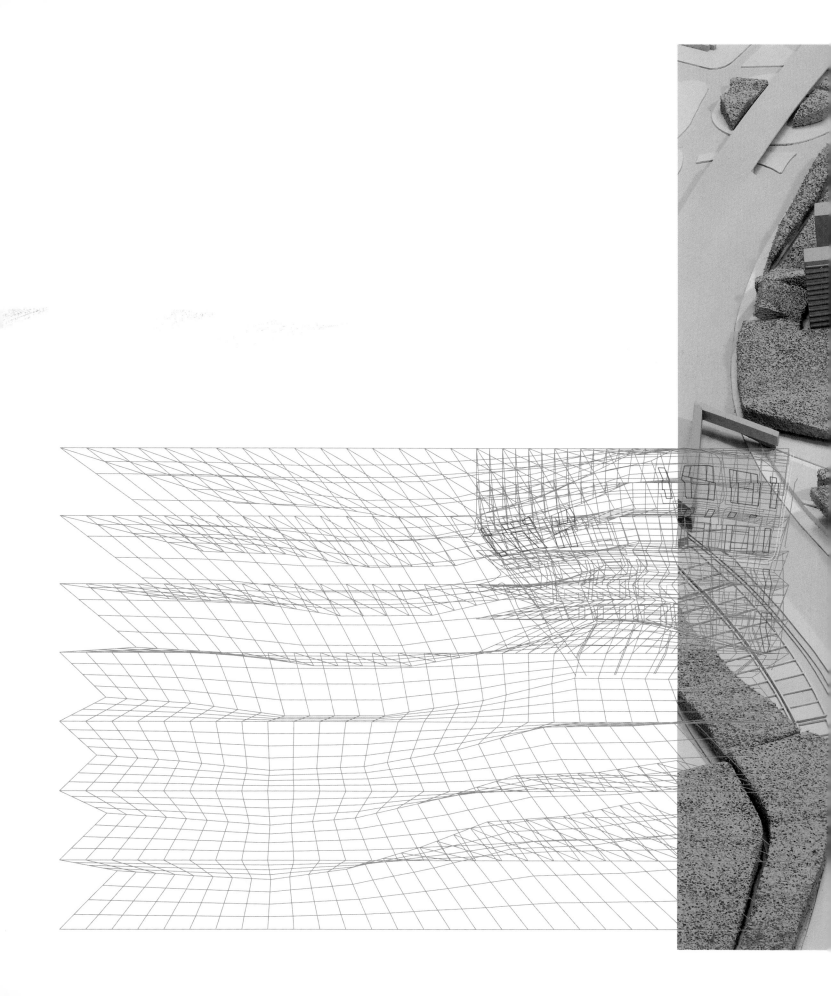

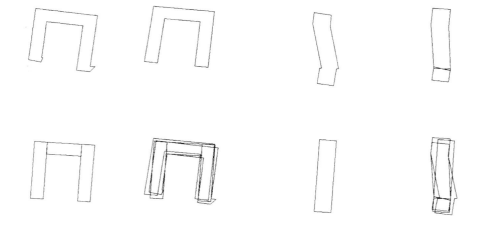

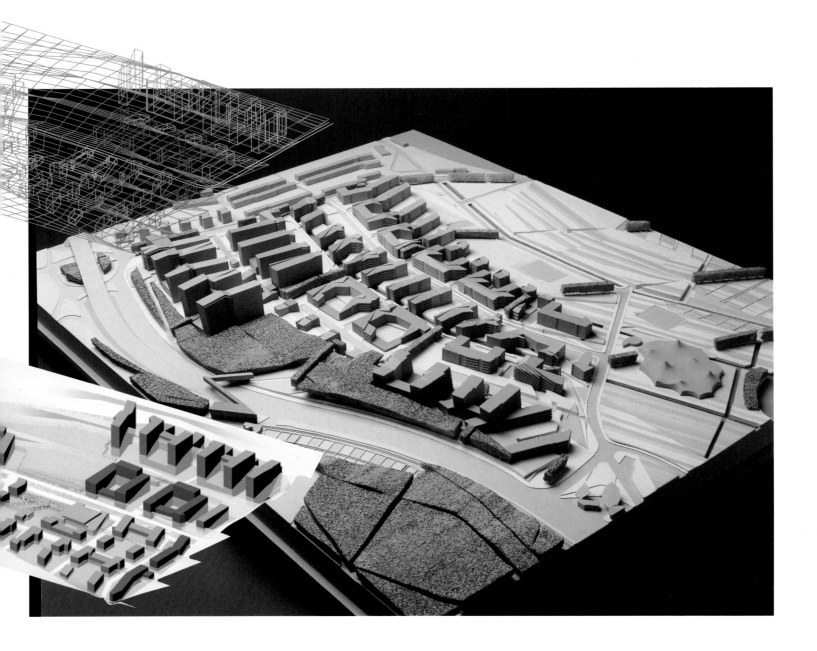

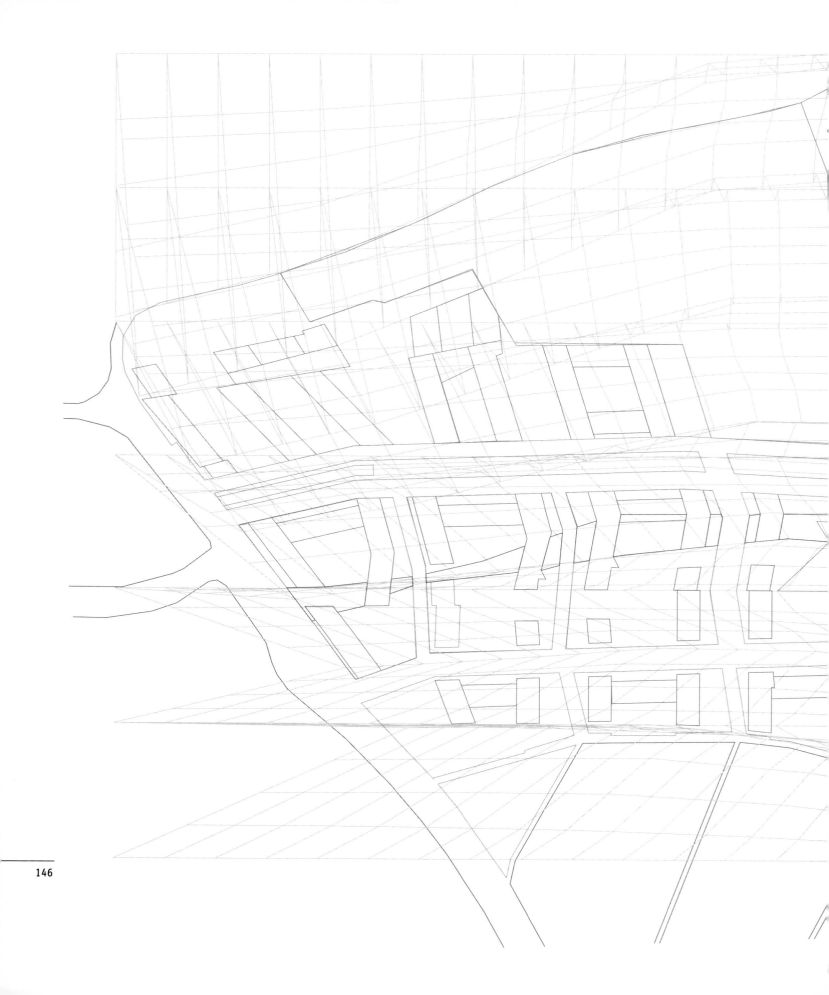

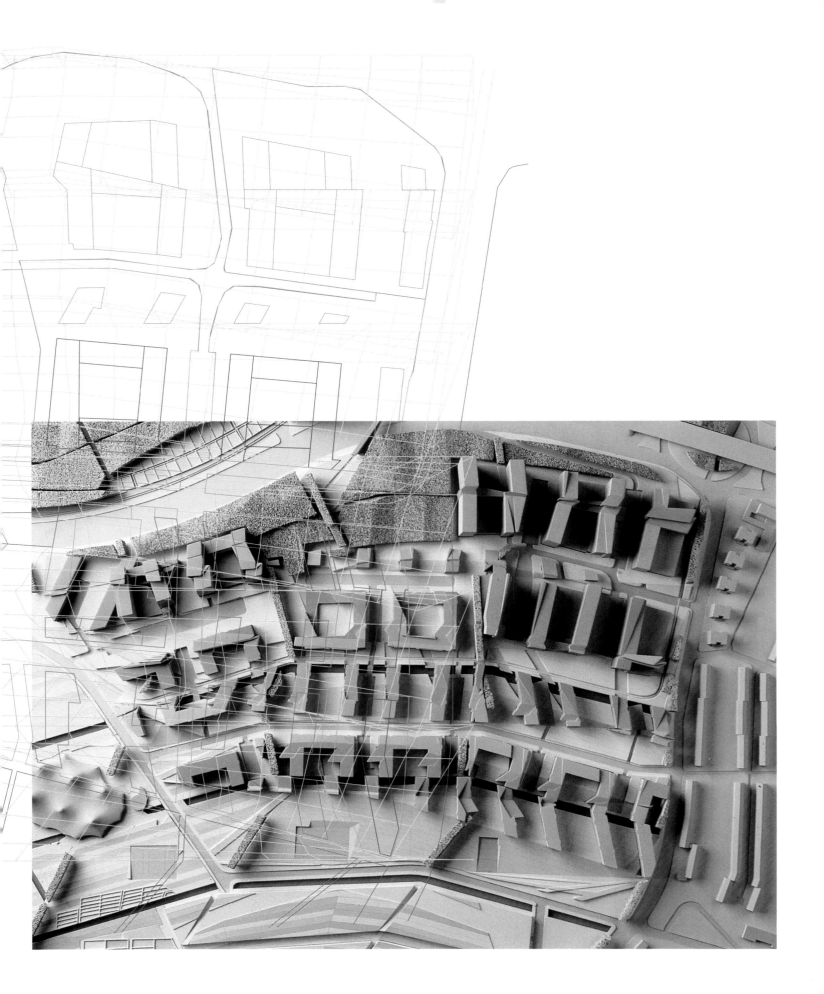

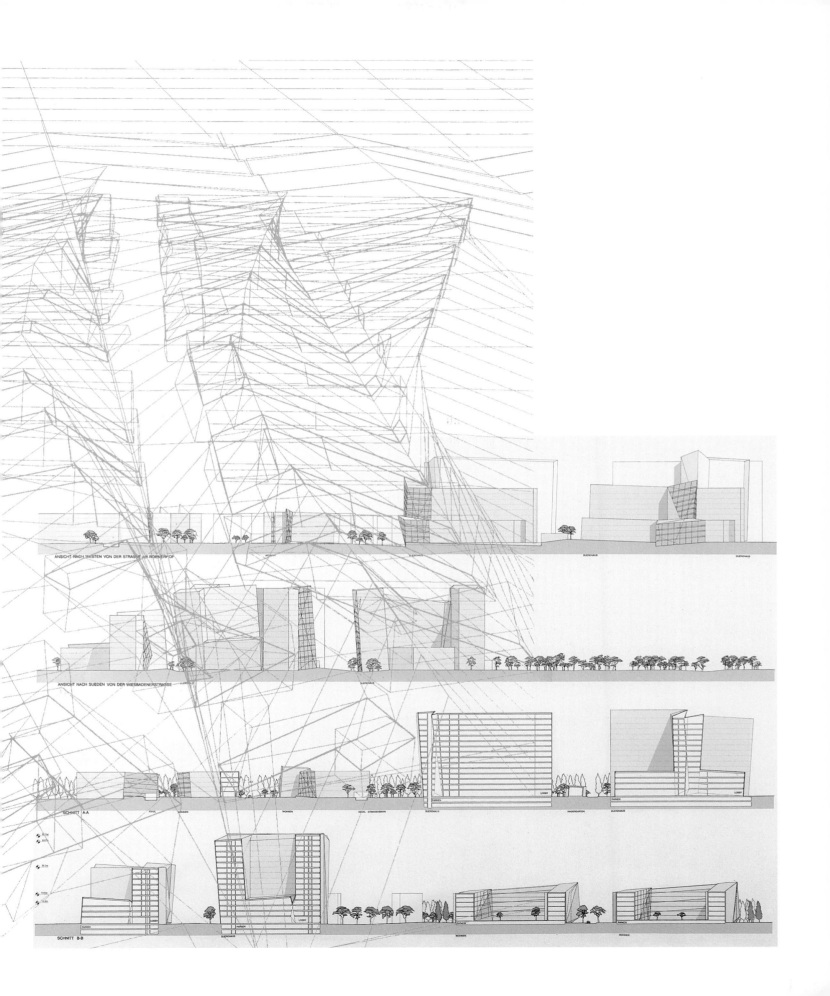

ANSICHT NACH WESTEN VON DER STRASSE AM ROEMERHOF

ANSICHT NACH SUEDEN VON DER WIESBADENERSTRASSE

SCHNITT A-A

SCHNITT B-B

Perplications: On the Space and Time of Rebstockpark

John Rajchman

Nothing is more disturbing than the incessant movements of what seems immobile.
—Gilles Deleuze, *Pourparlers*

It can happen, as in the baroque, that an architectural invention is enveloped in a larger event, implicated in a larger question that arises in our space, complicating it and our vision of it. A formal trait in architecture may then become part of the crystallization of something unknown that is knocking at the door, something unforeseen that we can only experiment with or play with in our seeing, our thinking, our creations.

Peter Eisenman's proposal for Rebstockpark, a residential and commercial development on a 250-acre site on the outskirts of Frankfurt, is about *the fold* – the folding of architectural and urban space and the folding of that space into others. The fold is more than a technical device: it is the central Idea, or Question, of the project. But then, what is a question – what is "the Question" – in architecture?

"Folding" is the name that Eisenman gives to the central formal technique employed in the generation of the design, and in this respect it plays a role analogous to that of the superpositioning of the L grid in earlier works. The nature and the scale of the project, however, allow Eisenman to think in urbanistic terms. In Rebstockpark he wants to depart from the urban contextualism that rejected the modernist isolated point block or linear slab and made the perimeter block the basic unit of postmodernism. In

"folding" the Rebstock plot, Eisenman hopes to "index" the complexities in urban space that have unfolded since the war, and that contextualism has been unable to treat.

The starting point for the folding transformations is an imagined *Siedlung* in the prewar style of Ernst May – the once revolutionary style that supplanted the perimeter housing that the late 18th and early 19th centuries had carved out of the city and what is now seen as its rather corrosive effects on the urban fabric. The formal transformation then consists in successively putting this imagined design through the net of a folding operation derived from a modified version of a René Thom butterfly net. This "folding" of the complex is meant to introduce another sense of space and time within the urban landscape than that of the revolutionary tabula rasa of the modern or the kitsch, sentimental context of the postmodern.

But this is not the only sense in which the Rebstock project is a project of "the fold." Rebstockpark is folded in many senses and many times over – many things are implicated in it or implied by it. To explicate what it implies, or to unfold what is implicit in it, one must unravel the general questions of space, time, vision, technology, and architecture that its Idea involves. For, in architecture as elsewhere, an Idea is never exhaustively or integrally realized in a single work; in any given case, there are always "complications." And that is why, as Leibniz knew, in explicating something it is always difficult to know where to begin and how to end.

Rebstockpark is then about folding in architecture. But what is the fold, and what is it to fold? Gilles Deleuze, in his philosophy and his reading of the history of philosophy, has developed perhaps the most elaborate conception of folds and foldings, which he sets forth in *Le pli*. The book is a study of Leibniz and the baroque, and it ends with these words: "What has changed is the organization of the house and its nature. . . . We discover new ways of folding . . . but we remain Leibnizian since it is always a question of folding, unfolding, refolding."[1]

One may say that *Le pli* is Deleuze's most architectural book, for it envisages Leibniz's philosophy as a great baroque edifice and supposes that his philosophy formulates the ideas of such edifices: the idea of folds endlessly passing over into other folds, folding into folding to infinity. Yet in terms of the new ways of "folding, unfolding, refolding" that *we* continue today, Deleuze discusses *l'informe* in music, painting, and sculpture but makes no reference to contemporary architecture. We may thus regard the "folding" of Rebstockpark as Eisenman's attempt to take up the question about contemporary architecture and urbanism that these last sentences implicitly raise, discovering thereby something unnoticed, implicated all along in his own work and thought: as Deleuze invents a new philosophy of the *informe* or an *informel* art of thinking, so with Rebstockpark Eisenman invents an architecture of the *informe*, or an *informel* way of building and designing.

INTENSIVE READING

The Rebstock project may then be taken as a reading – an intensive reading – of *Le pli*, and *Le pli* of it. What Deleuze calls an "intensive reading" is not an internal formal reading or an external contextual one but rather an experimental encounter. An intensive reading releases unnoticed "complicities" between two spaces that remain divergent and singular or common "implications" between two things that remain "differently" folded or constitut-

ed. One example is the use that Deleuze himself makes of the passage from Bernard Malamud's *The Fixer,* which serves as an exergue for his book on the practical philosophy of Spinoza, in which an old Russian Jew explains before an Inquisition authority that he read a few pages of Spinoza's *Ethics* and then "kept on going as though there were a whirlwind at my back."[2] This "whirlwind" becomes important for Deleuze's conception of Spinoza as a "practical philosopher" and for his concept of the intensive encounter in Spinoza's philosophy. In discussing the fold, Deleuze uses the term again to describe the sort of "multilinear ensemble" through which, by intensive encounter, philosophy connects with history and with something like architecture: such foldings of philosophy and architecture as *Le pli* and Rebstockpark into one another "would be like the detours of a movement that occupies the space in the manner of a whirlwind, with the possibility of emerging at any given point."[3]

PLICA EX PLICA

Deleuze explains that the arts of the *informe* are about two things: textures and folded forms. The baroque invents one possibility of fold and texture: there are the textures through which matter becomes "material" and the enfoldings of the soul through which form becomes "force." In the baroque, as in Leibniz, the metaphysics of formed matter is replaced by a metaphysics of materials "expressing" forces. The baroque thus opens, without prefiguring, possibilities of texture and fold taken up in other ways by Mallarmé and Heidegger. For example, Deleuze finds that the release of garment folds from the contours of the body shown in baroque painting and sculpture is unexpectedly continued in a different way in the mad theory of veils proposed by Clérambault, the French psychiatrist whom Jacques Lacan (who maintained a special affinity with the baroque) took as his master.[4]

But there is also a linguistic point: the words belonging to the texture and the fold family have a philosophical use and lineage for the weaving or *plex-* words (like *complexity* or *perplexity*), and the folding or *plic-* words (like *complication* or *implication*) define, in modern European

1 Gilles Deleuze, **Le pli: Leibniz et le baroque** (Paris: Minuit, 1988), 188.

2 Gilles Deleuze, **Spinoza: Practical Philosophy** (San Francisco: City Lights, 1988).

3 Gilles Deleuze, **Pourparlers** (Paris: Minuit, 1990), 219.

4 On Lacan and Clérambault's veils, see Joan Copjec, "The Sartorial Superego," **October** 50 (fall 1989); on Lacan and baroque vision, see Jacques Lacan, **Encore, 1972–1973** (Paris: Seuil, 1975), 95ff., and Christine Buci-Glucksmann, **La folie du voir** (Paris: Galilée, 1987).

languages, a family whose members include terms like *imply* and *explain* with important places in the philosophical lexicon. Indeed, the last words of Deleuze's book might be read as saying, "We are still implicating, explicating, replicating." But there is one member of this family – whose lineage goes back to a Latin "enfolding" of the Greek and thus to the Greek or dialectical fold – of which Deleuze is fond above all others, and through whose eyes he sees all the others: the word *multiple*. Thus on the first page of his book Deleuze declares: "The multiple is not only what has many parts, but what is folded in many ways."[5]

A defining principle of Deleuze's own philosophy is that the Multiple comes first, before the One. In this sense, states of affairs are never unities or totalities but rather "multiplicities" in which have arisen foci of unification or centers of totalization. In such multiplicities what counts is not the terms or the elements but what is in between them or their disparities; and to extract the ideas that a multiplicity "enfolds" is to "unfold" it, tracing the lines of which it is composed. Multiplicity thus involves a peculiar type of com-plexity – a complexity in divergence – where it is not a matter of finding the unity of a manifold but, on the contrary, of seeing unity only as a holding together of a prior or virtual dispersion. Complexity thus does not consist in the One that is said in many ways, but rather in the fact that each thing may always diverge, or fold, onto others, as in the ever-forking paths in Borges's fabled garden. A "multiple" fabric is such that one can never completely unfold or definitively explicate it, since to unfold or explicate it would only fold or "complicate" it again. Thus, while it may be said that for Deleuze there are folds everywhere, the fold is not a universal design or model; and indeed no two things are folded in just the same way. The multiple is thus not fragments or ruins supposing a lost or absent unity any more than its incessant divergence is a dismemberment of some original organism.

In this image of complexity-in-divergence and the multiplex fabric, we may discern one complicity between the Deleuzian and Eisenmanian folds: the Idea of a folding together, or complication, which does not reduce to relations among elements in a space-time parameter but which supposes a strange invisible groundless depth from which irrupts something that creates its own space and time. By reference to such "intensive" complexity, the two attempt to depart at once from Cartesian space and Aristotelian place. As Deleuze puts it, "I don't like points. *Faire le point* [to conclude] seems stupid to me. It is not the line that is between two points, but the point that is at the intersection of several lines."[6]

PERPLICATION

Deleuze, of course, is not the first to raise the question of complexity in architecture or the first to connect it to mannerism and the baroque. On the contrary such discussion itself belongs to an entangled historical nexus, which includes, in the first generation of the Frankfurt School, Walter Benjamin's study of the baroque *Trauerspiel,* to which Deleuze returns in *Le pli.* But more important for Peter Eisenman's background, and for his generation, are two authors to whom Deleuze does not refer: Robert Venturi and Colin Rowe. Deleuze not only has a different view of "manners" from these authors – not a mannered decoration attached to an essential shed or habitation, but rather manners detaching themselves from a habitation no longer seen as essential, something like the flowing folds of baroque garb that detach themselves from the body – but he also starts from a different conception of "complexity" itself. His is not Venturi's notion of a contradictory or "difficult" whole; it is not Rowe's image of cubist collage and gestalt perception. For the first reduces complexity to the totality and simplicity of compositional elements, and the second reduces depth to the simultaneity of figure and ground. Thus they eliminate what makes complexity multiple and divergent and what makes depth intensive and ungrounded. They assume a bounded or framed space in which discrete elements may be associated with one another, more or less ambiguously; and so they subordinate diversity to unity, rather than seeing unity as a contingent operation holding together a potential divergence. That is why their thought leads to the sort of liberal-minded empiricist "toleration of ambiguity" that they oppose to the revolutionary-minded rationalist promise of a new order. By contrast, Deleuze's concep-

5 Deleuze, **Le pli**, 5.

6 Deleuze, **Pourparlers**.

tion of complexity-in-divergence leads to the Question; it leads to the practical ethic of not being unworthy of what is disturbing the spaces we inhabit – of this Other who is knocking at our door. It involves a notion of "distance" or "distantiation," which allows Deleuze to find something baroque in constructivism, as well as in Foucault's idea that the only sort of perplexity worth pursuing is the one that takes us from ourselves. Deleuze thus speaks not only of implication, explication, and replication but also of what, in *Différence et répétition*, he calls "perplication" – a folding through or folding across.[7]

"Perplications" are those "cross-foldings" that introduce a creative distantiation into the midst of things. Such distance is the holding apart – what Deleuze calls the "disparation" – of a space that opens in it the chance of a "complex" repetition (not restricted to the imitation of a given model, origin, or end) or a "free" difference or divergence (not subordinated to fixed analogies or categorical identities). Perplications are thus what allows one to trace the diagonal lines in a fabric that cut across it so as to fold it again. They are the times of "the question," for it is just when a question comes into a space that the space discovers its free complexity; and conversely, when a space freely complicates itself it always opens itself to question. This perplexing sort of complication is thus not a matter of resolving a contradiction, as with Venturi, but rather of what Deleuze calls "vicediction" or the weaving together of a multiplicity. It is concerned with a kind of depth that is not a ground, as with Rowe, but rather the "groundless" depth of an intensive space in the extensive one that includes or frames it. Perplications are thus the foldings that expose an intensive multiple complexity in the fabric of things rather than a contradictory framed one; they unearth "within" a space the complications that take the space "outside" itself, or its frame, and fold it again. For Deleuze this deep or groundless complexity is always *virtual* – disparation is always a virtuality in a space, a sort of potential for free self-complication. But such virtuality cannot be a *dynamis* any more than such actuality can be

an *energeia;* for otherwise complexity would be reduced to the unity of pregiven origins and ends. "Intensity" is rather a nondynamic energy; and actuality always occurs in the midst of things, just as virtuality is always to be found in their intervals. Thus the virtual space that a line of actuality exposes in a fabric is not at all a possibility or a design to be integrally realized within a fixed frame, but rather the movement of a question that opens onto new, uncharted directions.[8] That is why the times of perplication that hold a space apart are times of a peculiar sort – not times of the instantiation of eternal Forms, not times of the continuation of traditional customs, but the "untimely" moments that redistribute what has gone before while opening up what may yet come.

In such perplicational terms one may then read Eisenman's motto, reported by Tadao Ando: "In order to get . . . to a place, you have to . . . blow it apart . . . you have to look inside it and find the seeds of the new."[9] One must disparate a space or blow it apart to find the complexity of which it is capable; and conversely, the deep or intensive complexity of a space is shown in those moments that hold it apart, taking it out of itself, so that it can be folded anew. In Eisenman's words: one must make "present" in a space its implicit "weakness" or its "potential for reframing." The principles of his perplication are then that there is no space and no place that is not somewhat "weak" in this sense; and that weakness is always imperceptible, prior to the point of view that one normally has on the space or the place. Thus where architectural or urban vision for Venturi and Rowe remains a matter of discovering an imperceptible unity in a perceptible diversity of elements, in the Rebstock project it becomes a matter of "indexing" an imperceptible disparation in what presents itself as a perceptual totality.

THE REBSTOCK FOLD

What then is an "architecture of the *informe*"? One of Eisenman's words for it is "excess." An architecture of

7 Gilles Deleuze, **Différence et répétition** (Paris: Presses Universitaires de France, 1968), 324–30, 359–60.

8 Deleuze proposes the terms **virtual** and **virtuality** in a special way. With these terms he is not referring to what architectural criticism calls "virtual space" or what Rowe also terms "illusionism" in architecture. Nor is what Deleuze calls "virtual" to be confused with what Silicon Valley has decided to call "virtual reality," even though it is part of Deleuze's view that virtuality, unlike possibility, is always real. Perhaps the closest term in Peter Eisenman's own idiom would be "immanence." Deleuze introduces his sense of the virtual in his **Bergsonism** (New York: Zone Books, 1988), 96–103, distinguishing it from the possible. "Virtuality" is not the "possibility" of something that might be "realized"; it is already real, and it does not stand in a representational or mimetic relation to what "actualizes" it. Rather, what is virtual is always a "multiplicity"; and it is actualized through a free or creative "divergence." This theme is further elaborated in **Différence et répétition** (269–76) in relation to Leibniz, before being taken up again in **Le pli**. In that work it is also linked to "perplication"; the "perplication of the Idea" is defined as its "problematic character and the reality of the virtual that it represents" (324).

9 **Tadao Ando: The Yale Studio and Current Works** (New York: Rizzoli, 1989), 19.

the *informe* is one that exposes its containing grid as "constraining" or "framing" something that is always *exceeding* it, surpassing it, or overflowing it. The grid has always been a central element in Eisenman's architecture and architectural discourse,[10] and in the Rebstock project, it does not disappear; it is not, and cannot be, abolished. The strategy is rather to introduce something into – or more precisely, to find something "implicated in" – the gridded space, which it cannot contain, which leaks or spills out from it, linking it to the outside. In this way the grid becomes only a dimension of the folding of the space in which it figures.

Eisenman uses the term *frame* to discuss the grid, as that term has been elaborated by Jacques Derrida, notably in his work on "the truth in painting": much as Derrida says that the dream of a completely unframed space is vain (and that "deconstruction" is not that dream), so one might say that there is no such thing as gridless architecture. Yet there exists a "complexity," or a potential for folding, that is not contained within any frame or grid; on the contrary, a frame or grid only exists within a larger virtual complexity that exceeds it. What is thus implicit in a space, which it cannot frame, may at any point or moment break out of it and cause it to be reframed. "Reframing," in other words, is a virtuality in all "framed" complexities.

For Eisenman, in the case of architecture this means that there exists something that exceeds Vitruvian commodity, firmness, and delight – something that cannot be simply read as the adequation of Form to structure, site, or function but that allows Form to detach itself from such determinants and freely fold: namely the intensity that releases an "excess" that takes a space outside its bounds or through which it becomes "beside itself." The condition of the *informe* would then be that of this intensive space that seems to break out of the intervals of the articulating elements of the bounded space and the traditional place in which it occurs with a free, smooth "rhizomatic" energy that exceeds the framing of site, plan, and program.

This cluster of ideas is then what distinguishes the folding of Rebstockpark from Eisenman's earlier attempts at superposition. Superposition still preserves the simultaneity

of figure and ground, and so does not yet find or invent a groundless, smooth depth. In Rebstock, Eisenman starts to work instead with a type of com-plication that is no longer a matter of linear juxtaposition in an empty space or "canvas" but rather assumes the guise of a great "transmorphogenic" irruption in three-dimensional space. Rebstock is a smooth, folded space rather than a striated, collaged one and so no longer appears rectilinear or Cartesian. Thus the Idea of the project (as distinct from its program or plan) passes from a punctual dislocation of a Place to a multilinear smoothing out of a Site, and from notions of trace and archaeology to notions of envelopment and actuality – to the attempt to release new points of view or readings of the "context" that would be imperceptibly implicit in it.

In Rebstockpark, the housing and commercial units no longer figure as discrete extrusions out of a planar gridded space but appear to have been deformed through an intensive *intrusion* that seems to have come from nowhere and to take one elsewhere. They appear as though they were the remains of an irruption that had broken out of the ground and returned to it, suggesting that such a "catastrophic" occurrence might again arise anywhere in the calm solidity of things. The Rebstock fold is thus not only a figural fold as in origami – not a matter simply of folded figures within a free container or frame. Rather the container itself has been folded together, or complicated, with the figures. Rebstock is folding in three dimensions. Hence one is not dealing just with an urban "pattern"; rather the urban "fabric" on which the pattern is imprinted is folded along this line, becoming thereby more complex, more multiplex. The periphery of the plot thus ceases to be its defining edge and becomes instead one dimension of an uncentered folding movement that overtakes the site, pushing through and out of it like a sudden whirlwind.

Thus the units or their juxtaposition no longer define the spaces in between them as more or less filled voids. On the contrary, the space in between the units has come alive, for the "crease" of the fold intrudes from the midst of them. The crease line – an intrusive or fault line – now seems to differentiate or distribute the units in a noncontiguous continuity, where each unit becomes singular or

10 On the grid in Eisenman's early work see Rosalind Krauss, "Death of a Hermeneutic Phantom: Materialization of the Sign in the Work of Peter Eisenman," in **Peter Eisenman: Houses of Cards** (New York: Oxford University Press, 1987). See also her "Grids," in **The Originality of the Avant-Garde and Other Modernist Myths** (Cambridge, Mass.: MIT Press, 1985); this book also includes two original essays on the index.

disparate, even though it "coimplies" the others along the line. The crease is thus not a coordinating, containing, or directional line – it does not resolve an inner contradiction, establish a "difficult whole," or juxtapose figures as in a collage. It is rather a free, vicedictory line that instead of going from one point to another traces a multidimensional space, without fixed points of beginning and ending, of which one can never be quite sure where it has come from or where it is going.

The Rebstock fold is thus an intensive line, energetic without being dynamic, dimensional without being directional. But it is also a perplicational or perpletic line. It does not follow the "strong" determinations of the program, structure, or site alone but tends at the same time to take one "outside" them. For while in functional terms the crease of the fold is the connecting space between the various activities to be carried on in the modules, in architectural terms it offers the sense of the sudden emergence in the site and its activities of another free space that escapes them. It has the look of the arrested moment of an irruption whose cause is unknown or external to the site and its uses and the feel of an explosive energy that seems to come from somewhere else. Thus the fold distances one from one's habitual perception or reading of the space, as if to transport one to this "elsewhere" where things go off in unimagined directions or are folded again.

Because Rebstock is in this way folding in three dimensions, its flowing movement cannot be wholly captured in a figure/ground plan. The plan is only one point of view, one aperture or opening onto a movement that, since it is "smooth," cannot be "drawn" as in a coordinated projection. Indeed Eisenman thinks that the whole relation to projective drawing changes. Folding cannot be projected from a combination of plan and section but requires a topographical model and involves another kind of sign: the index. In this case the proverbial index finger points to something unseen, to a virtual movement that would not destroy the site but would "reframe" it, setting it off in other directions. For the deep complexity of a site is always "implicit" – imperceptible in space, virtual in time. That is why to discover it one must "blow the place apart." In Deleuze's idiom, one might say that the index

points to something that cannot be "mapped" but only "diagrammed" – the intensive space within the extensive one or the smooth space within the striated.

What Eisenman calls weak urbanism may then be defined as the attempt to provide for a moment of urban "envelopment" in urban development or to provide a place for urban diagrammatization within the space of urban planning. The idea of the Rebstock fold is to become this surface on which urban events would be inscribed with an intensive actuality. It thus involves a particular point of view on the city.

LIGHT REGIMES

One can imagine different points of view or perspectives on the city: that of the cartographic photo from the plane above, which gives the impression of a god's-eye view; that of someone who knows his own district or neighborhood so well that he can see the whole city refracted in it; or that of the flâneur – the perspective of the Baudelairean walk or the situationist *dérive* (drift). Implicit in Deleuze is another idea: the point of view of the implications and perplications of the city. With this conception of complexity goes an art of seeing.

Folding and seeing, complexity and clarity, perplexity and illumination – it has long been asked how these go together. In Neoplatonism, the One is a Lumens Divinis, faintly shining through the complications in everything, always waiting to be read again. Via Gershom Scholem, one can find something of this tradition in Walter Benjamin's account of baroque allegory. But in the Deleuzian multiplex, complexity is such that things can never be folded back to a first seeing, to a single source or "emanation" of Light. Rather than a god's-eye view on everything, there are only new points of view always arising everywhere, complicating things again. For light is not One but multiple, and one must always speak of *les lumières*. Illumination or clarification is thus never a complete reduction of complexity to obtain an uncomplicated or unfolded planar surface or transparency. On the contrary, in the first instance, it is the multiple complications in things that illuminate or clarify, redistributing what may be visible and what obscure.

Thus, according to Deleuze, it is just when, in Leibniz and the baroque, space becomes "folded" or acquires the sort of "texture" that can express force that there is a dual departure at once from Cartesian logic and Cartesian optics – from the regime of the "clear and distinct." There arises another "regime of light" in which things can be inseparable or continuous even though they are "distinct" and in which what is "clear" or "clarified" is only a region within a larger darkness or obscurity, as when the figures emerge from a "dark background" in the baroque painting of Tintoretto or El Greco. Thus the windowless monads illuminate or clarify only singular districts in the dark complexities of the world that is expressed in them; and Leibniz becomes a "perspectivist" philosopher for a world that has lost its center or can no longer be illuminated by the Sun of the Good.

But our own *informel* foldings involve no less a type of seeing or perspectivism, for one can never see the deep intensity or virtual complexity of a space without changing one's point of view on it. To inhabit the intervals or disparities of a city, tracing a diagonal line in its fabric, is to see the city as never before: to see something not given to be seen, not already "there." Divergences are what permit "subjective" points of view or perspectives and not "subjective" views of an unchanging, uncomplicated space that permit perspectival variation. That is why Deleuze says that the "there is" of light is not given by the subject or his field of vision; on the contrary, the subject and his visual field always depend on the light that there is. For illumination or enlightenment always comes from the midst or intervals of things; and the disparation of a space is always a kind of illumination or enlightenment. It is as if, through the crevices of the city and the cracks of its edifices, light were always seeping in, illuminating the lines of its becoming other. In its intervals and imperceptible holes, *la ville* is thus always virtually *radieuse;* and that is why the free folding of its fabric is always illuminating.

DISPARATE VISION

The Rebstock fold implies a peculiar sort of architectural vision: an art of light and sight whose principle is not "less is more," but "more or less than what is there." Folding is an art of seeing something not seen, something not already "there." For the jumbled lines and tilted planes of the folding irruption, which deflect its surfaces onto its angular remnants, do not translate a free-flowing or transparent space. They do not possess even what Colin Rowe called "phenomenal transparency": they do not fit in a "pictorial" space where light is cast on a complex of clear and distinct forms for an independent eye standing outside their frame. Yet if Rebstock has a different feel from a free-flowing modern transparency, it is not achieved by enclosing the units and attaching to them a kitsch set of contextualizing or historicizing symbols. Rather the fold creates a different kind of "flow" – the flow of an energy that the bounded space seems to be impeding, that is spilling over into its surroundings, interrupting the calm narrative of its context and so opening new readings in it.

The heraldic and emblematic imagery of baroque and mannerist art presents visual enigmas that interconnect images and signs, seeing and reading. What Eisenman calls the index is not exactly such an allegory, yet it uncovers a complexity in things, a complication that is prior to what is given to be seen or read, or that lies "in between" the things that are seen or read: this free region where the visible and the readable are implicated in one another and the fabric folded anew. Thus, in Rebstock the eye is no longer directed, as in modernism, to an uncomplicated and unadorned space, where clarity is distinctness; it is no longer shown an "illumination" of structure and use so pure that all reading would be eliminated. But the eye is not shown a cluster of allusions to tradition, nor is its reading historicist. Rather Rebstock complicates the space in which forms might otherwise freely flow and so intrudes into its site, unfolding unnoticed implications. It works thus as an index that points to a diagrammatic rather than a programmatic or nostalgic reading of the site – an illuminating disparation in the midst of things.

The "vision" of modernism meant a *replacement* of what was already there; the "vision" of contextualism meant an *emplacement* with respect to what was already there. What Rebstock would give to be seen is rather a *displacement* or "unplacing" that would be free and complex, that would instigate without founding, that would open without prefiguring. It is just when vision becomes multiple, complicating, and "perspectival" in this way that Hermes becomes nomadic, inhabiting the intervals and the midst of things rather than carrying messages from one place – or one master – to another. No longer content simply to reestablish the "hermeneutic" places, sites, or contexts of messages, Hermes creates his own space, his own lines of flight or creative divergences, rather as *le pli* can refer to the envelope in which a message is sent – something, of course, that facsimile transmission would dispense with.

URBAN ELECTRONICS

Rebstockpark is to be the first thing one sees heading from the airport for downtown Frankfurt, now announced by the Helmut Jahn tower – a new gateway to the city. Once the home of a great critical-philosophical school, Frankfurt has become the finance capital and, afterward, a kind of "museum capital" of the *Wirtschaftswunder*, the German postwar economic "miracle," museum and capital having discovered a new type of interconnection and, with it, a new type of architecture.[11] Site of a former Luftwaffe airport, a tabula that was literally rasa by the war (and that neither client nor architect finds worth "recalling" in the project), the Rebstock plot is now, in the post- and post-postwar period, internationally noted for its proximity to the site of the annual Frankfurt Book Fair. One implication of the Rebstockpark fold is then the way in which it supplies a sort of contortionist vision of the whirl of this postindustrial capital of the *Wirtschaftswunder*.

Among the vectors that have transmogrified urban space, those of transport and transmission have performed a key role: in some sense it is the automobile and the airplane that killed or complexified the rational grids and the radial city of 19th-century industrialism. Such processes supply the starting point for the analyses of urbanist and philosopher Paul Virilio, who, like Eisenman, thinks that to understand the complexities of the city, we must depart from a "static urbanism" and view the city instead in terms of the movement, rhythm, speed, in a word the "timespaces," that the various modes of transport and transmission make possible.

Along such lines Virilio proposes to analyze the intrusion into the urban environment of a "timespace" rooted in electronics technology, spread out yet interconnected through the likes of facsimile transmission and closely tied to the finance capital with which the Rebstock development is linked in so many ways. The result is what Virilio calls "the overexposed city." But if this "overexposed" city is unlike the "collage" city brought about through the transformations of 19th-century industrialism, it is because its complexity is not so much that of a Lévi-Straussian bricolage of distinct elements as of a Deleuzian texture or interweaving of disparities. The overexposed city is an intensive or explosive city, not gridded – a city in which incessant "movement" is prior to the apparent immobility of traditional place or planned space.

Philosophers of science once debated what it meant to "see" electrons, and so whether such "theoretical entities" were real or only inferred. Today everyone tacitly counts them as real, because without ever seeing them, one nevertheless cannot but "inhabit" the space of what their ever miniaturized and transportable manipulation makes possible – a manipulation that is becoming ever more direct, interactive, or "live." Toward this space which "exposes" the city and to which it is "exposed," Virilio adopts the critical attitude of what he calls "nonstandard analysis." In the Rebstock project, Eisenman seems to adopt what might be called an attitude of perplectic analysis. For there is a sense, at once spatial and historical, in which the Rebstock site is "framed" by the railway and the highway lines that lead into the city, where museums now cluster about the old river Main, which the Franks eponymously crossed. By contrast, the electronic space in which we move and make moves "exposes" the city to something that can no longer be read as a structuring or framing network or seen through the materials and locations that realize it. For it is in itself invisible and unlocalizable; it no longer requires the sort of physical displacements that provided the sense of mobility and congestion captured in the progressivist and futurist imagination.

The energy of Rebstock is thus not a directional "dynamism" racing toward a sleek new future; rather it belongs to a sort of irruptive involution in space; and this multilinear nondirectional energy takes one out of the traditional

---

11 On the connection between contemporary museums and finance capital see Rosalind Krauss, "The Cultural Logic of the Late Capitalist Museum," **October** 54 (fall 1990); the problem of banking and finance plays an important role in the analysis of capitalism that Deleuze proposes in collaboration with Félix Guattari, as well as in a short text, "Postscriptum sur les sociétés de contrôle," in **Pourparlers**. It would seem timely to analyze along these lines the centrality of the museum as a type in contemporary architecture.

gridded city. Rebstock gives neither a futuristic nor a nostalgic sense of our electronic moment but an "actualistic" one. Its attitude toward the new electronic technologies is neither rejection nor nostalgia nor the manic embrace of a California cybercraze. It is rather an attitude of this perplexity of the multiple "elsewhere" that the technologies introduce into our ways of inhabiting spaces. Rebstock is not about the arrival of a new technological order any more than it illustrates the postmodernist sense that nothing can happen anymore, that all that will be already is, as though history had come to an end in the self-satisfaction of the health club or the shopping mall. It is rather about this implicating, explicating, replicating energy that is always escaping or exceeding the space and the locale in which it is implanted, introducing a distance that allows one to look back upon the gridded or collage city with the mixture of nostalgia and horror with which one once looked back *from* it to the country.

Perhaps one might thus speak of a new relation between architecture and technology. The Bauhaus sought to display in architecture the preelectronic industrial engineering that had made possible a new program of "rational" building and construction, artist and engineer joining in the new figure of the architectural *Gestalter*. But "postindustrial" electronic technology shows itself architecturally in a different manner: in terms of a free excess in formal variation that still remains compatible with structure and use and that is made possible by invisible means. It is shown in an exuberant detachment of form, in the sort of contortions between the random and the regular that electronic modeling makes possible. Thus from the Bauhaus aesthetic of geometric abstraction one passes to the electronic aesthetic of "free" abstraction, where an intensive line goes "all over," released from its subordination to the grid – a passage from formal juxtaposition to *informel* smoothing out, of the sort that Deleuze associates with Klee rather than Kandinsky, in the points, lines, and inflections of the Bauhaus painters.

METROPLEX

We thus inhabit the metroplex. There is no completely rational space, no completely adequate place, and the alternative between topia and utopia no longer defines our possibilities. That is why the Rebstock style is neither "international" nor "regional," "elitist" or "populist," but rather moves in a space in between. While it always remains "now-here," it seems to come from "nowhere," for, in the words of Deleuze, while there are folds everywhere, the fold is not a universal design. Rather, singular or new foldings somewhere in the social fabric provide the chance for the emergence of this *peuple à venir,* this "people-to-come," that is no longer identified by a rational space or an adequate place, of which Deleuze declares the architect always has need, even if he is not aware of it.

Deleuze presents the baroque as marking a moment when the collapse of the old heliocentric *cosmos,* where man imagined he had his place and his task, gives rise to a decentered perspectival *mundus,* where each monad has a particular point of view on the world it includes or expresses – the moment when the traditional separation into two different realms is replaced by a single edifice with two stories in which there is a "new harmony" between an enclosed interior and an inflected exterior. But our own "foldings" no longer transpire in such a baroque *mundus* any more than in an ancient *cosmos,* for "the organization of the house, and its nature" have changed. Our manners of coexistence can no longer be held together through the principle of the baroque house – the greatest or most complex variety in a single compossible world – for the world we inhabit is multiplex. We no longer have – we no longer need to have – the good cosmos or the best world, the illumination of the form of the good or the clarifications of the principles of the best. Our foldings, our own "mannerisms," have dispensed with the single best world, turning rather to the complicities and complexities of the disparation through which things diverge into others; our invention of new "manners" of being comes in response to events that disrupt our contextual frames, complicating things again, introducing new enfoldings, or free spaces of implication. From the good city and the best world we have passed to an intensive cityspace or metroplex, where we are no longer supposed to find the identity of context or of reason, of tradition or of eternity, but are instead free to practice an art of inhabiting the intervals where new foldings arise to take our forms of inhabitation in new and uncharted directions. And so, in the place of the cosmopolitan or universalist thinker, "citizen of the world," there arises a strange new ubiquitous nomadic community of *metroplexed* thinkers, perplectic inhabitants of our contemporary "chaosmos."

GAMES OF CHANCE

What then is "complexity," what is "the question" in architecture today? In the drama of philosophy, Deleuze finds the invention of various philosophical protagonists: there is Hume, the inquirer, or Kant, the judge at the tribunal of reason. In *Le pli* Leibniz figures as the defense attorney of God, a great inventor of "principles" in philosophy, a whole Jesuitical jurisprudence to account for the incessant emergence of perplexing cases. Leibniz was the genius of principles, and the principle of Leibnizian jurisprudence was inclusion in the best world that God selects, and that, in some sense, we ourselves are "inclined without being necessitated" to select, even though that means that some of us must be damned. Deleuze calls Leibnizian Principles "cries of reason" in the baroque world that theology seems to have deserted.

But as we today in our "post-Enlightenment" times find a multiple intensive complexity in things prior to simplicity and totality of compositional elements, the perplexing case – the question – acquires a positive capacity to reframe or re-create our principles, our jurisprudence itself; and there emerges a new type of player in the game of the complexities of thought. Deleuze sees Nietzsche as announcing a new protagonist in philosophy, one who starts to play the game in the new way as given by the two Whiteheadean principles that Deleuze makes his own: the abstract or the universal is not what explains but what itself must be explained; and the aim of the game is not to rediscover the eternal or the universal but to find the conditions under which something new may be created. In our folding, unfolding, and refolding, we no longer inhabit the two-story baroque house where, on the heights of the windowless walls of the interi-

or, would be heard the elevating reverberations of the cries of Beelzebub below. For complexity no longer occurs within a house governed by the principles of such an "elevating" illumination but rather becomes a matter of a multiplex play at once within and without the house – of this *pli*, this "folding," which is a matter of an inexplicable chance, prior to principles, prior to design, yet always virtual in them. The figure of our post-baroque or *informel* complexity is thus a player – the player of the new game of perplication.

It would seem that Eisenman tries to introduce just this sort of game into architecture and architectural discourse, for, anterior to yet inseparable from the requirements of the program and the site and the space of the drawing plan, he discovers the play of the idea or the question. Eisenman's architecture plays a game where chance becomes an inextricable part of design, and not something that design must master or eliminate – a game whose object is to maintain the play of chance within the space of design. Deleuze distinguishes two ways of playing the game of chance. Pascal, in his wager, exemplifies the bad way, where the game is played according to preexistent categorical rules that define probabilities and where one calculates gains and losses. The true player (like Nietzsche or Mallarmé) does not play the game in this way. Rather the table itself bursts open and becomes part of a larger, more complex game that always includes the possibility of new rules; and to play the game one must thus, in making each move, affirm all of chance at once. Thus a game of "nomadic" or "smooth" distributions replaces a game of categorical or striated ones; chance itself ceases to be tamed or hypothetical and becomes free and imperative. It is then this free multiplex game of chance that the Rebstock Fold tries to play in urban and architectural space.

The baroque fold, for Deleuze, is unlike the oriental fold, which weaves together or com-plicates empty and full spaces, voids and presences. For in the baroque, "holes" only indicate more subtle foldings, and the principle is that there are no voids, that everything is included in a single expressive continuum, as in the principle of the Leibnizian best that the greatest number of folds be fit within the same com-possible world. Thus Derrida once wrote that Leibniz's God, in selecting the best world, experiences nothing of the anxiety of the Jewish God, who must create out of nothing, out of the void; and that baroque plenitude is thus symptomatic of an avoidance of the "pure absence" that a Mallarmean sort of writing would suppose and that would be incompatible with anything like a "built visible *architecture* in its locality."[12] Yet the free play of chance that Eisenman's Rebstock fold tries to introduce in design is not a "pure absence" – not a lack or void from which everything would have come. It is rather the virtuality in a space of what is "more or less than what is there," of something that exceeds the space and that it cannot integrally frame. As Deleuze remarks, "to speak of the absence of an origin, to make the absence of an origin the origin is a bad play on words. A line of becoming has only a midst."[13] In the perplication game, untamed chance is not a place, not even a void or absent place, but rather the virtual space of the free line in the midst of things.

The supposition of the game in Eisenman's perplicational architecture is thus not "absence" but "weakness" – the complex chance of a space to be folded, unfolded, and folded again. It is in this sense that Rebstock remains a "full" space – it is "full" just because it is weak, or is "filled by" its weakness. For the fold, which fills up the space, is at the same time what takes the space out of itself, bursting it open and smoothing it out, releasing an intensive energy that is neither theological nor mystical, neither baroque nor oriental, neither elevating nor quieting. Rebstock is rather "full with" a "distantiation," an unsettling question that clears out a space offering the chance of a complex repetition or a free divergence. It fills its space in a manner different from the baroque and from the checkered pattern of voids and presences defined by the modern slab or *Siedlung* – through the intervals of which a new *lumière* peers, from an intensive depth prior to figure and ground, and with a diverse complication that spills over into history and context with a perplexing tension. That is what Eisenman calls "presentness." Presentness is the splendor of the fold in the house that we have come to inhabit, where the game of creation is played not *ex nihilo* but *ex plicatio*.

12 Jacques Derrida, "Force et signification," in **L'écriture et la différence** (Paris: Seuil, 1967), 28. By "pure absence" Derrida means "not the absence of this or that – but the absence of everything in which every presence is announced" (17). This text first appeared in **Critique** in 1963, at a time when Derrida was still trying to work out a phenomenological contrast between geometric and literary "ideality." It is a review of a book by Jean Rousset, a central figure among those who, referring to Heinrich Wölfflin and Rudolf Wittkower, tried to establish the existence of a "baroque age" in literature. In **Le pli** Deleuze refers on several occasions to Rousset, remarking that those who have written best about the baroque are those most skeptical of the category. Rousset's account of the attempts to discover a baroque age includes reference to the rediscovery of the English metaphysical poets and, in this sense, lends support to Geoffrey Bennington's impression that "Mannerist and Baroque buildings are to Venturi [in **Complexity and Contradiction in Architecture**] what the English Metaphysical Poets were to Eliot." In 1963 Derrida took Rousset's "baroquism" as only one instance of something called "the structuralist passion," and he went on to advance the more general argument that the attempt to find "spatial" or "architectural" metaphors for literature is ultimately vain, since there is something inherent in "literary ideality" that "excludes" this sort of description "in principle" ("Force et signification," 29). After 1963 one of course finds in Derrida's continuing reflections a more complex (not to say baroque) discussion of the theme of absence, and the theme has an important part in his writings on the architecture of both Eisenman and Bernard Tschumi. Yet it might be argued that Derrida preserves from his early work the general problematic of the literary and the spatial, or the textual and the architectural. Deleuze, by contrast, is never motivated by a search for a phenomenological contrast between literary and geometric ideality; instead, he invents a singular kind of spatial idiom in philosophy, using it in his readings of literature. Thus, he comes to the view that there is a sense in which architecture, regarded as a "framing of territory," is the **art premier**.

13 Gilles Deleuze and Félix Guattari, **A Thousand Plateaus** (Minneapolis: University of Minnesota Press, 1987), 293.

John Rajchman is a philosopher and teacher in New York City. This essay was first published in the catalog **Unfolding Frankfurt** (Berlin: Ernst & Sohn, 1991).

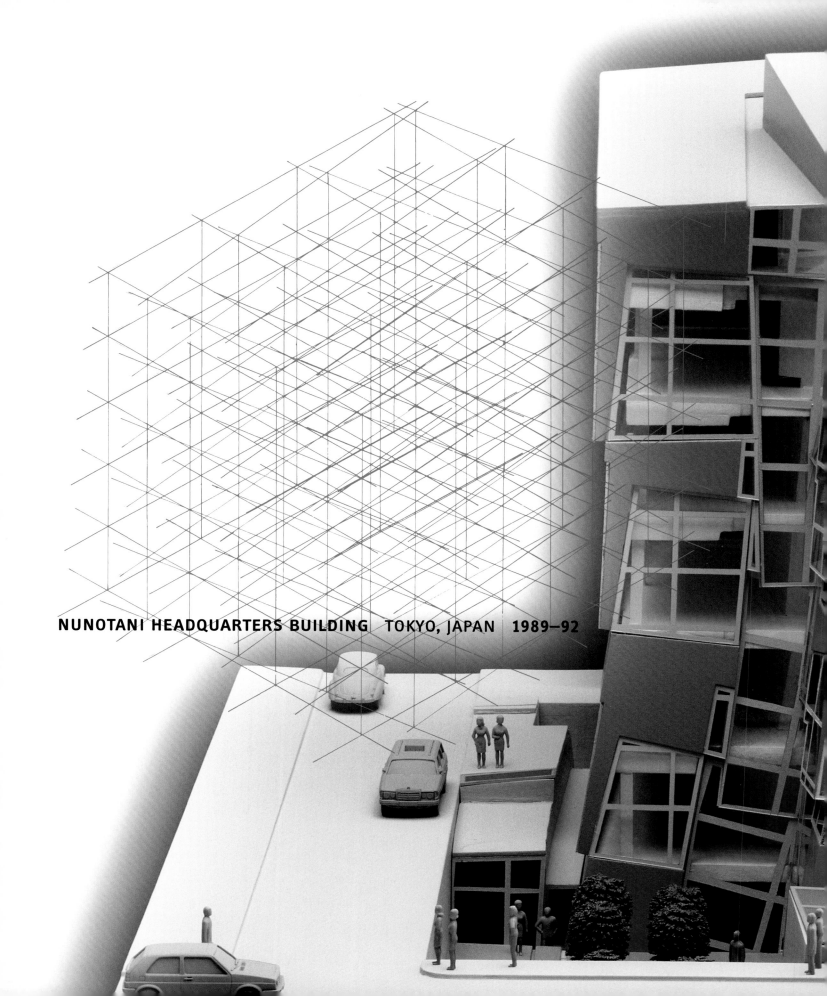

NUNOTANI HEADQUARTERS BUILDING | TOKYO, JAPAN | 1989–92

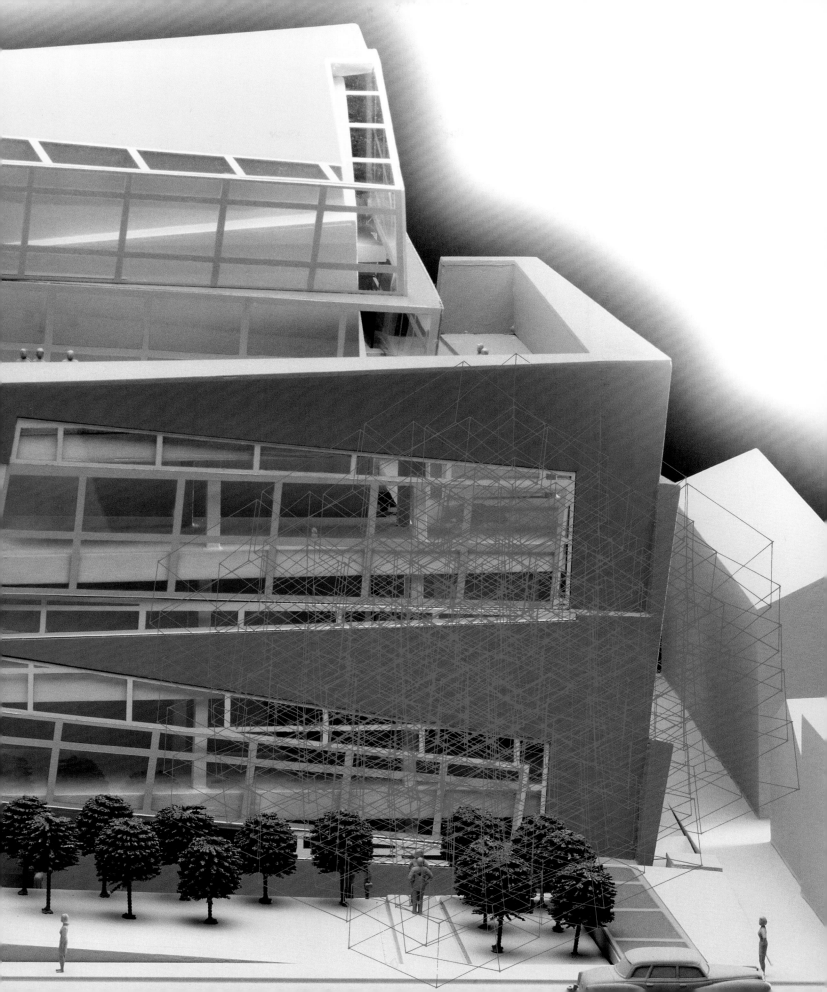

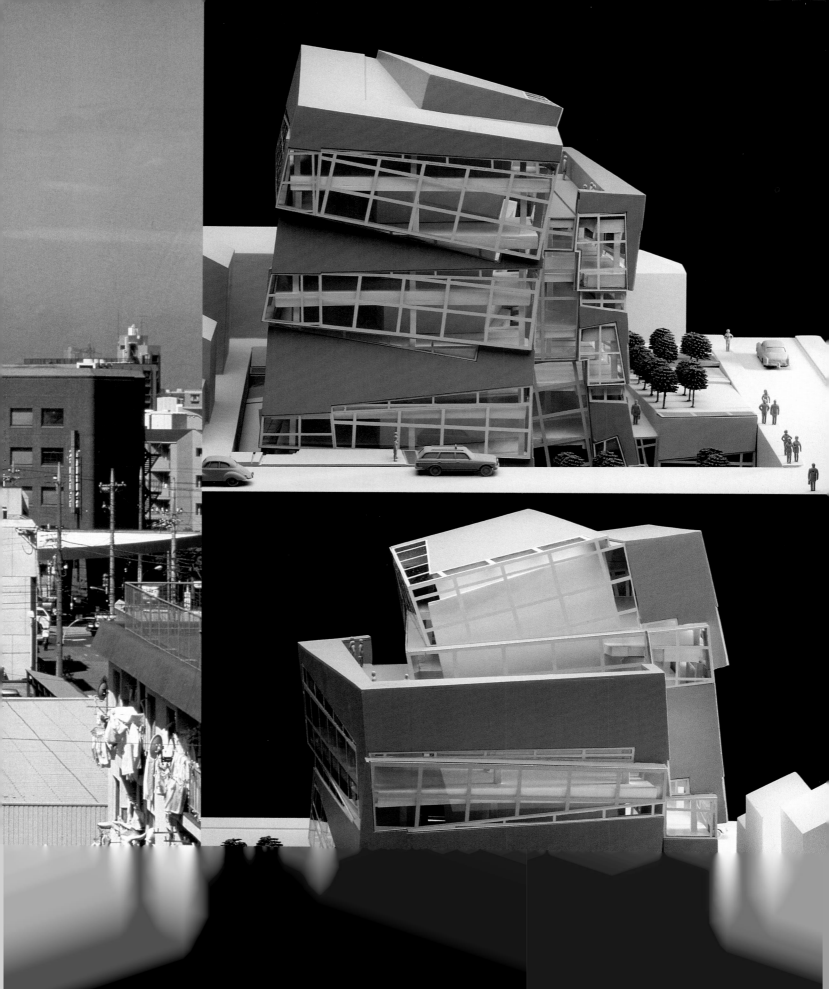

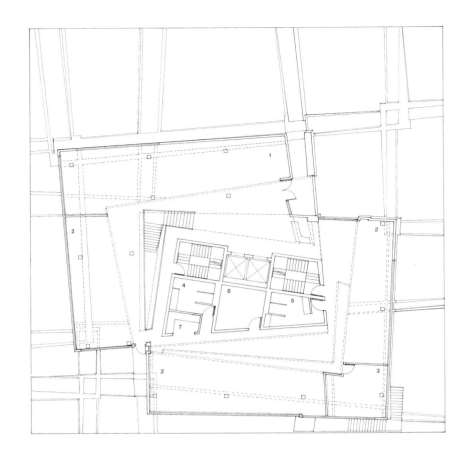

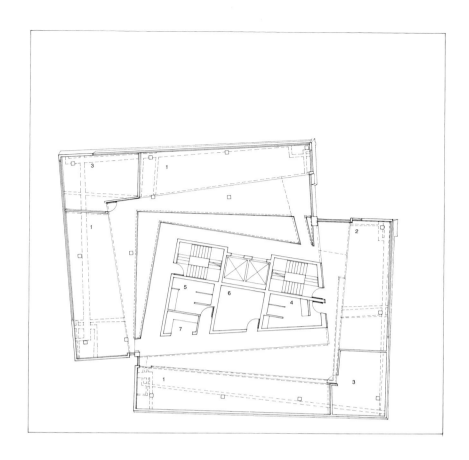

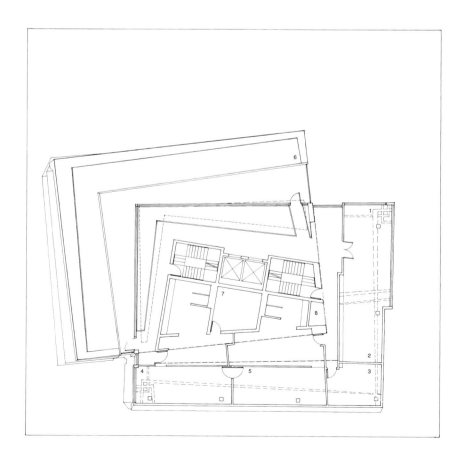

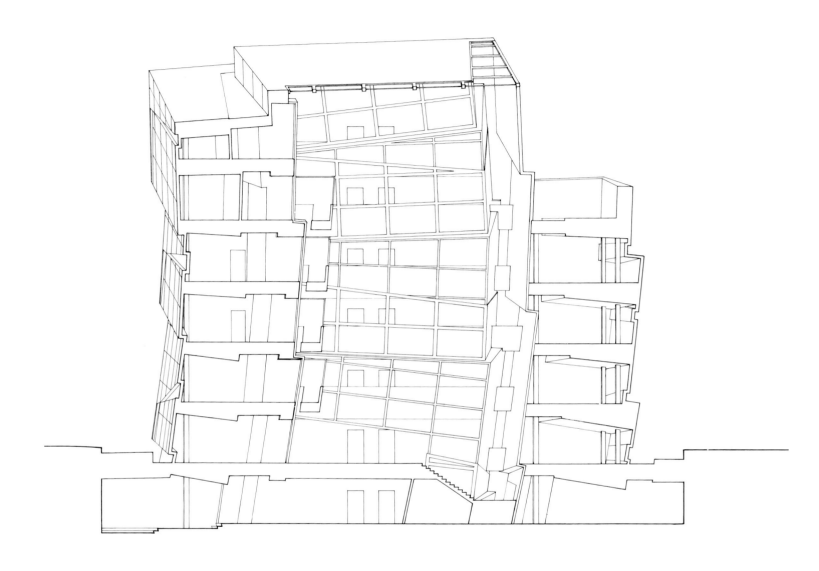

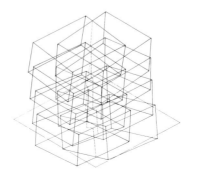

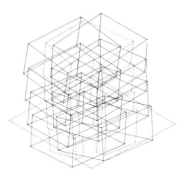

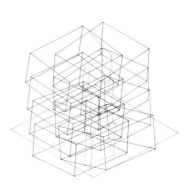

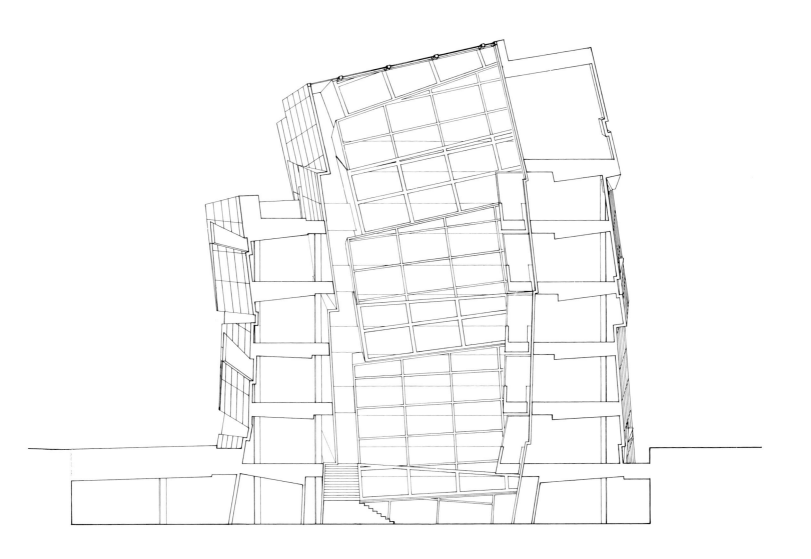

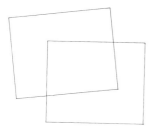

A Game of Eisenman Seeks
Cynthia Davidson

In Kobo Abé's novel *The Box Man*, the unnamed protagonist takes up residence in a heavy cardboard box that was originally used for shipping a new refrigerator. The box is both transformed and transforming when it becomes, as a shell is to a snail, a transportable shelter for its human occupant. Within this oddly architected structure, the itinerant "box man" paradoxically both finds his identity and preserves his anonymity in the world at large.

With his legs visible beneath the box as he propels it and himself along the street, the box man is a strange and threatening sight, not so much because of the box, which is still recognizable as such, but because the box offers its architect (author) and occupant a perverse voyeurism and suspect anonymity. This is achieved by cutting a tiny slit into one side of the box to make an observation window, which is then covered with two pieces of overlapping frosted vinyl. When the box is vertical, the vinyl serves as a screen. When the box is tilted, the vinyl swings away from the slit and a clear opening appears, permitting the box man to see out. Hence, because of the tilt, the occupant of the box can see yet remain unseen, observing a world altered by his new perspective. But the world has not changed; the man in the box and his and our perceptions of him and, ultimately, of the box itself have changed. The tilted box becomes the metaphoric possibility of reseeing and rethinking the world both for the box man and for Abé.

Peter Eisenman's headquarters building for the Nunotani Company in Tokyo presents an equally unsettling paradox. This too is a box, but not the standard-issue vertical office block that comprises the Edogawa district on the city's outskirts. Rather, like Abé's container, Eisenman's tilted box is a metaphor for questions about transformation, movement, and identity. The architect uses a box – or stack of tilted boxes – to displace the traditional notions of shelter and enclosure and to rethink its metaphoric possibilities. Painted pink and rising seven stories, this box is not about the anonymity of its occupant; this client wanted an arresting building image that would be featured on a magazine cover, thereby giving his company great visibility. But neither is it the strange anthropomorphized box of Abé, for Eisenman's tilted structure represents his attempts to deny both anthropocentrism and the identifying signature of the human author, while at the same time desiring recognition not simply as another kind of box but specifically as another kind of architecture. For Eisenman this means an architecture that is not dependent upon the traditional assumptions of commodity, firmness, and delight – that is, not dependent on looking like it could stand up – but rather is a device for expressing new methodologies of thinking about and building architecture.

Like the writer Abé, the architect Eisenman pushes the paradox of a functioning box/building as a metaphor for an altered state of existence to an almost intolerable limit. *The Box Man* requires the reader to suspend a system of beliefs – for example, that a cardboard box is not a habitable structure – and then psychologically to cohabit a box with an anonymous man. What begins as a novelty grows increasingly difficult to tolerate as the story becomes claustrophobic with despair. Likewise, while the tilting elevations of the Nunotani building generate a certain excitement and tension, that tension is problematized when one realizes it is necessary to suspend traditional notions of structure in order to accept the slumped appearance of the project. This is not so easy to do. At the dedication of the completed headquarters, the homeowner who lived next door asked Eisenman, in all seriousness, whether the building would topple onto his house.

In pursuing their respective disciplines, Abé and Eisenman have found themselves to be figuratively boxed in – Abé by the form of the novel, Eisenman by an architectural tradition that constantly seeks to reaffirm the order of the status quo. Their respective methodologies of reworking both the metaphorical and literal "box" require the suspension of a certain common belief as to what that box – whether literature or architecture – not only is but could become.

"Actually a box, in appearance, is purely and simply a right-angled parallelepiped, but when you look at it from within it's a labyrinth of a hundred interconnecting puzzle rings. The more you struggle, the more the box, like an extra outer skin growing from the body, creates new twists for the labyrinth, making the inner disposition increasingly more complex," Abé writes. This inner disposition is more psychological than structural, both for Abé, who constructs the box in order to blur the voice of the narrator, and for Eisenman, who invents a narrative outside of architectural tradition to blur the reading of the box. In fact, Eisenman's architecture must be approached through a seemingly arbitrary text, or diagram. In this case the diagram is one of colliding plates, which, like the labyrinth of Abé's box, creates literal twists as it rises in the building's section.

For the Nunotani structure, sited at the corner of an urban intersection, the challenge was to build vertically without the iconography of the vertical, that is, without needing to "look like" it could stand up. An early proposal dealt with the idea of shifting in a way that produced a massing scheme with an arched and plated "back" that was neither roof nor wall nor the spine of upright man. Rather, the massing resembled a heavily plated armadillo, akin to the earthshaking monsters made famous in Japanese B movies. This earlier, prehensile version of the building succeeded in blurring the iconography of verticality, but it also produced an unexpected second image that Eisenman did not want. While it created a sensation of uncertainty due to its seeming state of restlessness and movement – the very antithesis of the notions of permanence and stability embedded in the iconic necessity of architecture – it also looked animate. There was, however, no sense of imminent collapse. Rather, the shifting could be construed as a metaphor for movement away from the traditional and away from the identifiable. Thus a change was required.

The second, and built, Nunotani project is no armadillo. This is a box that appears to be suspended between stasis and collapse. Two overlapping grids of wall and window slip past one another, blurring verticality and, with it, stability. In addition, the detail of the gridded facade and the very scale of the tilting planes take the emphasis away from the horizontal datum of the ground plane. On the exterior the overlapping and imprinting of each grid create an unreadable building scale, whether on the windowless back and side facades that look into the block or on the partly glazed facades that overlook the street corner. For a passerby, it is virtually impossible to declare with any certainty the number of floors within. As the building reads less and less as a traditional work of architecture, its strangeness as a work of architecture – its lack of the anthropocentric traditions associated with architecture, such as horizontal datum, floor height, and human scale – simultaneously gives the project both its anonymity – the anonymity of the unknown – and its identity (including the unique cover image so desired by the client).

As is true of all of Eisenman's architectural investigations, built and unbuilt, architectural form and space are the result of a complex layering of many different factors and influences not traditional – that is, not seen as "natural" – to the discipline. In his efforts to break free of the tyranny of the functional diagram, to break free of the dictum that form follows function, Eisenman continuously seeks to invert the commonplace, to displace the timeworn methodologies of making architecture. With the Nunotani project, we find what might be considered the first three-dimensional expression of his theoretical work on "weak form," which for Eisenman is a metaphorically nonanthropomorphic form. Precisely because it withstands gravity without a direct bond or relationship between its structural function and the iconography of a vertebrate form, it becomes, in C. S. Peirce's terms, indexical. Eisenman argues that architecture, more than any other sign system, has traditionally had a strong relationship between form and signified because form and signified exist as one and the same presence. Weak form attempts to move the sign from an iconic to indexical, or secondary, condition.

In the Nunotani project, the icon of structural necessity is reduced to a secondary role. This is because the building's tilted planes and overlapping transparent slots appear to be precariously piled one on top of another without the seeming benefit of traditional modern skeletal construction. In its place is what Eisenman calls a "limp erection," a metaphorically nonvertebrate structure that is shifted in such a way that it is never parallel with any wall or corner. While a grid of columns rises through the floor plates much like the system that supports every modern office building, here it no longer supports a dominant phallocentric identity. At first glance this imagery seems to be a one-liner, but several other narratives are at work that contribute to the idea of weak form. Part of Eisenman's idea is to weaken the sign and thereby its meaning so that there is no one reading from the final image. In other words, the work is not about signaling information or significance but rather, as in all of his recent work, the nature of the architectural sign.

In this regard, Eisenman can easily move from phallocentrism to plate tectonics to explain the seeming "aftershock" quality of the Nunotani's tilted double grids. In this instance he can claim that the ever-shifting geologic structure of the Japanese islands is invoked in the genesis of the building's tilts. For in fact the islands of Japan are located over the point of collision between the Western Pacific continental plate and the Pacific

oceanic plate. The movement of these plates and the activity of undersea volcanoes both formed these islands millions of years ago and today continue to compress and expand the continuous plate structure of the Edogawa district. Thus, within this zone, another narrative of the Nunotani building could be seen as what the architect called "a metaphoric record of the continuous waves of movement as the plates overlap." No longer is the form simply the result of a process of formal transformation. Now it has a diagrammatic basis. This form is not platonic but plate-tectonic. This is an important shift from Eisenman's earlier diagrams, such as the transformations of line, plane, and volume that occurred in his 1970s explorations of the cube.

Eisenman could make up any number of narratives to explain the appearance of the Nunotani building and they seem plausible, in part because the aesthetic of the structure – its arrested massing and strangely tantalizing pinkish color – is so displacing that we no longer begin to read the architecture from the facts of structure, shelter, and function. This is not the case with the box man, whose cardboard container seems to have only these conditions without any aesthetic aura. This aura is what ultimately moves Eisenman away from Abé.

Near the end of Abé's story, the box man is enticed into coming out of the box to make physical contact with a woman he has been observing for some time. Throwing off his mantle of cardboard, he emerges nude, except for a pair of boots, in an obvious expression of vulnerability not only of the protagonist but of the author as well. The Nunotani building puts Eisenman in an equally vulnerable position in a profession where change or displacement has been virtually impossible, but his is not a displacement of despair. Here the act of throwing off the traditional box challenges the accepted canons of aura in the making of architectural form. While Eisenman's critics may say this returns him to the status of the emperor and his new clothes, he would argue that it is the affective experience of the building that provides the possibility of a new aura. If we undertake such an exploration of affect, perhaps then we will find what Eisenman seeks.

Cynthia Davidson is an architecture editor and writer in New York City. An earlier version of "A Game of Eisenman Seeks" appeared in **A+U** 252 (September 1991).

EMORY UNIVERSITY CENTER FOR THE ARTS ATLANTA, GEORGIA 1991—93

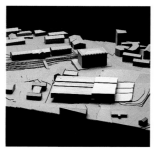 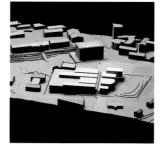 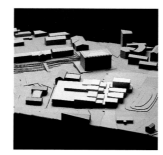 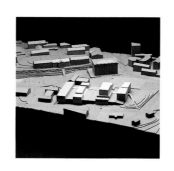 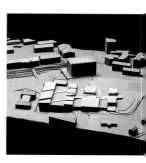

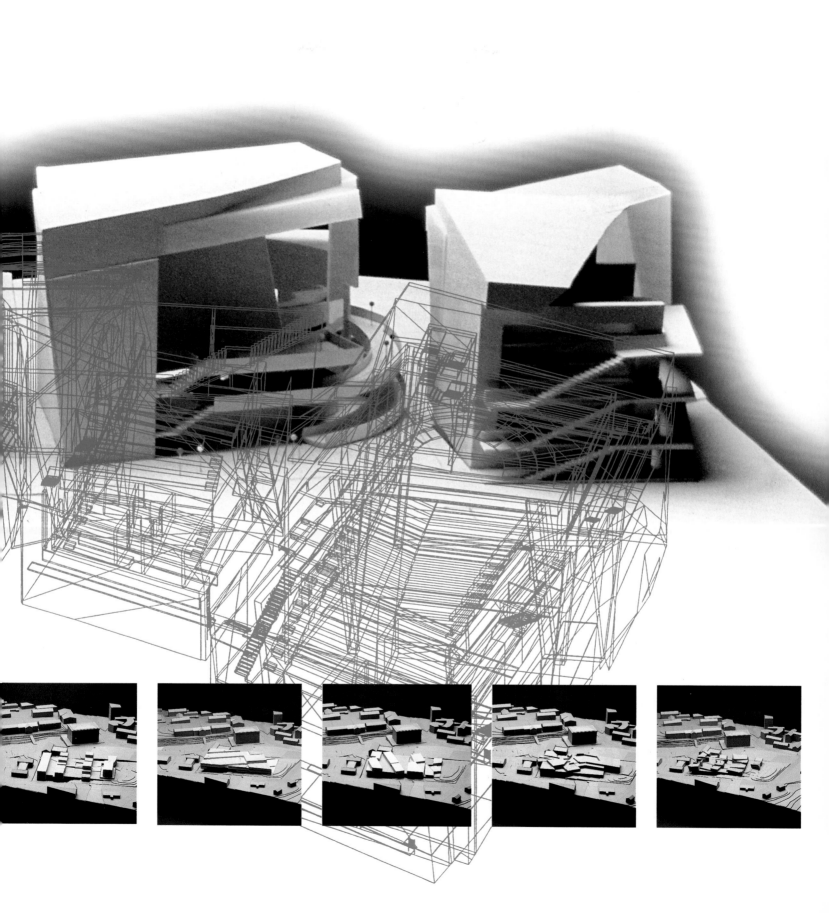

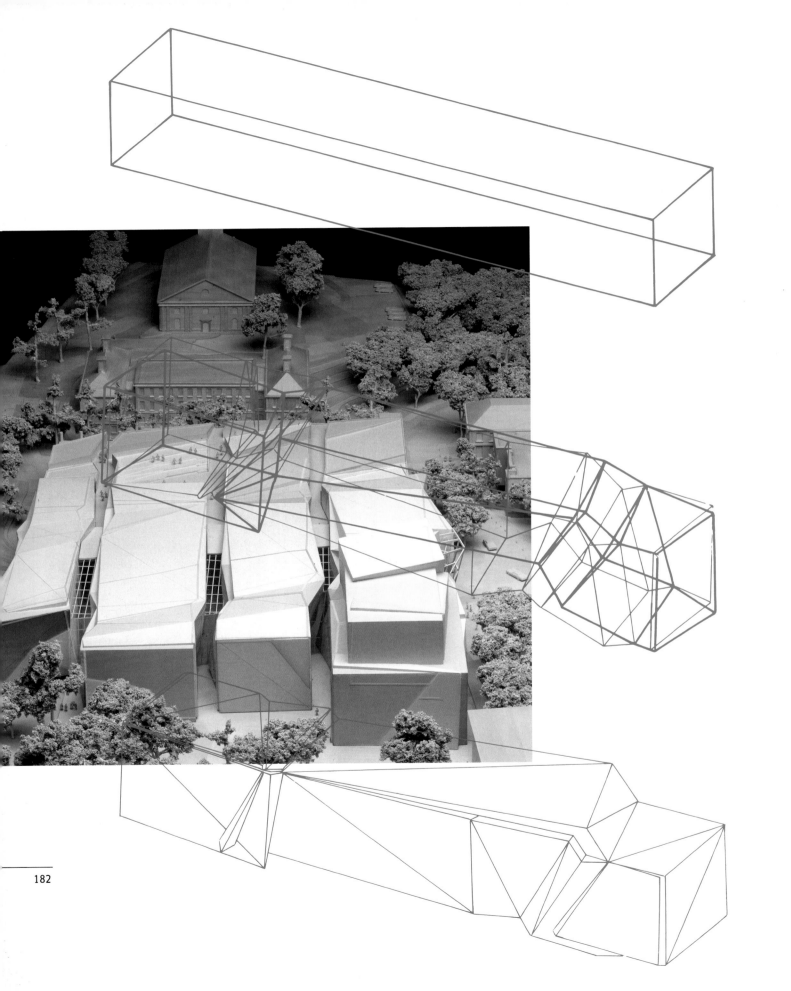

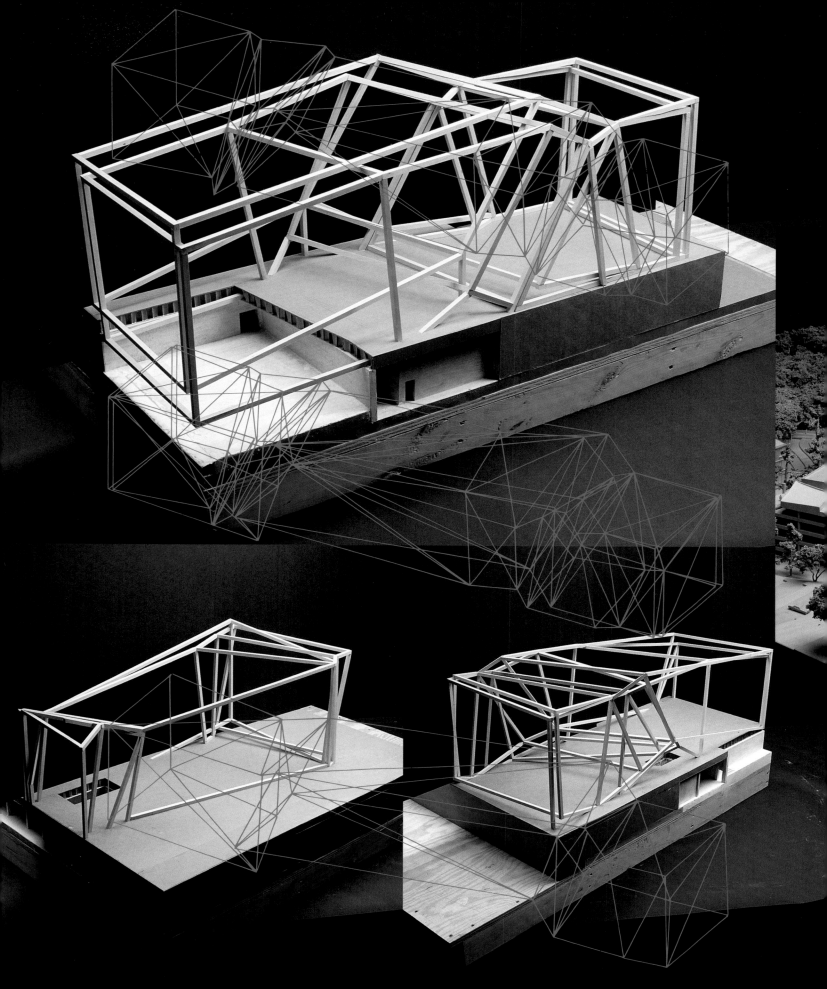

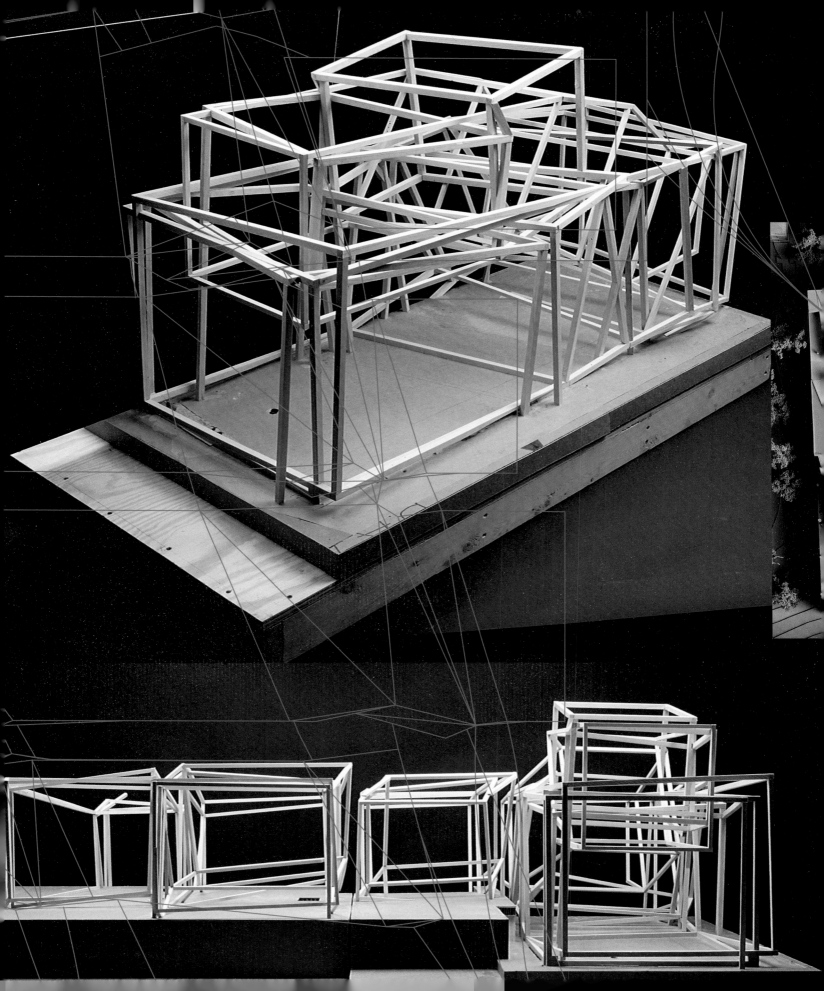

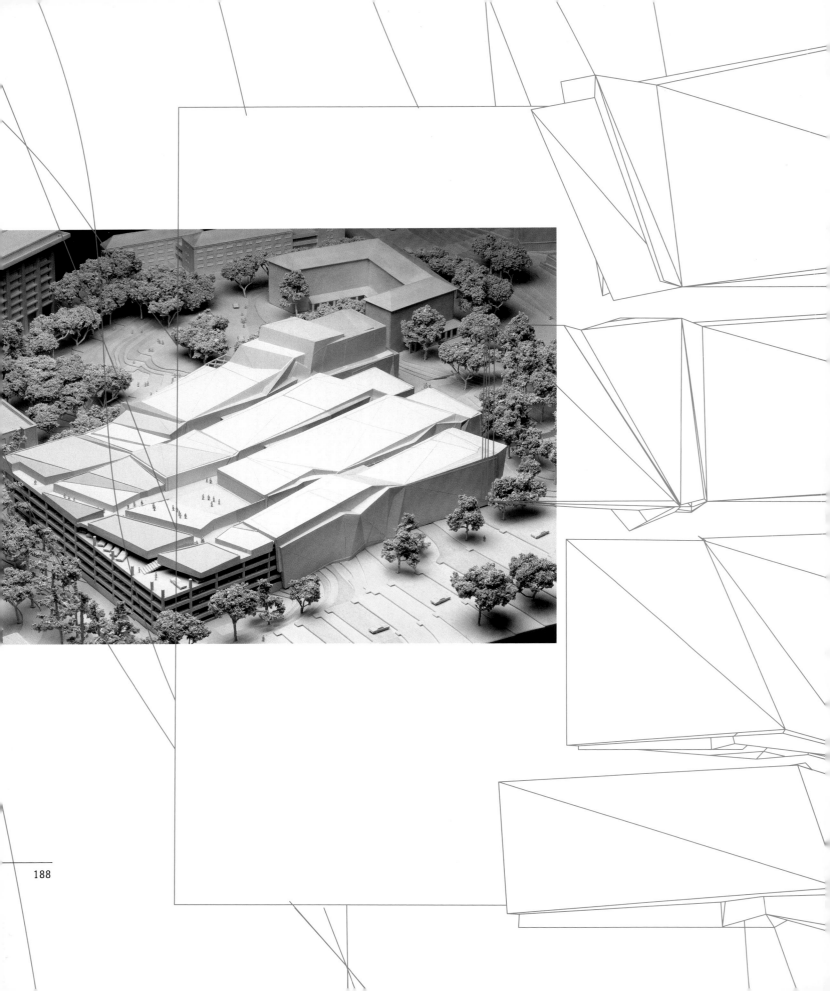

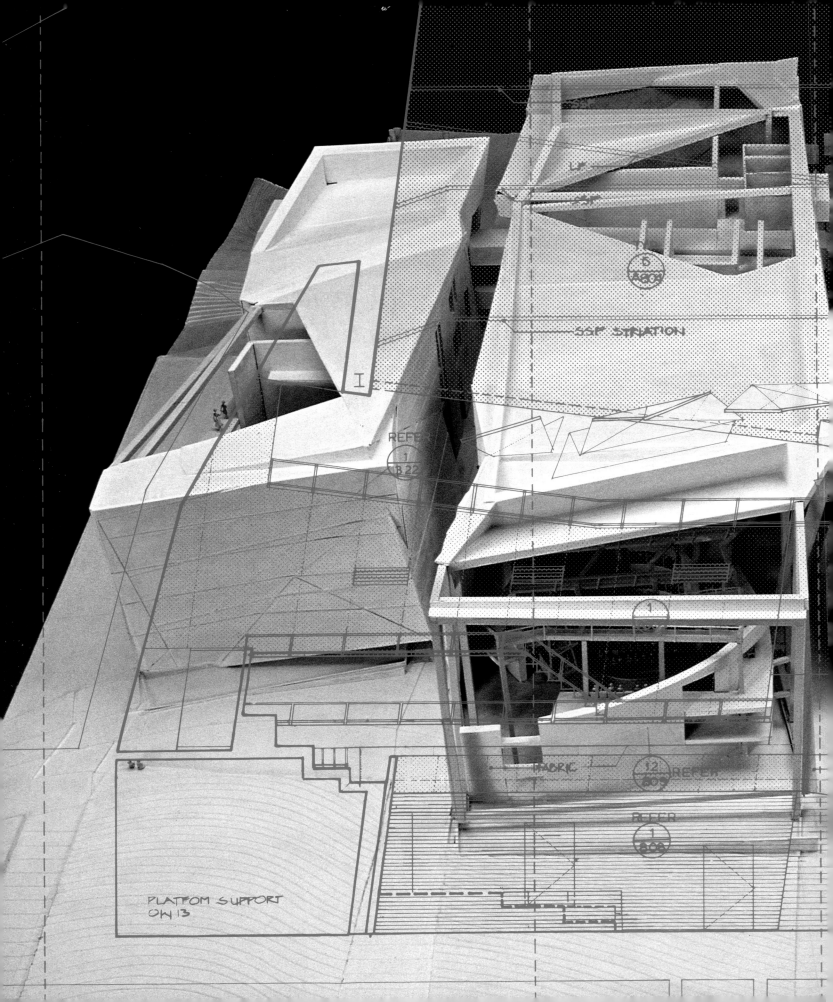

PLATFOM SUPPORT
OW 13

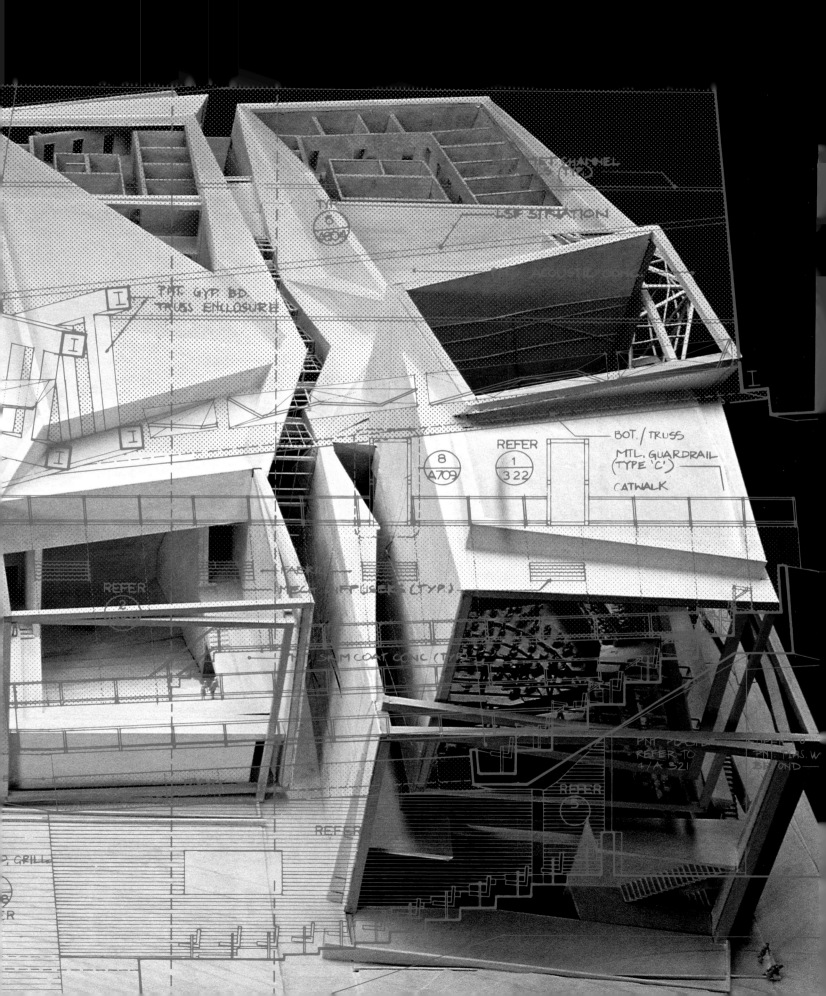

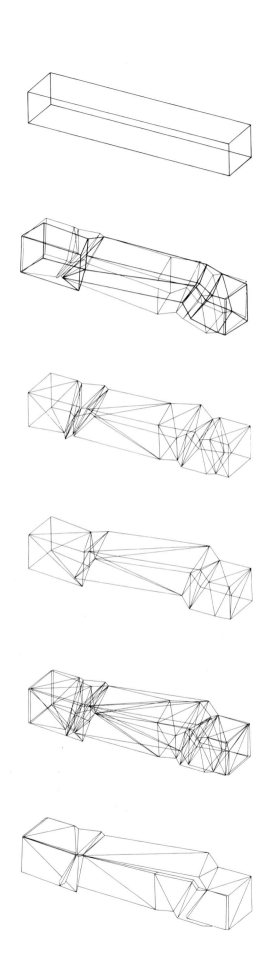

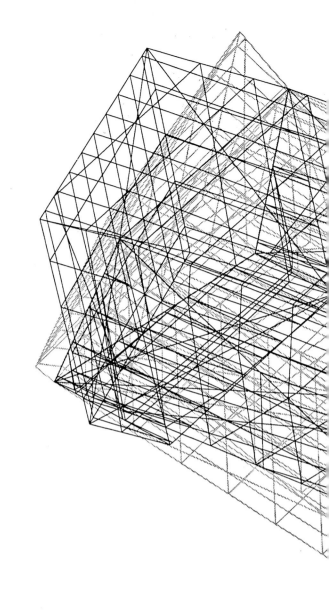

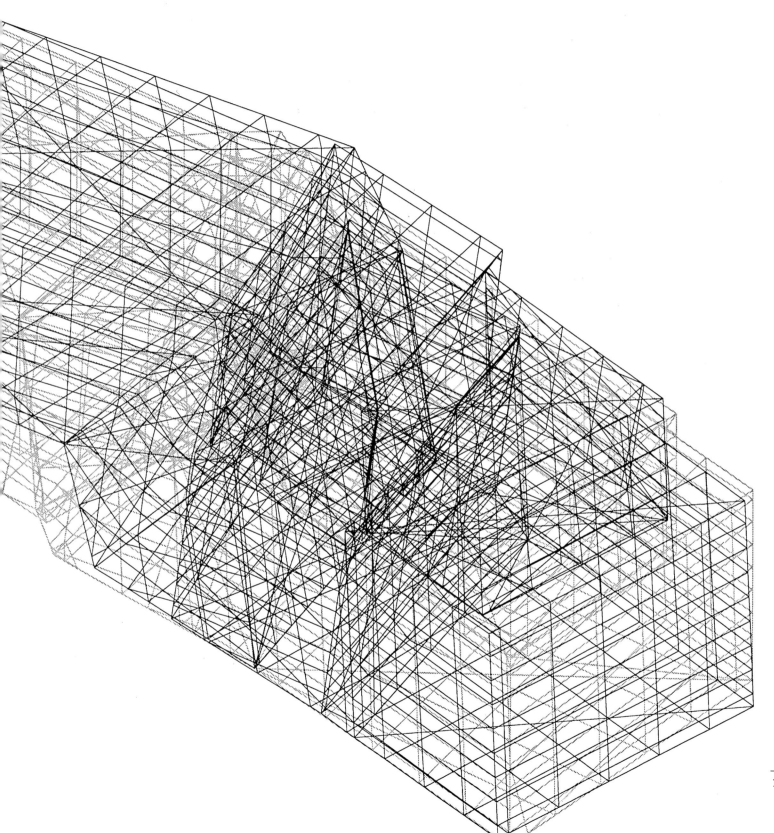

193

Woodruff Library

Asbury Circle

Hopkins Hall

Rich Business School

Fishburne Drive

Proposed
Business School

Service Drive

Center for the Arts

North Decatur Road

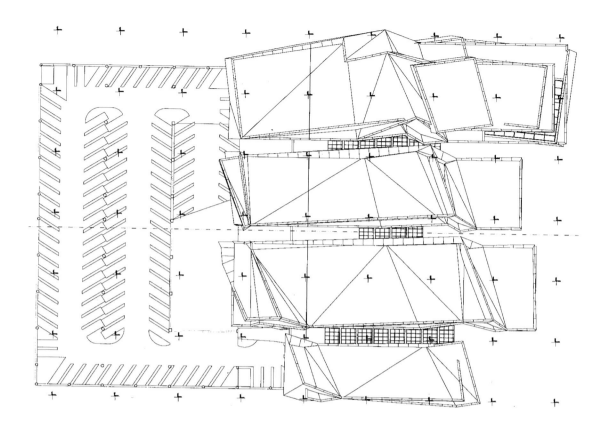

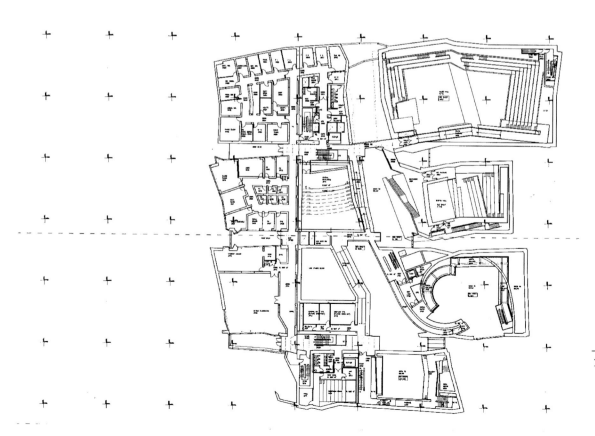

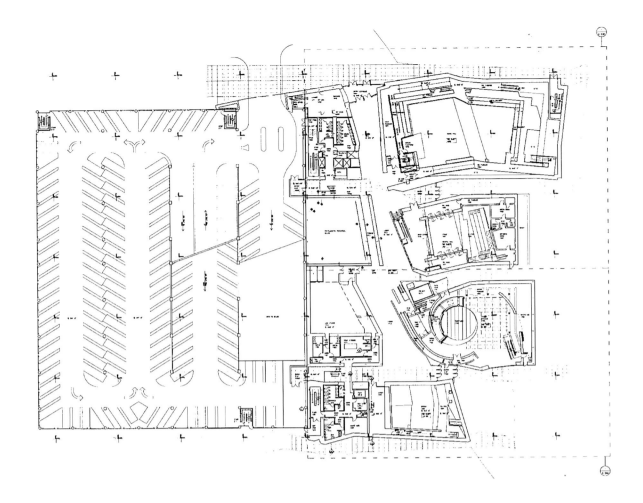

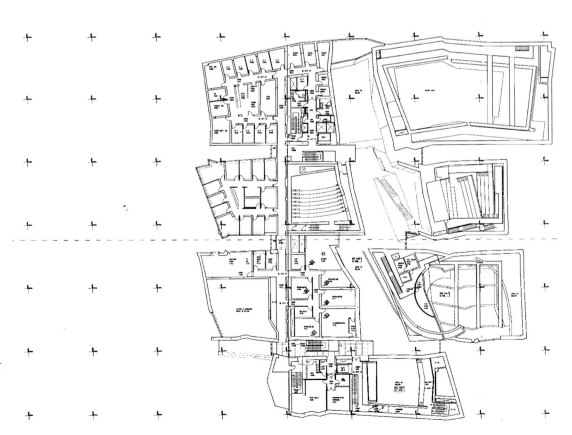

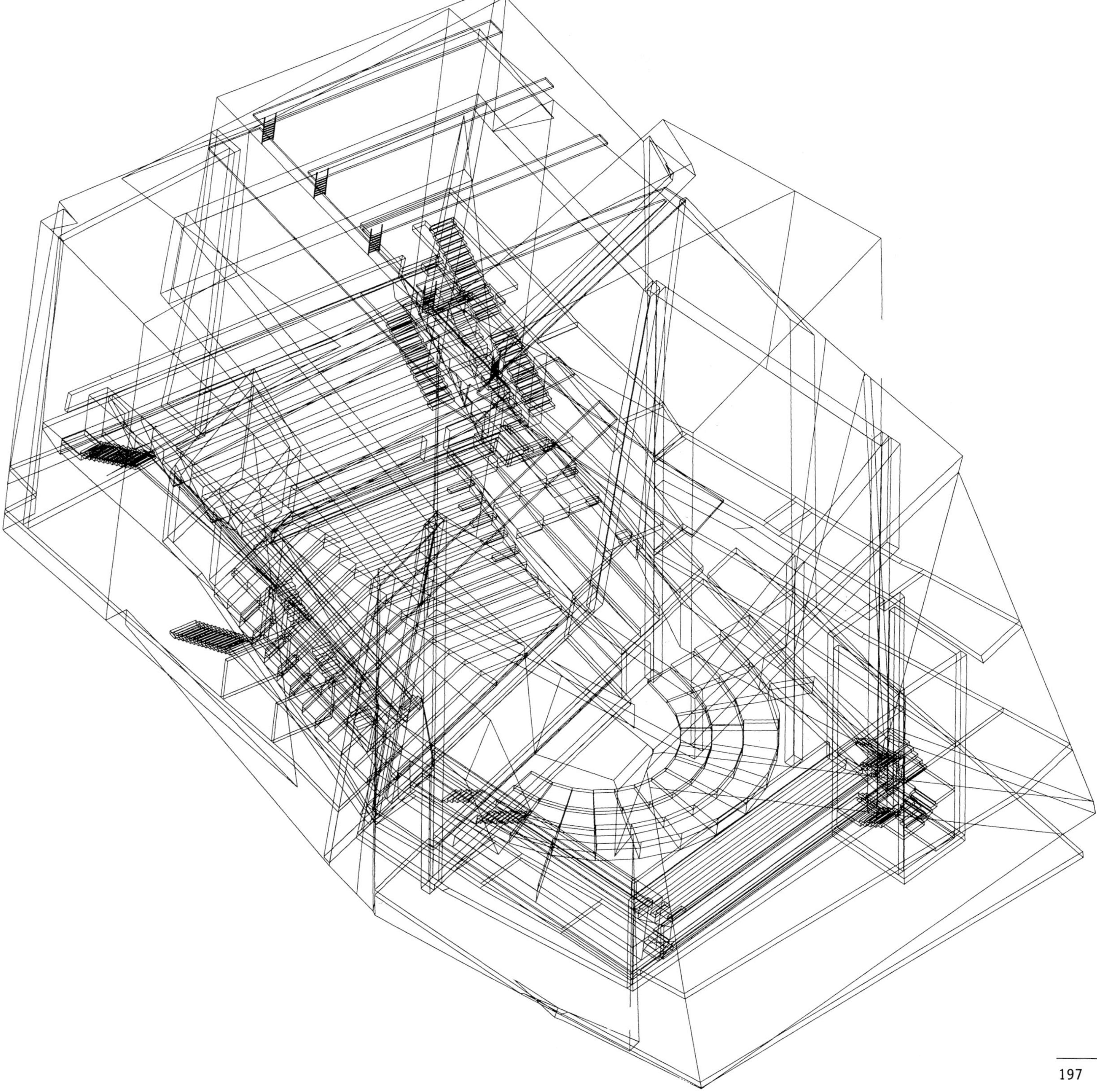

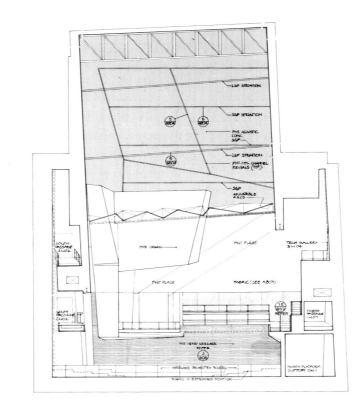

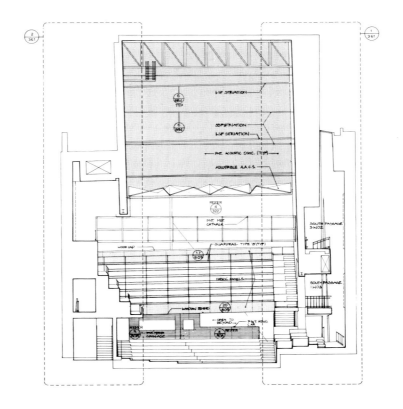

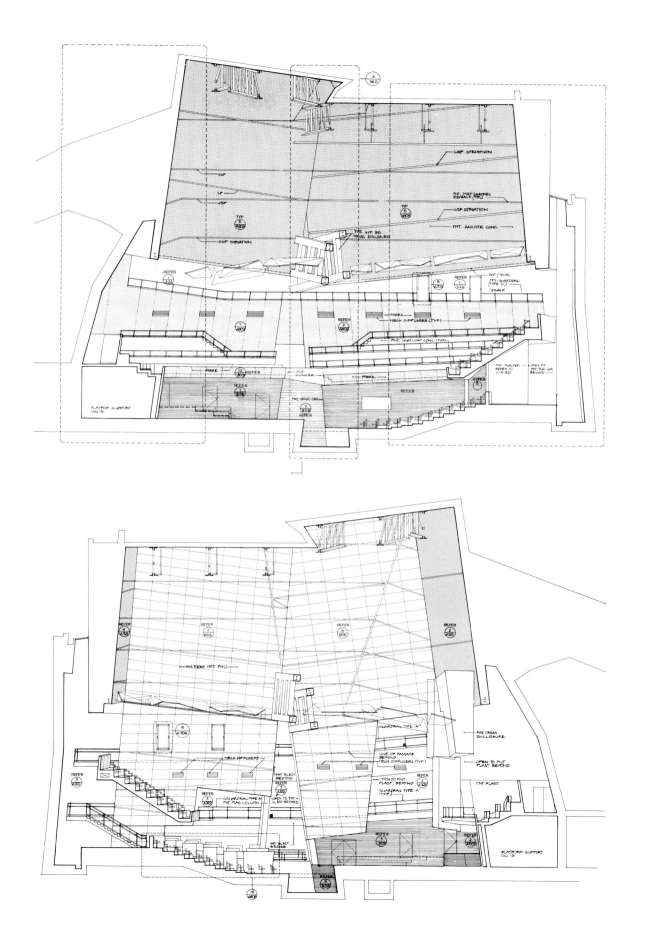

199

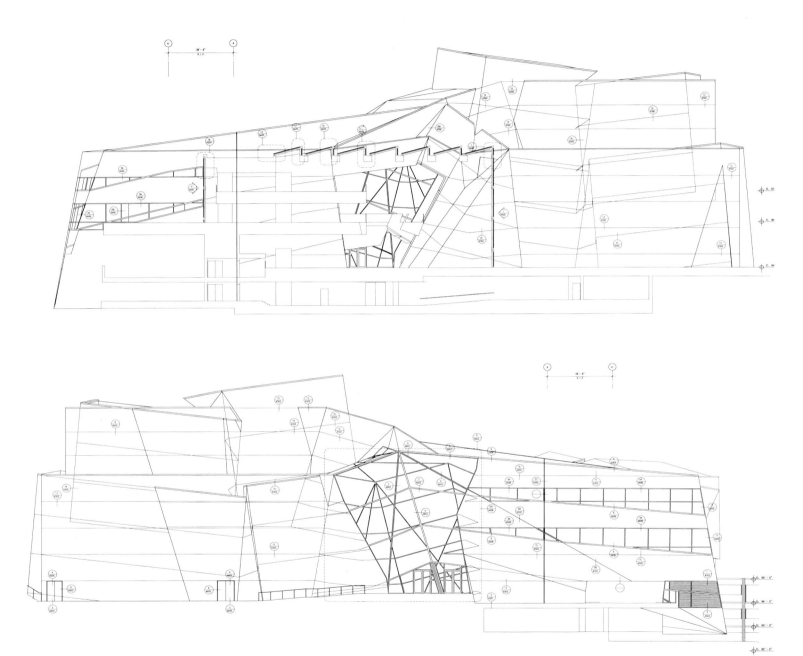

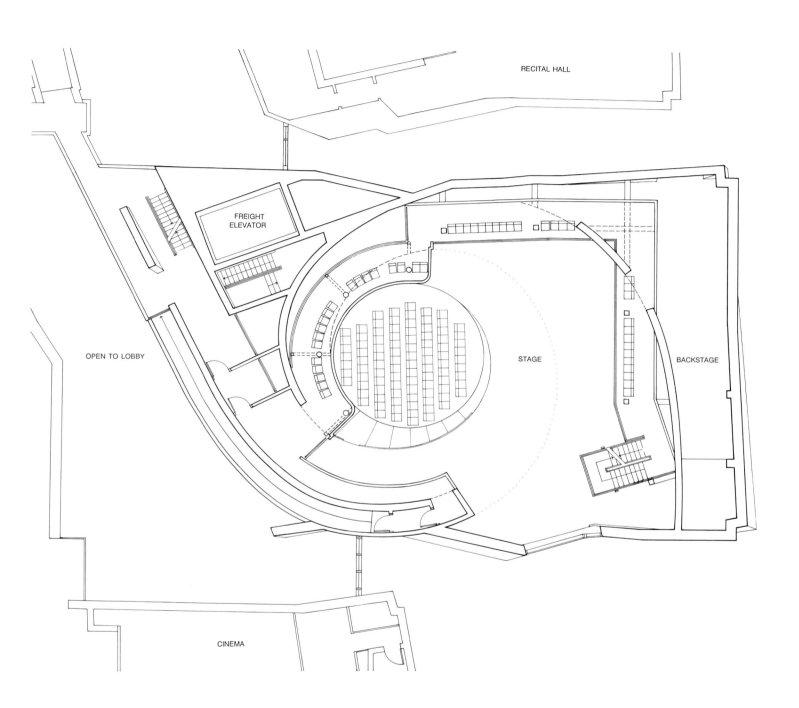

RECITAL HALL

FREIGHT
ELEVATOR

OPEN TO LOBBY

STAGE

BACKSTAGE

CINEMA

201

WHOSE M EMORY?
K. Michael Hays

A new generation, that of the spoilt children of the crisis, whereas the preceding one was that of the accursed children of history.
—Jean Baudrillard, *Cool Memories*

Two of Peter Eisenman's ghosts paid a visit to Harvard's Graduate School of Design in the fall of 1993 for Eisenman's Eliot Noyes lecture and the opening of his *M Emory Games* exhibition: Colin Rowe and Manfredo Tafuri. They appeared as the rock and the hard place of architecture theory, two intolerable but inescapable destinies of the architectural legacy that, for some time now, Eisenman has been trying to supersede.

Rowe stands for affirmative formalism. On this view, there is possible a liberal reconciliation of a disciplinary structure given by architecture's own history, and an individual architectural freedom to endlessly recombine the elements of the system. *Collage City* – the governing grid and the fragmented incidents it contains – is the sign and the technique of that liberal reconciliation, the establishing of a social consensus through formal conventions while at the same time a distancing of autonomous formal operations from the grit and grind of everyday social life.[1] For Rowe, structural systematism (like that of Palladio or Le Corbusier) tends to become aesthetic value, and formal satisfaction produces its own consensus. What disrupts the system are cross-modal affiliations (like, say, Robert Venturi's pop promiscuity) except to the extent that they can be brought back into the consensual aesthetic mix.

Tafuri stands for negational materialism. On this view, the material basis for modern architecture's social meaning has been progressively eroded by modernity itself; consensus is no longer possible and the history of modernism is the story of architecture's retracing of that fact, from the expressionists' yearning for subjective immanence to the rigorist technicians' giving form over to the very transcendent systems (from myth to technology) that overwhelm the last remnants of individuality. For Tafuri, the entire project of modernism, including Eisenman's neo-avantgarde, seems not much more than an idealization of capitalism and its representations – putting the best face on rationalization and consumption, providing experiences and spaces heretofore uncharted that capital can now colonize and profit from.

Eisenman's retelling of this story at the opening of the exhibition of Emory University's Center for the Arts project gives the effect another turn of the screw. For what Eisenman wants us to imagine is the double negation of these mutually conflicting positions; and what he wants us to look for in the project for a performing arts center is the first step toward that overcoming. For my part, it is not only the theoretical significance of blending and negating these two separate architectural ideologemes, but also the

---

1 On Rowe's liberal ideology (which is an ideology that does not know itself to be one), see R. E. Somol, "One or Several Masters?," in **Hejduk's Chronotope**, ed. K. Michael Hays (New York: Princeton Architectural Press/Canadian Centre for Architecture, 1996).

particular mode of perception of the architectural genre of which the Emory project is one instance that I want to take up here in an attempt to articulate the problem of the audience for this particular genre.

At Emory, a grid derived from the original Henry Hornbostel campus plan and the ravine running through that grid are sampled for their salient morphologies and then mutually deformed in terms of aptitudes and frequencies that result in a set of contours resembling the sine curves of musical harmonies. Such deformations, though predicted theoretically by Eisenman's earlier work, such as the Guardiola House and the Aronoff Center at the University of Cincinnati, would be impossible practically without the computer software Form·Z (developed in Columbus, Ohio, as a result of Eisenman's prodding). Form·Z can systematically distort a uniform gridded plane by "hanging weights" on its line segments and triangulating the resulting deformation into planar facets or tiling patterns across a three-dimensional solid like the four functional boxes of the Emory arts center. As a result, the project is able to take the superposed grids of Eisenman's "artificial excavations" period and extend their spatial effects into their sectional and elevational aspects, whose deformations, in turn, are heightened by the lobby connector running across the grain of the four boxes and the parking garage grafted onto them, creating an experience of space and surface only hinted at in the earlier "handmade" (that is, pre-Form·Z) projects.

Now, with Eisenman's work the critic becomes accustomed not only to creating new readings of familiar objects but also to mobilizing familiar ideologies against new objects. Indeed, a hypothetical reader conversant only in Rowe's collage aesthetics could convert these formal manipulations into a honed-down version of the stylistics of structure/incident, frontality/layering, local symmetries, and so forth, that collage is famous for. After all, isn't this just the same sort of inversion and collage of figure and ground as Rowe's examples of 19th-century Parma and Le Corbusier's plan for St. Die, or of the Hôtel de Beauvais and Villa Savoye, except that now the image of the structure is privileged over the structure itself or, better, that the contingent figure (produced by Form·Z)

fully absorbs the once stabilizing ground? Isn't this – this Gibsonian wire grid that does not so much accommodate accidents as absorb and reprocess them as new syntactic material – just what *Collage City* would look like if taken to its zero degree?

Alternatively, an unreconstituted Tafurian could fit these histrionics of surface into one more advanced stage in the inevitable conversion of the avant-garde's formal research into a spectacle – working with the "garbage and throwaways of our daily and commonplace existence," employing "war surplus materials . . . discarded on the battlefield after the defeat of the Modern Movement."[2] Emory is surely resonant with other generic allusions and the problems of cross-media popularization and commercialization they evoke: most obviously, Eric Mendelsohn's department stores, Johannes Duiker's cinemas, and Hans Scharoun's Philharmonie, but also, and more tellingly, the *Merzbildern* and *Merzbau* of Kurt Schwitters, whose very titles (a truncation of the German word for "commerce") flaunt their affiliation with the emerging consumer culture that Tafuri would later pin to its historical destiny in postmodern anomie. For a Tafurian, the historical avant-garde was a premonitory aestheticization of precisely the subjective alienation and dispersion that would arrive fully geared up (or wound down to nothing) in the postwar consumer culture of America; and the neo-avant-gardes, Eisenman's included, are nothing but a bathetic replay of the avant-garde's self-destructive project.

One could read the Emory project through either of the two lenses that Eisenman wants to shatter, but it is not in the terms of their mutual differences but rather of their common ground that Eisenman, I believe, supersedes them. For as opposed as they might otherwise be, the positions represented here by Rowe and Tafuri share a recognition of the need for (and of architecture's various historical attempts at) the maintenance or construction of social-consensual meaning and a practical architecture theory for such meaning-production. *Collage City* proposes itself as just such a practical theory of consensus, of a liberal humanist kind, whereby individual incidents are reconciled within the structure of the regulating grid. Tafuri is resigned to the necessary suspension of the effort until such time as

2 Manfredo Tafuri, "L'Architecture dans le Boudoir: The Language of Criticism and the Criticism of Language," **Oppositions** 3 (1974): 38.

society itself has reconstructed the material preconditions for consensus and meaning. Until then, the architects who would try "to reconstruct a common discourse for their discipline" are "forced to rely on materials empty of any and all meaning . . . to mute signals of a language whose code has been lost."[3]

In contrast to these two positions, both built on the problem of social-consensual meaning – that is, on representation, on the question of how a class or a group constructs pictures of itself – perhaps the most notable thing about Eisenman's recent recommendation is not the abandonment of the project of representation (which, one could argue, was his mode of operating until recently) but rather the taking up of that project again on different architectural terms. It is the new terms of representation that will bring me to my question of audience after a brief detour through the matter of genealogy.

Eisenman's "cities of artificial excavation," the set of projects of superposed planimetric grids mostly for urban centers executed between 1978 and 1988, are one sort of culmination of the Rowean paradigm – a resolutely formalist dialectic between the governing structure of the architectural language (incarnated in the grid) and the production of random, elemental formal incidents.[4] By 1986 the excavations were on the verge of exhaustion, the technique's potentials of organizing form and space restricted to the most generalized plan overlays, scalar disjunctions, and morphological appropriations – including those that came to be called "mapping" and "grafting," in which two or more morphological or textual systems are transcoded and combined, resulting in a new system of continuous and articulate contingencies – with the occasional appropriated narrative floated over the formal system (e.g., Romeo and Juliet, the historical transformation of Berlin, the dialogue with Jacques Derrida and Bernard Tschumi).

It was left, albeit for a short time, to a younger generation of architects to take the geometrical research of Eisenman, synthesize it with the more overtly popular-culture and cinematic notations of Tschumi, and develop techniques of architectural production that joined geometrical complexities with scenographic allusions to the "look" of high media and information technology. Projects by Greg Lynn, Jeffrey

Kipnis and Bahram Shirdel, Hani Rashid and Lise Anne Couture, and others drew from Eisenman's own layering and scaling techniques developed after 1978 but pushed them away from fragmentation and contradiction and toward a suture that is not only formal but cross-media as well, involving film and video along with graphic design, computer imaging, mathematics, and biology. I will call this suture of form and modality "ideological smoothness" and mention just two of its aspects.

First was the renunciation of the contemporary efficacy of modernist practices of negation. To these young architects, negation came to be understood historically rather than programmatically, and Tafuri's pessimism regarding contemporary practice was jettisoned. Second was a refusal to privilege the structural linguistic paradigm that had remained canonical in architecture theory since 1970. The new "languages" of electronics, DNA, chaos, catastrophe, and the semiotics of mass culture itself seemed to escape the relational codes of structural linguistics; and Rowe's collage techniques were overloaded until they snapped. In some cases, architectural codes were almost completely displaced by others, the vertical surfaces of buildings conceived no longer tectonically or anthropomorphically but as blank screens for information. Greg Lynn now attributes this inquiry to nothing less than a paradigm shift from "deconstructivism" to "folding,"[5] from a dry and brittle practice of criticism and resistance to a supple, slippery ride on the wave of advanced media. One notes that the attributes of this paradigm are not formal only, for this new system of affiliations finds its social correspondents in practices as seemingly diverse as channel surfing and malling and gene splicing.

Emory's Center for the Arts project fits into this new paradigm, reappropriates it from its progeny, and pushes it another step beyond an affirmative representation of media. Feeling increasing pressure from theories of complex systems as well as from the technologies of information and communication, the Emory project seems to react by trying to become just those things – theories and media.

Let me make the point a slightly different way. Jeffrey Kipnis recently predicted the end of the architectural techniques of -*age*, that is, of collage, assemblage, and

3 Tafuri, "L'Architecture dans le Boudoir," 38.
4 See Jean-François Bédard, ed., **Cities of Artificial Excavation: The Work of Peter Eisenman, 1978–1988** (New York: Rizzoli/Canadian Centre for Architecture, 1994).
5 Greg Lynn, "Architectural Curvilinearity: The Folded, The Pliant and the Supple," in **Folding in Architecture,** Architectural Design Profile 102, ed. Greg Lynn (London: Academy Editions, 1993), 8–15.

montage, since they can only recycle material, can be only critical, and can never be projective. But Kipnis keeps distinct the new architectures of "DeFormation" – the grafting of abstract topologies especially to engender residual, incongruous sectional spaces – and "InFormation" – the deployment of monolithic forms and blank surfaces as screens for projected images.[6] What I want to suggest here is that the Emory project tends to collapse Kipnis's distinction, since in this project the topographical and topological material is itself deployed as a kind of superficial information. The hope of the Emory project seems to be that architecture's surfaces (as much as its spaces) will produce unexpected and spontaneous experiential effects, that the surfaces will engender virtual intensities whose manifestations as actual information or as programmatic activities emerge as a kind of après-coup. The building surface is to be read not as a projection screen but as a diagram of potentials for activity, a *dispositif* or distribution apparatus for differential forms, functions, contents, and expressions from incommensurable registers pressed together into a single tissue.

For the Rowe-minded reader, the Emory project achieves an involution of the technique of collage from within the conceptual space of collage, so to speak, which also means that the degraded popular waste products that such techniques were constructed to keep out (topographic banalities, noncompositional surfaces, architecture's affinities with mass media) have not so much contaminated as literally become the architecture itself. From Tafuri's vantage point, the negation of the negation is precipitated not by the liberal right but by the extremes of the aesthetic left. While Tafuri can see the formalist dialectics of Eisenman only as a kind of Barthesian "bleached writing," a stylistics from which all specific social referents are removed in an effort to escape the historical guilt of capitalist modernization, Eisenman's new ideological smoothness allows a historically synchronic reincorporation of "garbage and throwaways of our daily and commonplace existence" (or at least that part of commonplace existence directly invaded by computer technology, which is most of it) into what at first looked like nonreferential form. What is more, it re-auratizes the images of just those production

techniques – reiterative grids, cinematic surfaces, cyberspace – that were supposed to be auratic art's demise.

So Emory does construct something like a consensual meaning. My question is, for whom? The appeal of Eisenman's architecture to the two generations of architects after him and their appetitive response to his research in the formation of their own work are already a kind of answer. ("For they are the contemporaries of the new entrepreneurs and they are themselves wonderful media animals.")[7] Eisenman's architecture seems to achieve the expressive form of my own generation of baby-boomers and our just-younger siblings, who, through historical circumstance, have developed a very specific pattern of cultural production and consumption, one in which modalities of cultural expression have been blurred, in which high and low, hip and nerd, left and right, have all but lost their distinctions, in which surfaces do not conceal meaning but are meaningful in and for themselves. This, I suggest, is the social consensus Eisenman's architecture is made for.[8]

In the 1980s many of us came to think of any consensual meaning as synonymous with officially designated meaning, as a conciliatory "don't worry, be happy" kind of culture that Reaganism brought about. It appeared to us as bathos at best, at worst as a scam. In the meantime, we were training ourselves in a paradoxical sensibility that amounted to just such a consensus and that here I describe by example. It was the deindividuation in Laurie Anderson's album *Big Science* and the de-Oedipalization in David Lynch's television series *Twin Peaks,* both of which represented psycho-intellectual transformations and cross-media developments; it was the cultural credit card that enabled us to consume, not only with the same ease but also with the same means, music videos and Robert Wilson plays, Paul Simon's presumedly "low" appropriations of South African music and those of the high-end quartet Kronos; it was the ludic deconstructions of Andy Kaufman; it was the residual commitment to the liberating power of popular culture coupled with knowing better. It was too much education and a disproportionate control, through our sheer demographics, over the distribution of commodities.

---

6 Jeffrey Kipnis, "Towards a New Architecture," in **Folding in Architecture**, 41–49.

7 Jean Baudrillard, **Cool Memories**, trans. Chris Turner (London: Verso, 1990), 223.

8 Fred Pfeil has made a similar point about postmodern music and performance art in "Makin' Flippy-Floppy: Postmodernism and the Baby-Boom PMC," in **Another Tale to Tell: Politic and Narrative in Postmodern Culture** (London:Verso, 1990). My **Architecture Theory Since 1968** (Cambridge, Mass.: MIT Press, 1998) advances these suggestions more theoretically.

It was the smoothness with which uncertainty, estrangement, and deindividuation were converted into an affirmative project – a blending of bleakness with euphoria, extreme competence with resignation, and almost manic swings between exhilaration and contempt for the absolute ease with which the signifier could be loosened from its signified and endlessly redistributed. It was on these very specific paradoxes that we built up our reading habits.

At the beginning of the formation of the generational audience I am trying to delimit, architecture brought to a provisional close an Oedipal struggle it had already begun in modernism, involving both a resistance to and an internalization of the authority of external pressures such as social use, technology, mass culture, and media.[9] Modern architecture was at least partially constituted through a dialectic of struggle and submission to that difficult authority. By the time of the 1973 Milan Triennale, Eisenman's 1976 essay "Postfunctionalism" (which called for an architecture detoured away from both functionalism and humanism), and the formation of the New York–Venice–Milan axis,[10] we already understood that in its newly antagonistic relation to the positivist inquiries of functionalism, behaviorism, historical determinism, and consumer culture – in the very painfulness of that relation – architecture could achieve a degree of resistant autonomy. The affirmation of architectural form was the negation of the social status quo. And ideology had the scabrous surface of conflict.

During the 1980s, however, that autonomy began to be overwhelmed by an ever more direct incorporation of architecture into mass media, image technologies, and mass consumption.[11] Distorted into conformation in order to survive, architecture could only either clinch into an extreme and isolated self-involvement or relinquish its autonomy and reassert itself as the total fusion of these forces, coordinating them into a smooth experience of space and surface that dissolves the differences between wall and video screen, column and pixel, object and image. The developments of which the Emory project is a part, it seems to me, are attempts at the latter – a totalusion of media, in terms of both form and content – where the most basic architectural drives enter into collaboration with the superego of socialized representations.

An audience with some remaining memory of the faith in an engaged resistance (albeit at a formal level, which we called a "critical architecture") yet that can still be titillated by the ecstatic surrender of the architectural subject to the very forces that threaten its demise; an audience with a continuity of experience within which the punctual pleasure of disintegration can still be felt – this is the audience that the Emory project solicits. The historical fate of this brilliant but vulnerable compromise-formation may well be decided not by virtue of its inherent value but by the intellectual and cultural use we put this memory to.

9 Among the "primal scenes" of this struggle, wherein the trauma of the authority of mass culture was felt most profoundly, is the work of Alison and Peter Smithson ("We used to collect architecture, now we collect ads"), the Independent Group in Great Britain, and later Robert Venturi and Denise Scott Brown in the United States. On an earlier modernism and its struggles with mass culture and mass media, see especially Beatriz Colomina, **Privacy and Publicity: Modern Architecture as Mass Media** (Cambridge, Mass.: MIT Press, 1994), and also K. Michael Hays, **Modernism and the Posthumanist Subject** (Cambridge, Mass.: MIT Press, 1992).

10 Aldo Rossi, Massimo Scolari, et al., **Architettura razionale**, catalog for the fifteenth Triennale (Milan: Franco Angeli, 1973); Peter Eisenman, "Postfunctionalism," **Oppositions** 6 (fall 1976).

11 Which is to say, architecture's very autonomy was made ready for very different representational uses. Robert Hughes's cover story "U.S. Architects, Doing Their Own Thing," **Time**, January 8, 1979, was among the first signs of popular culture's reappropriation of "high" architecture. Disney was among the next.

K. Michael Hays is professor of architecture at the Graduate School of Design, Harvard University. "M EMORY GAMES" was first published in **M Emory Games: Emory Center for the Arts,** exhibition catalog (New York: Rizzoli/Harvard College, 1995).

MAX REINHARDT HAUS   BERLIN, GERMANY   **1992**

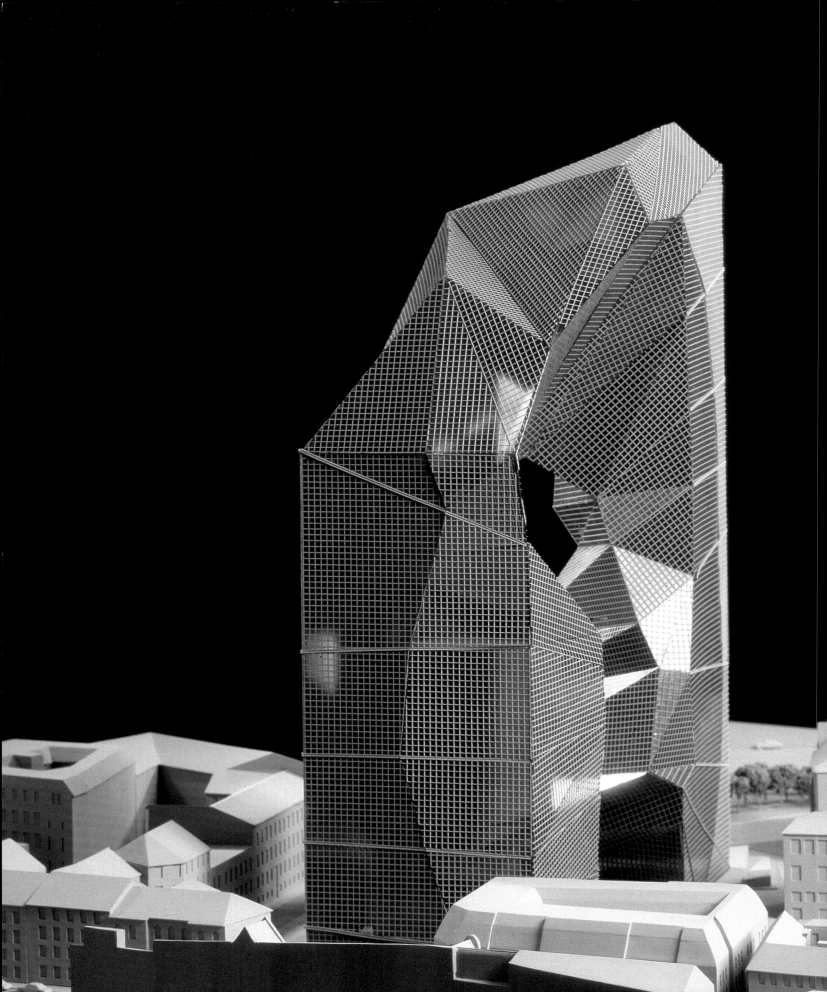

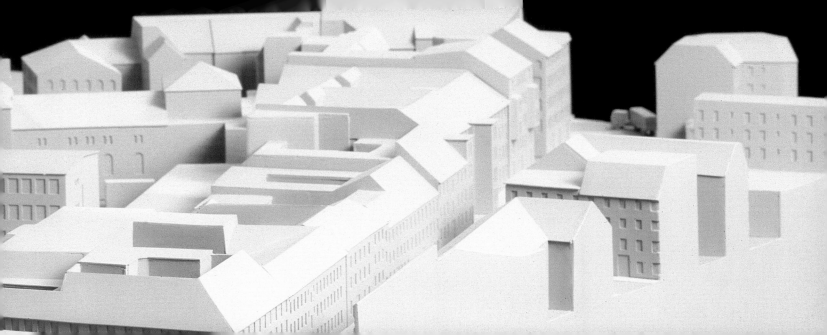

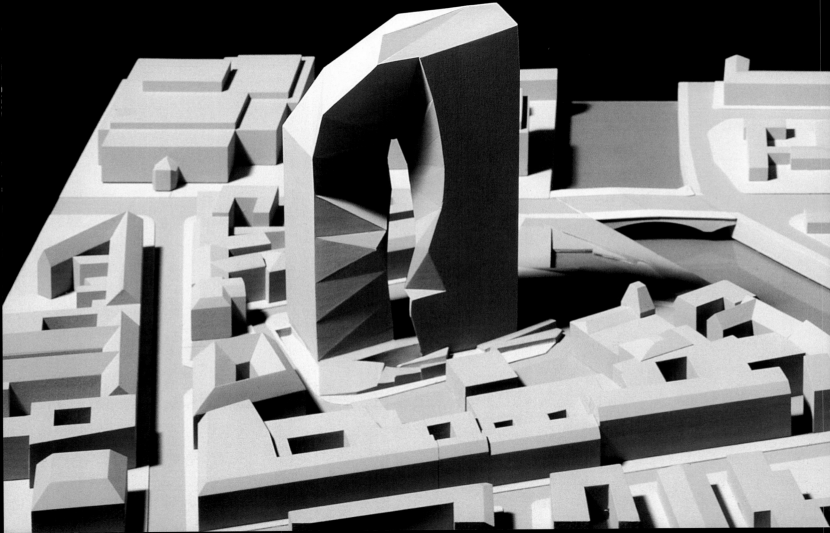

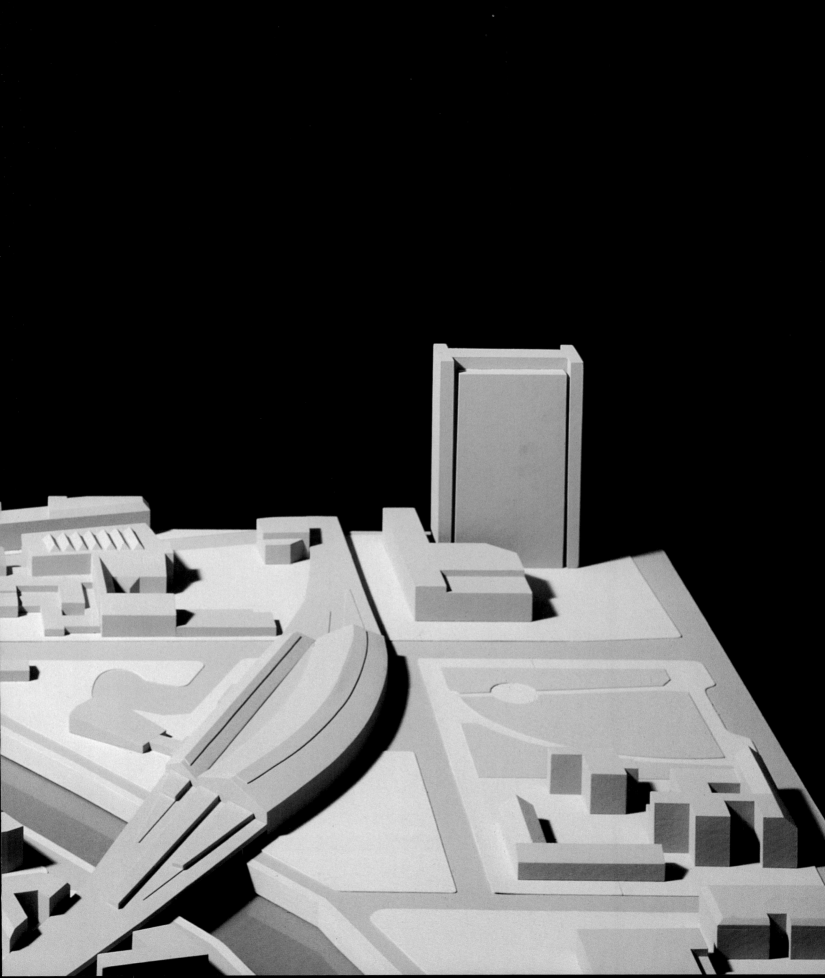

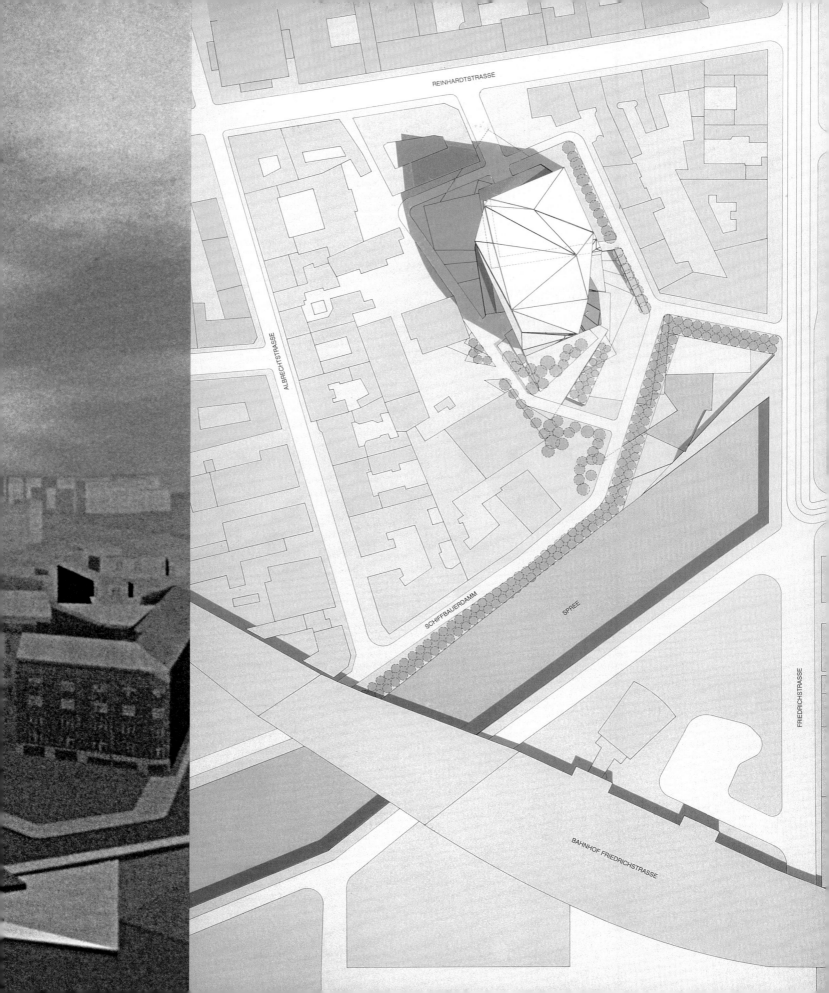

REINHARDTSTRASSE

ALBRECHTSTRASSE

SCHIFFBAUERDAMM

SPREE

FRIEDRICHSTRASSE

BAHNHOF FRIEDRICHSTRASSE

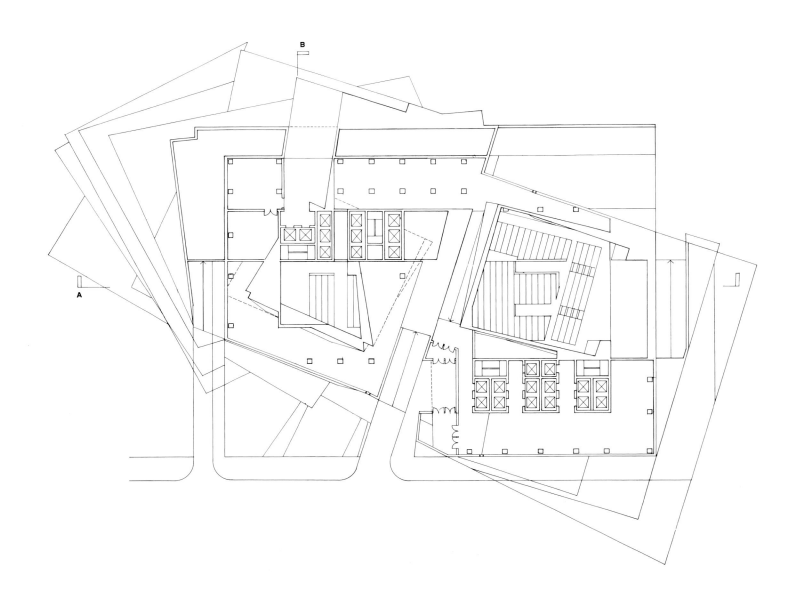

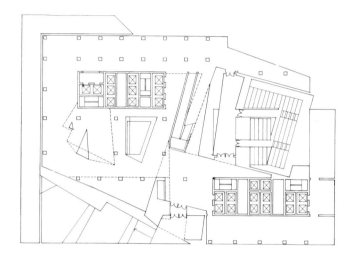

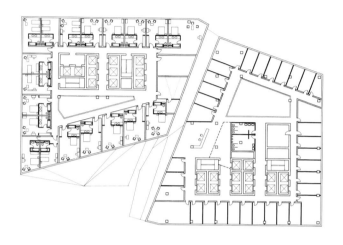

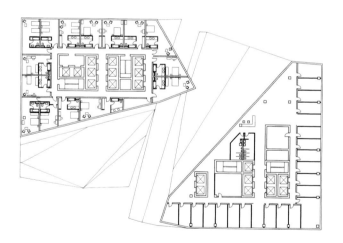

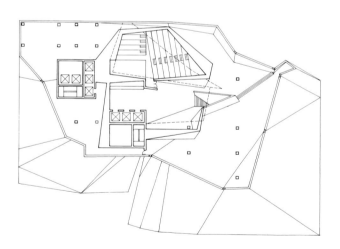

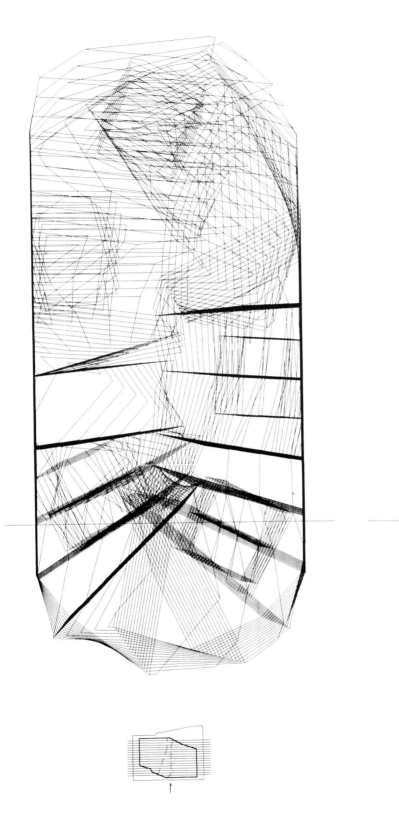

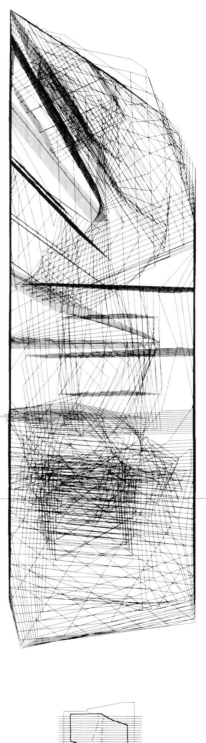

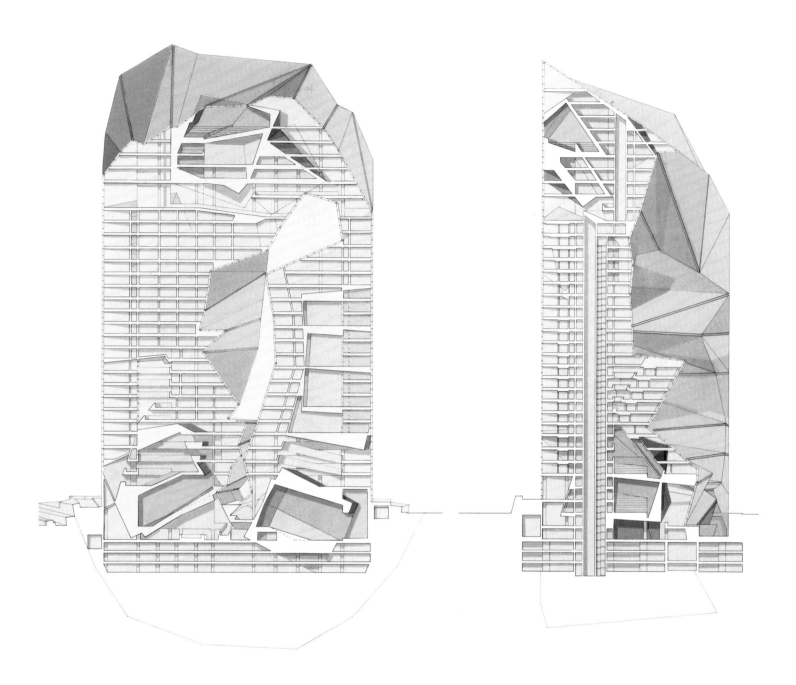

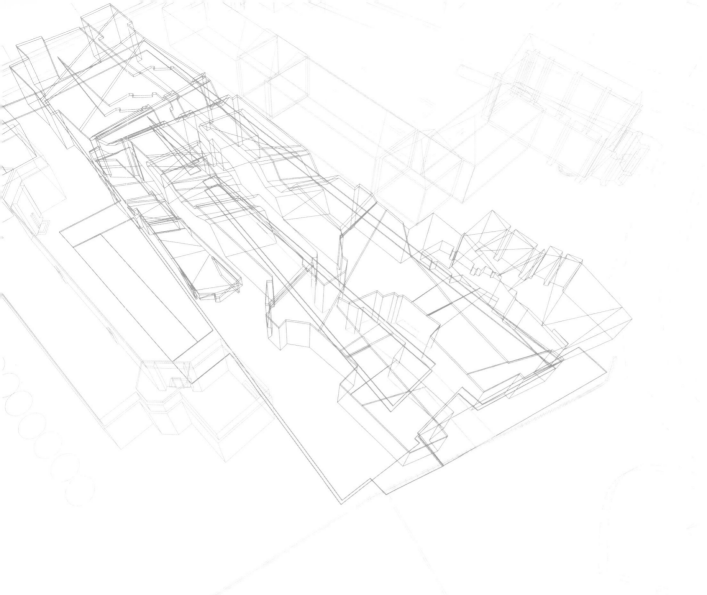

CONSERVATORY AND CONTEMPORARY ARTS CENTER TOURS, FRANCE **1993–94**

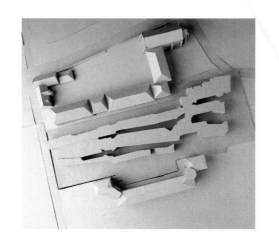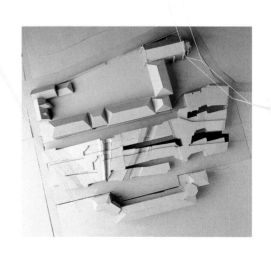

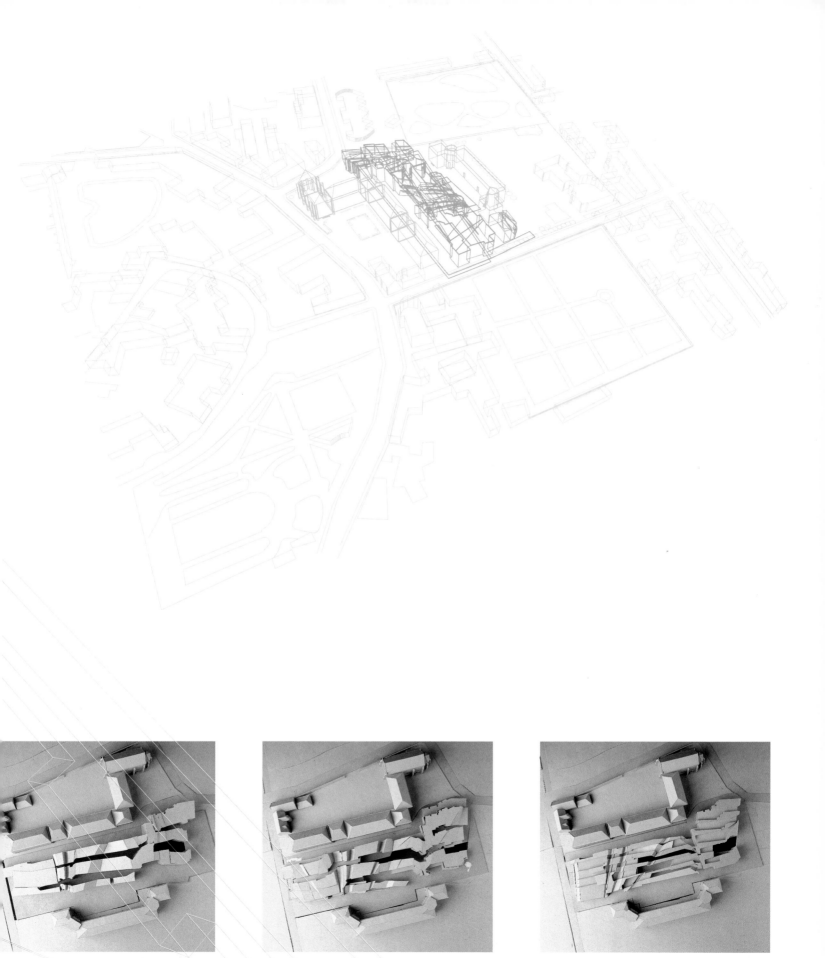

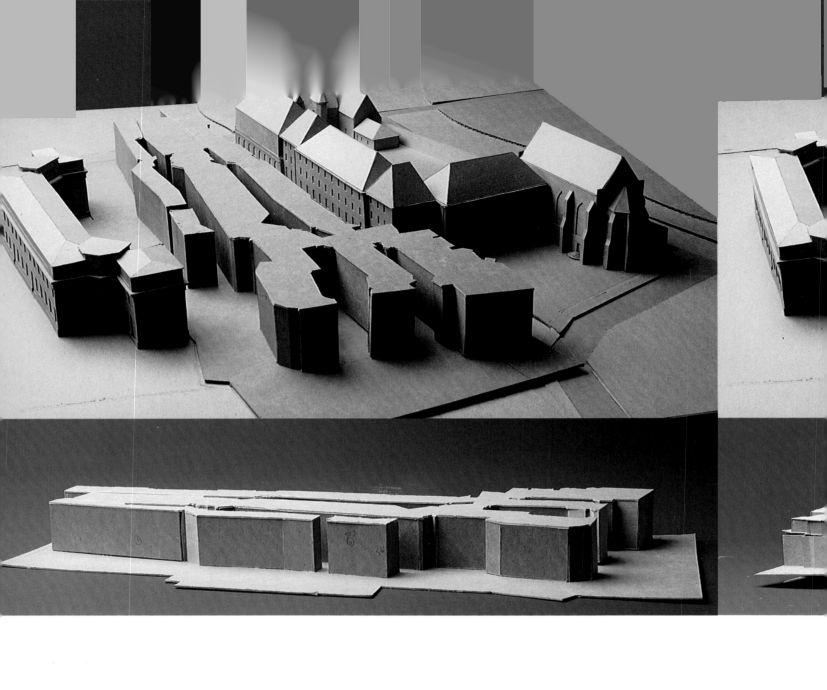

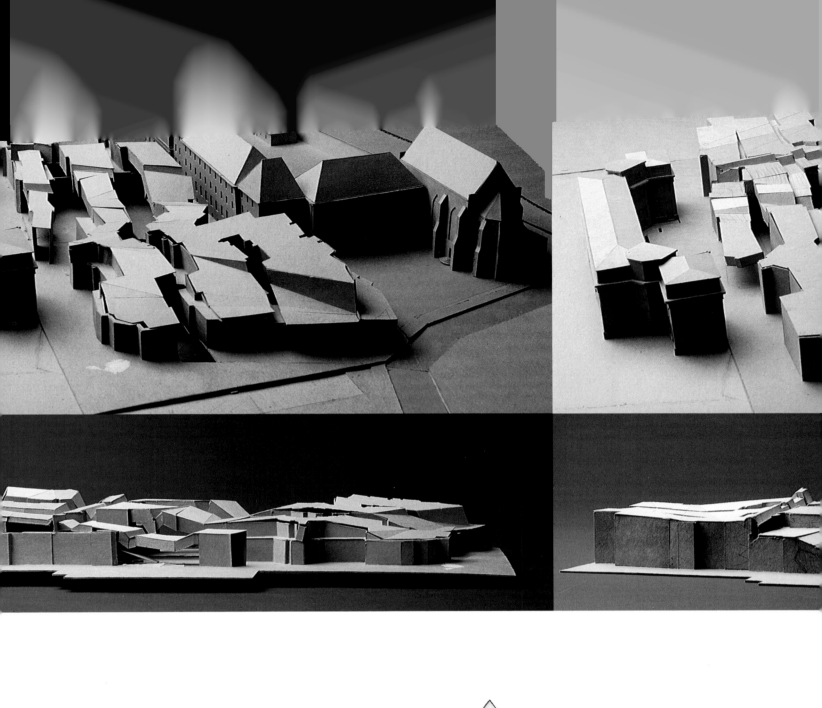

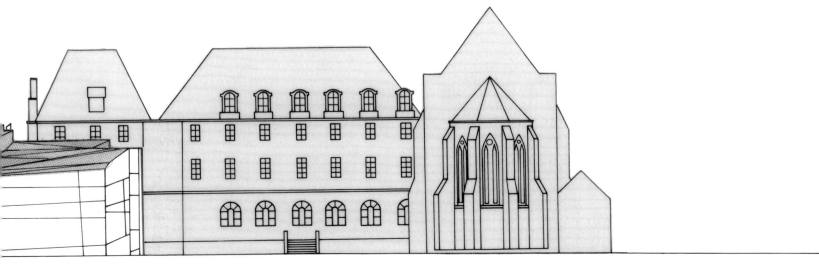

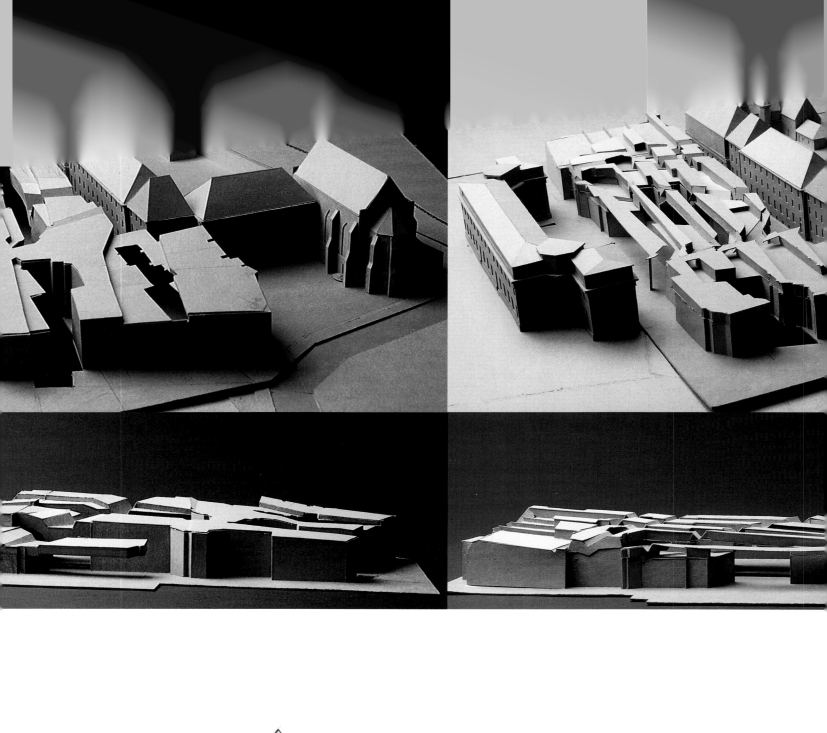

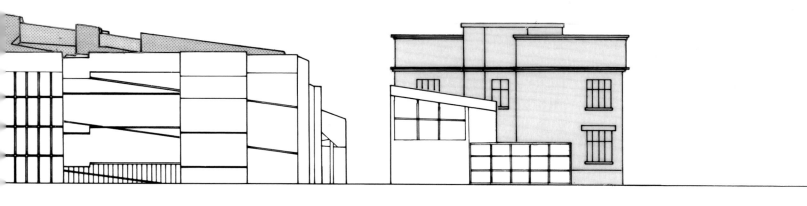

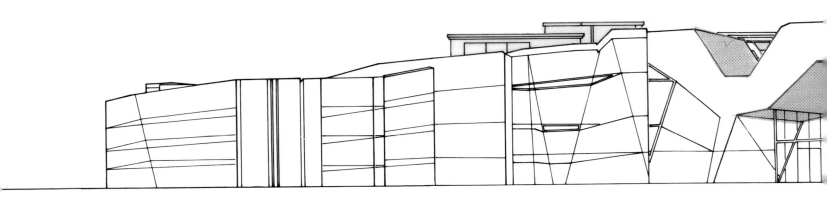

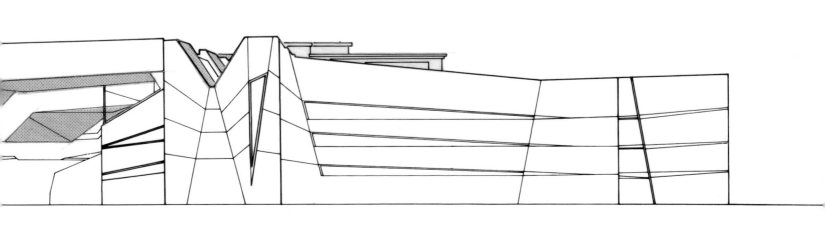

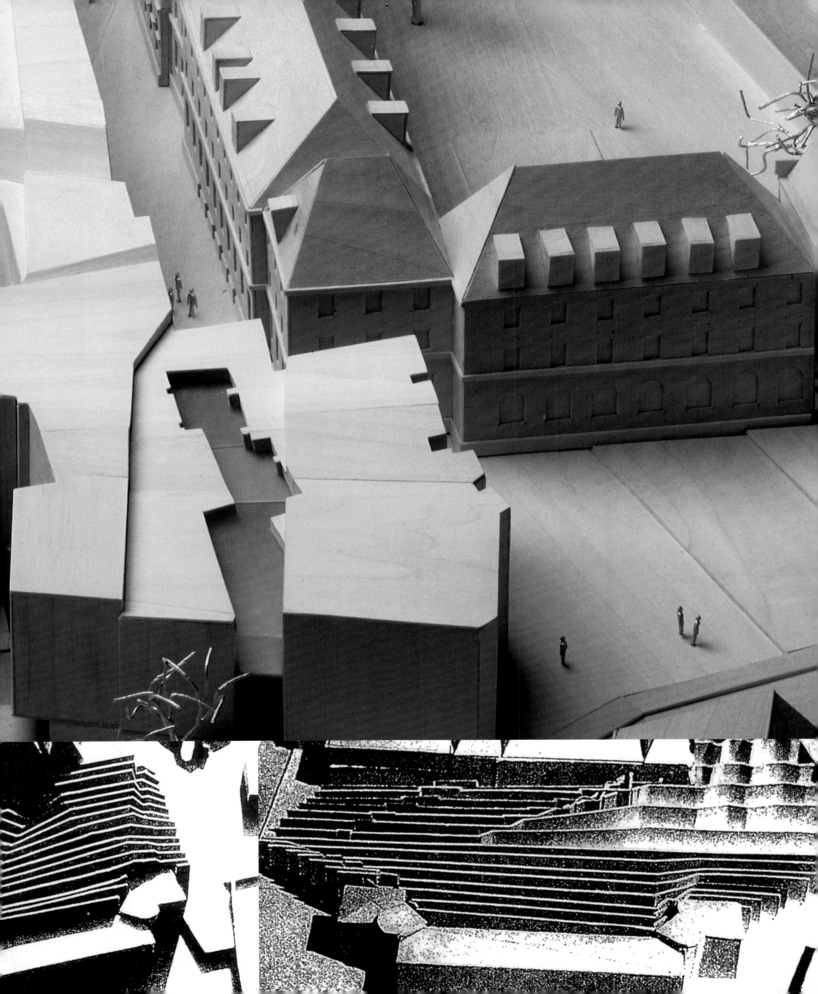

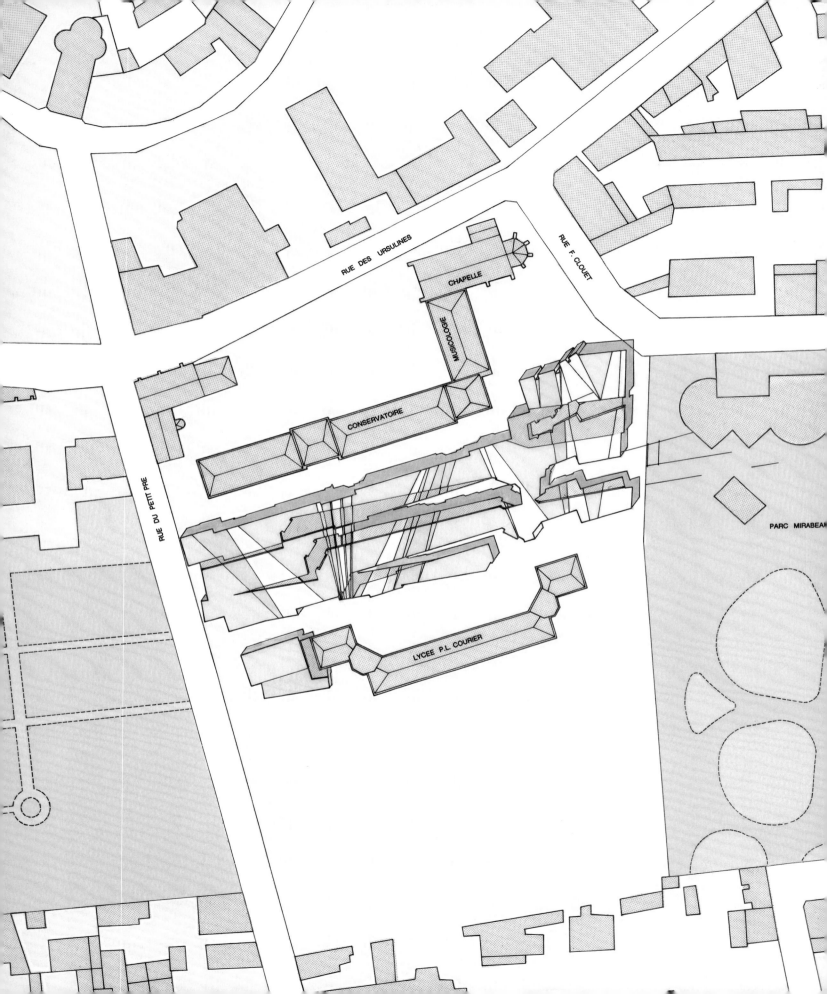

RUE DES URSULINES

RUE F. CLOUET

CHAPELLE

MUSICOLOGIE

CONSERVATOIRE

RUE DU PETIT PRE

PARC MIRABEAU

LYCEE P.L. COURIER

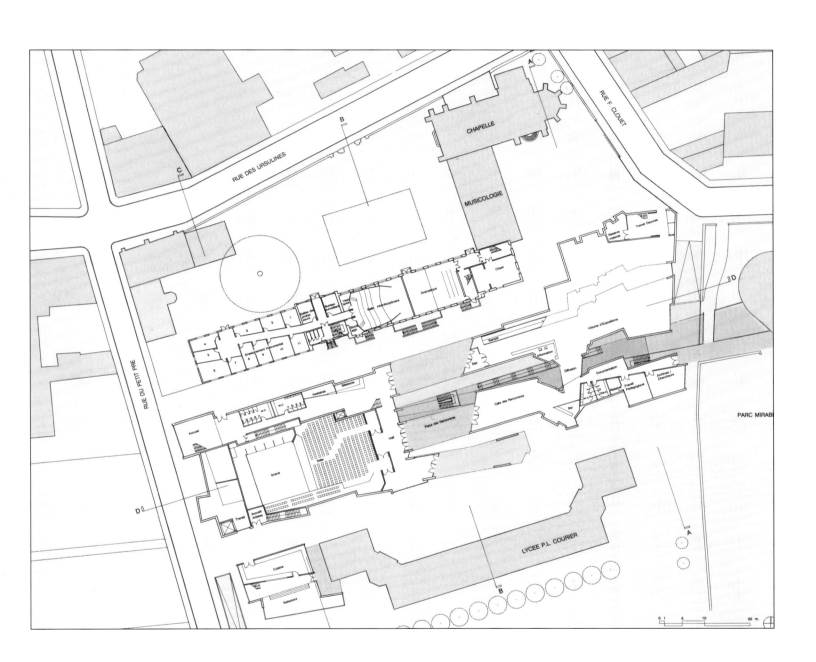

RUE DES URSULINES

RUE F. CLOUET

CHAPELLE

MUSICOLOGIE

RUE DU PETIT PRE

PARC MIRABE

LYCEE P.L. COURIER

233

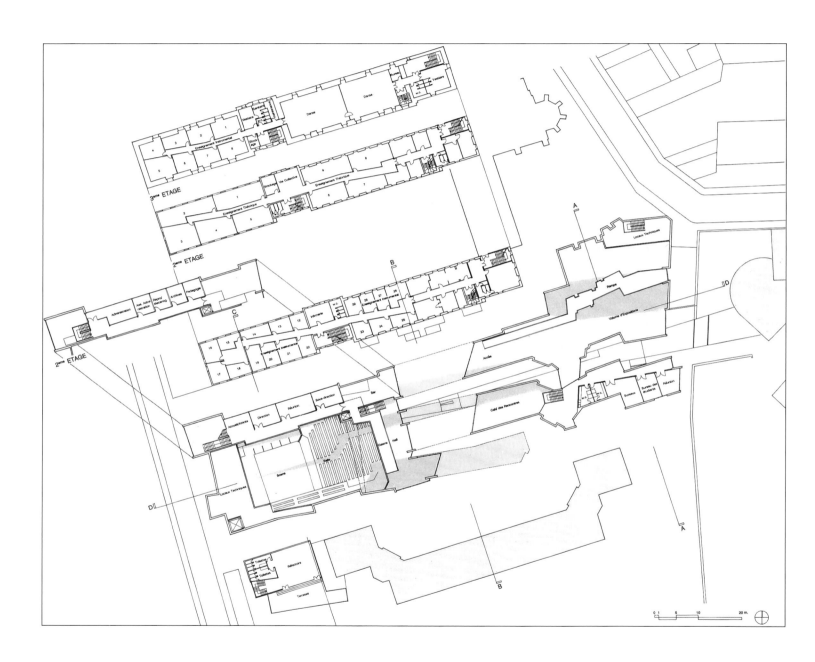

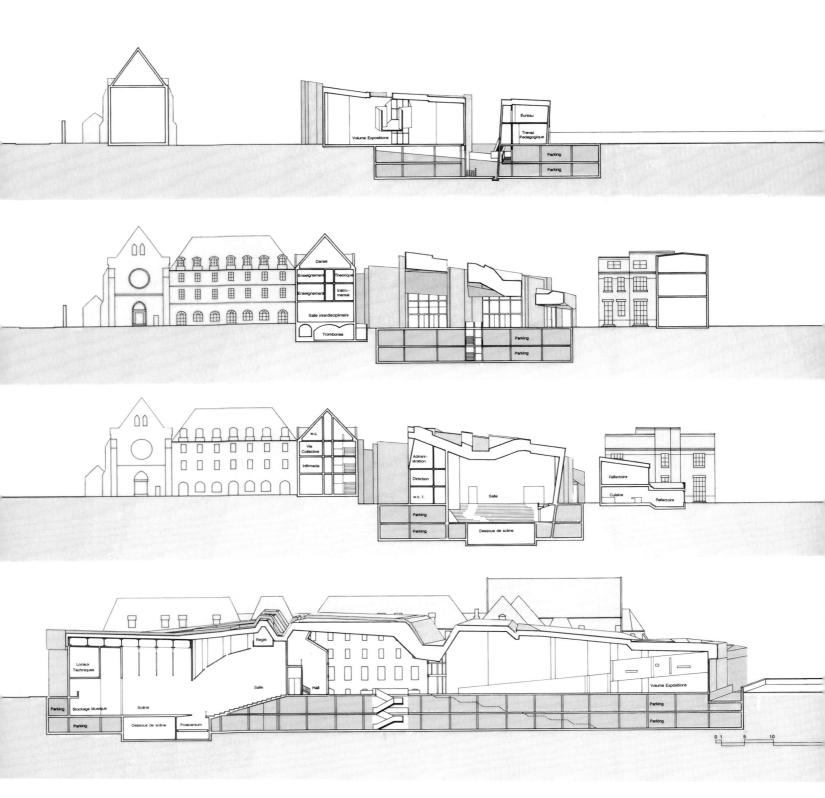

Bureau

Travail Pedagogique

Volume Expositions

Parking

Parking

Danse

Enseignement Theorique

Enseignement Instru-mental

Salle interdisciplinaire

Trombones

Parking

Parking

w.c.

Vie Collective

Infirmerie

Admini-stration

Direction

w.c. f.

Salle

Parking

Parking

Dessous de scène

Réfectoire

Cuisine

Refectoire

Regie

Locaux Techniques

Salle

Hall

Volume Expositions

Parking

Stockage Musique

Scène

Parking

Dessous de scène

Proscenium

Parking

0 1   5   10

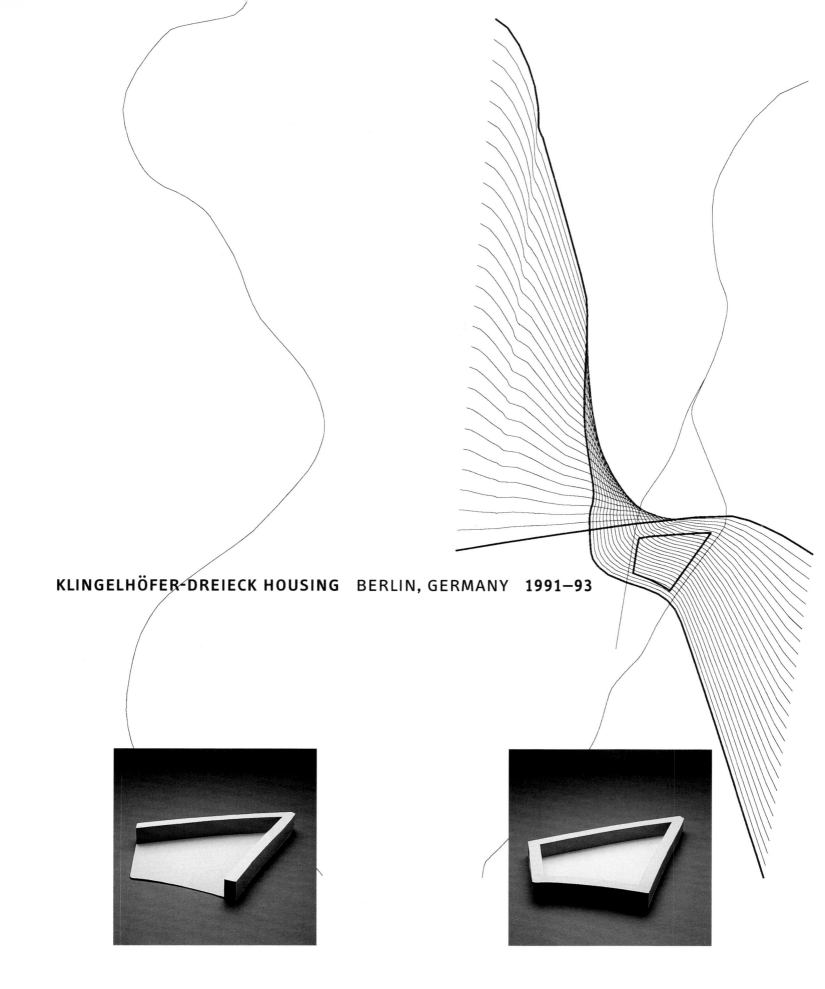

KLINGELHÖFER-DREIECK HOUSING   BERLIN, GERMANY   1991–93

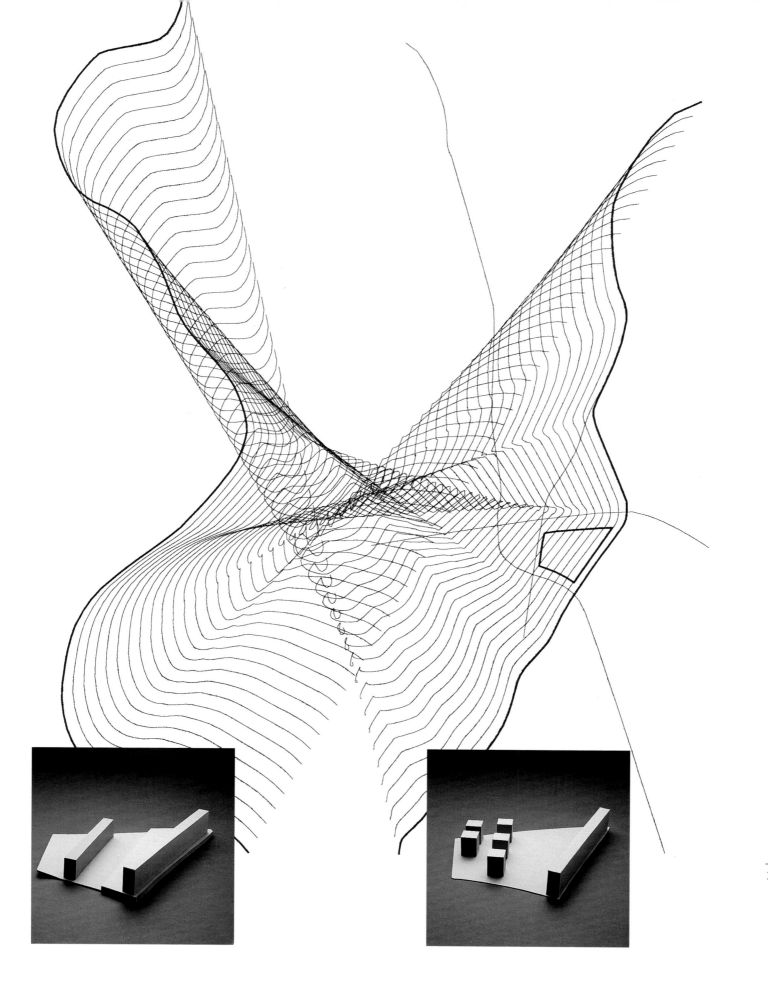

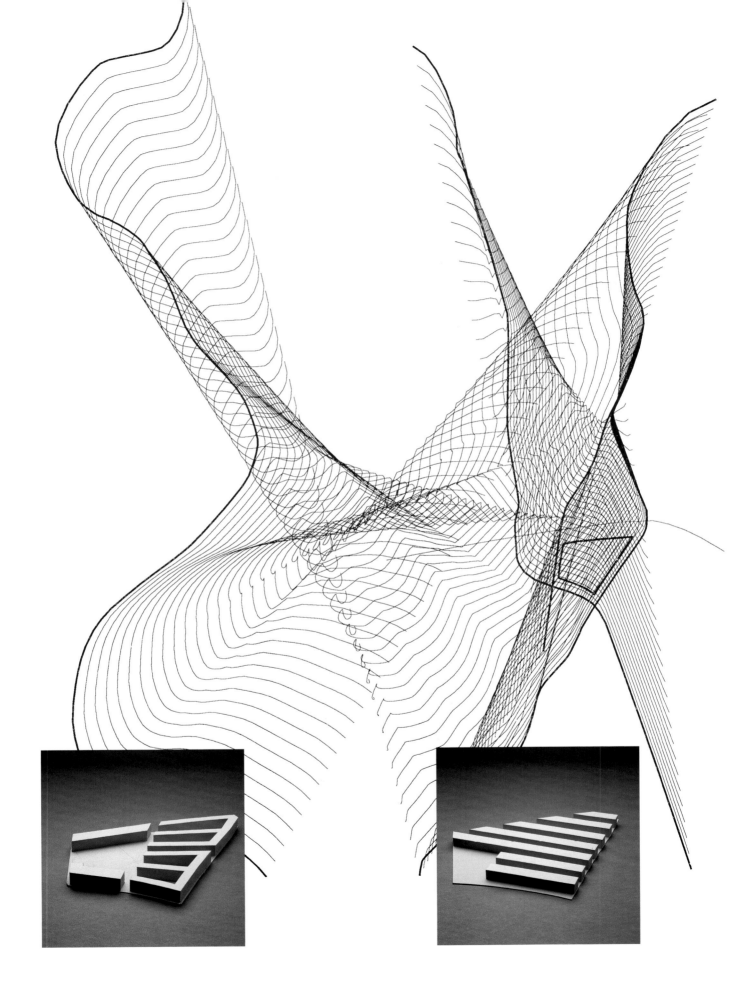

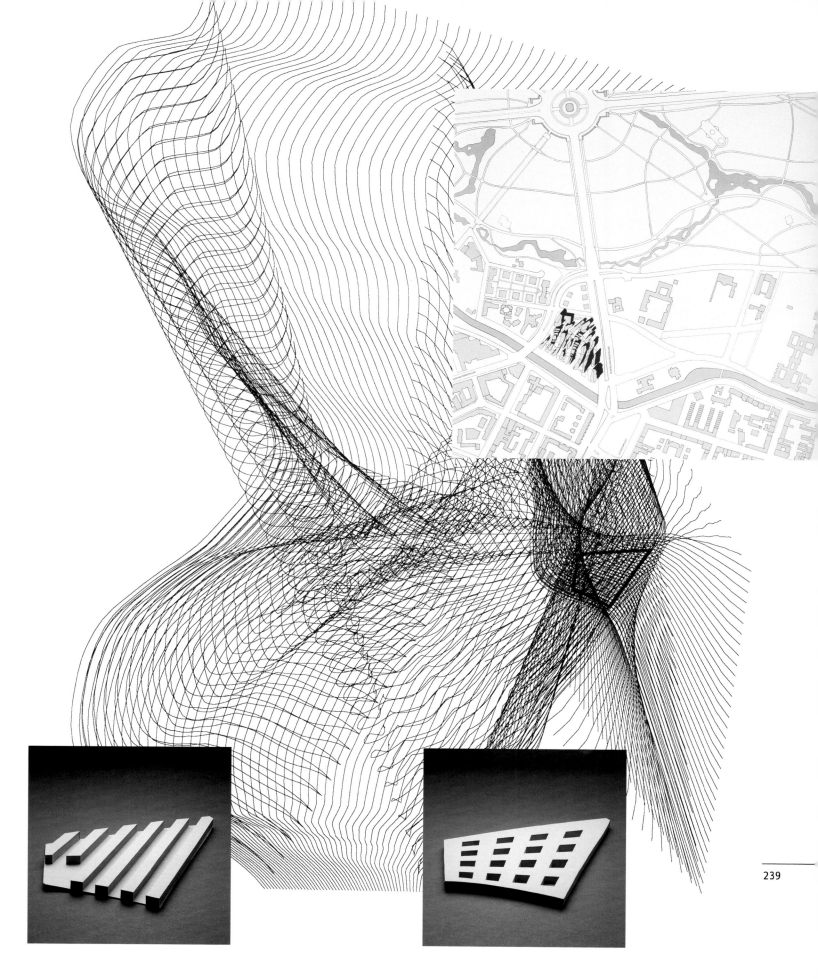

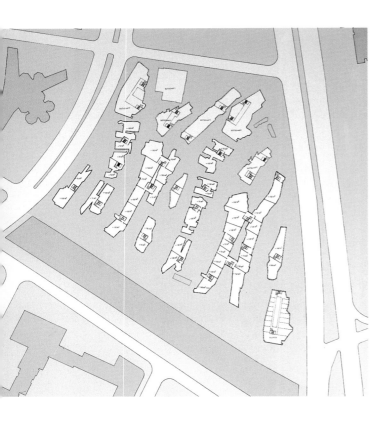

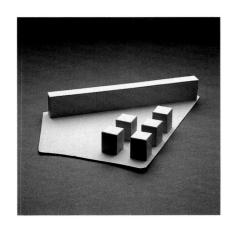

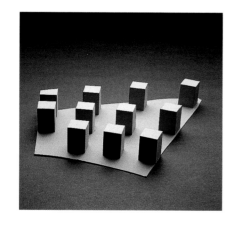

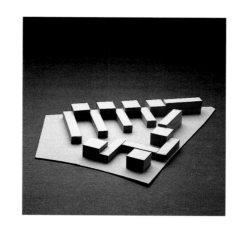

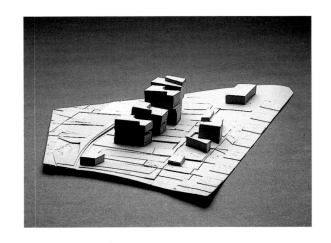

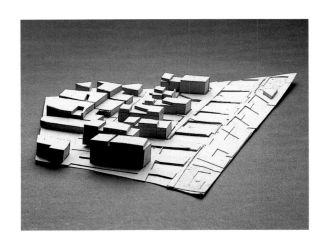

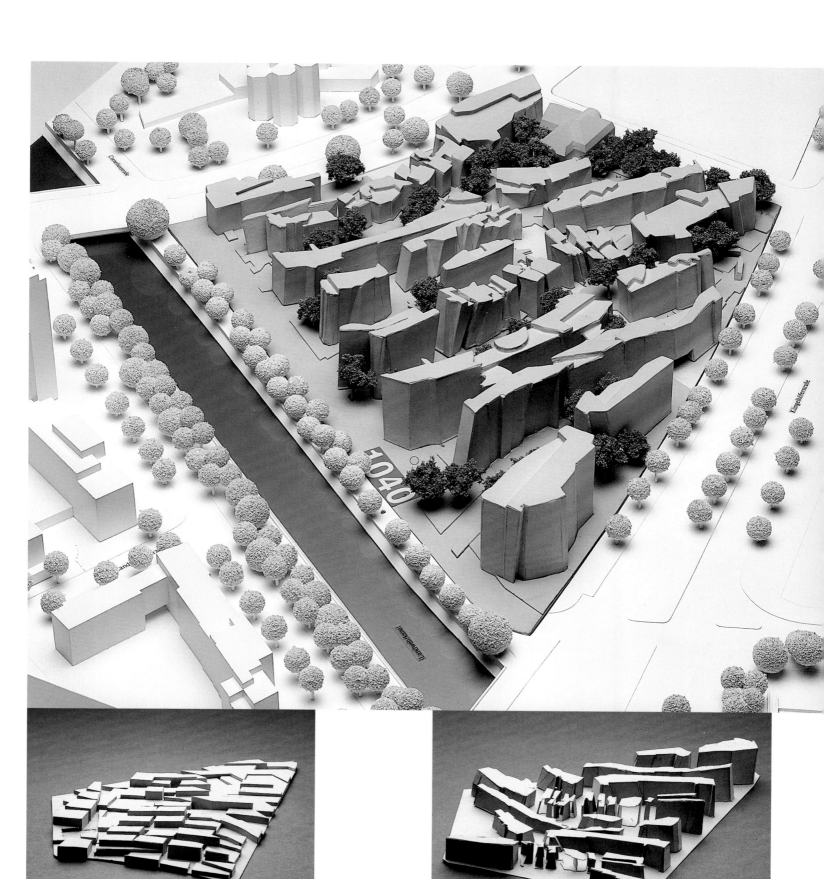

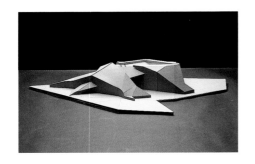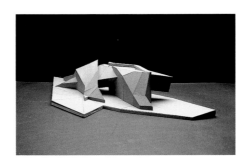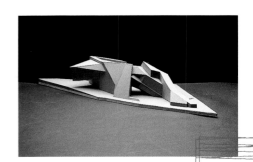

NÖRDLICHES DERENDORF MASTER PLAN   DÜSSELDORF, GERMANY   **1992**

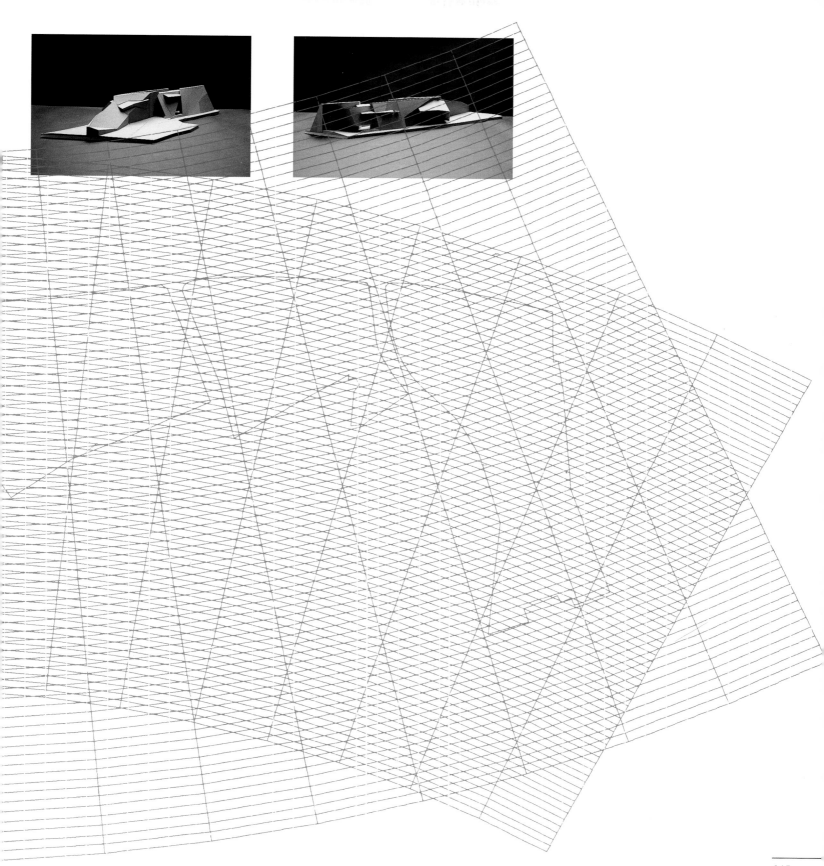

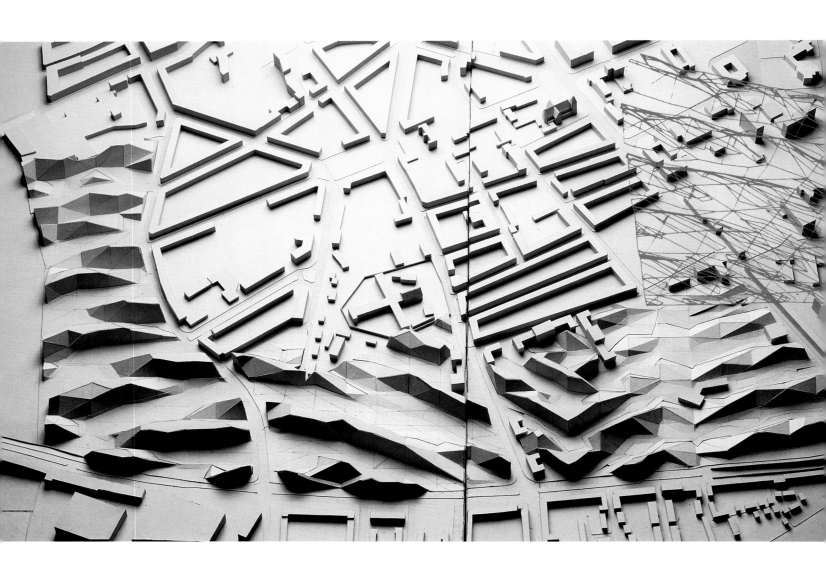

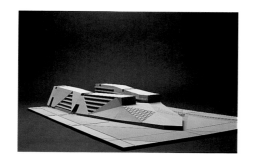

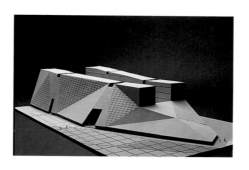

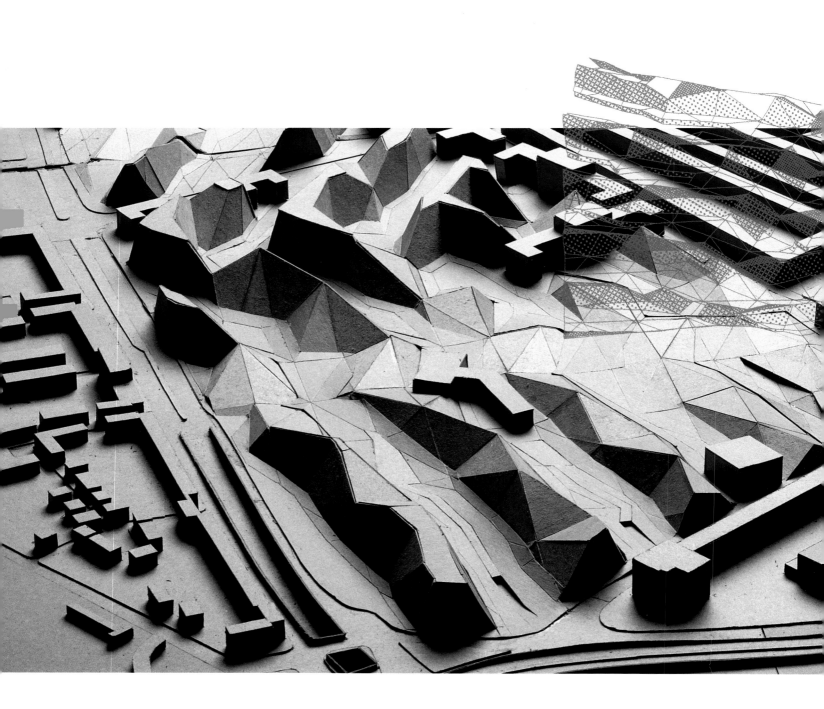

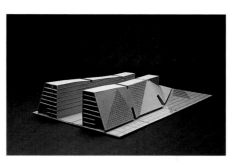

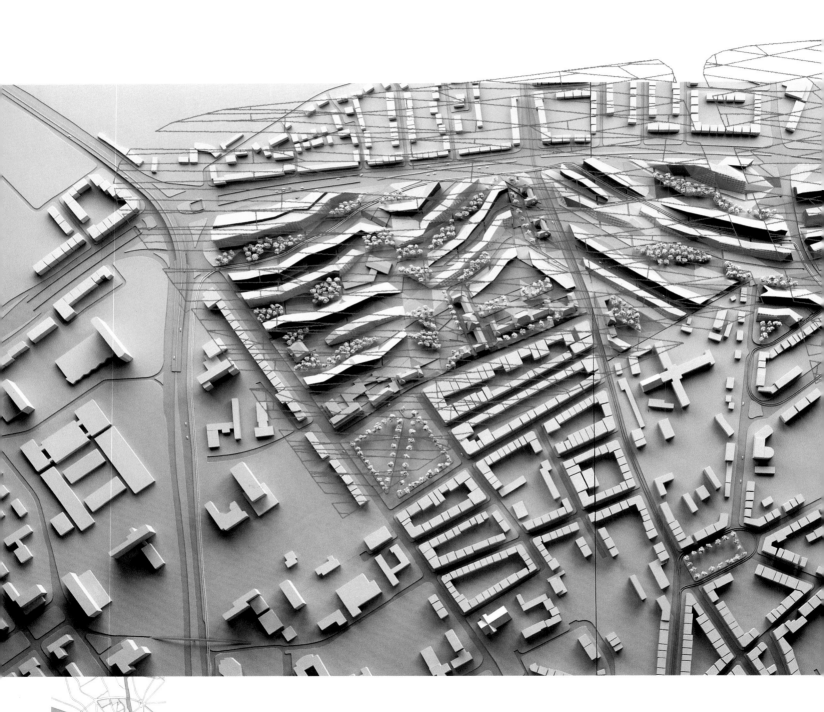

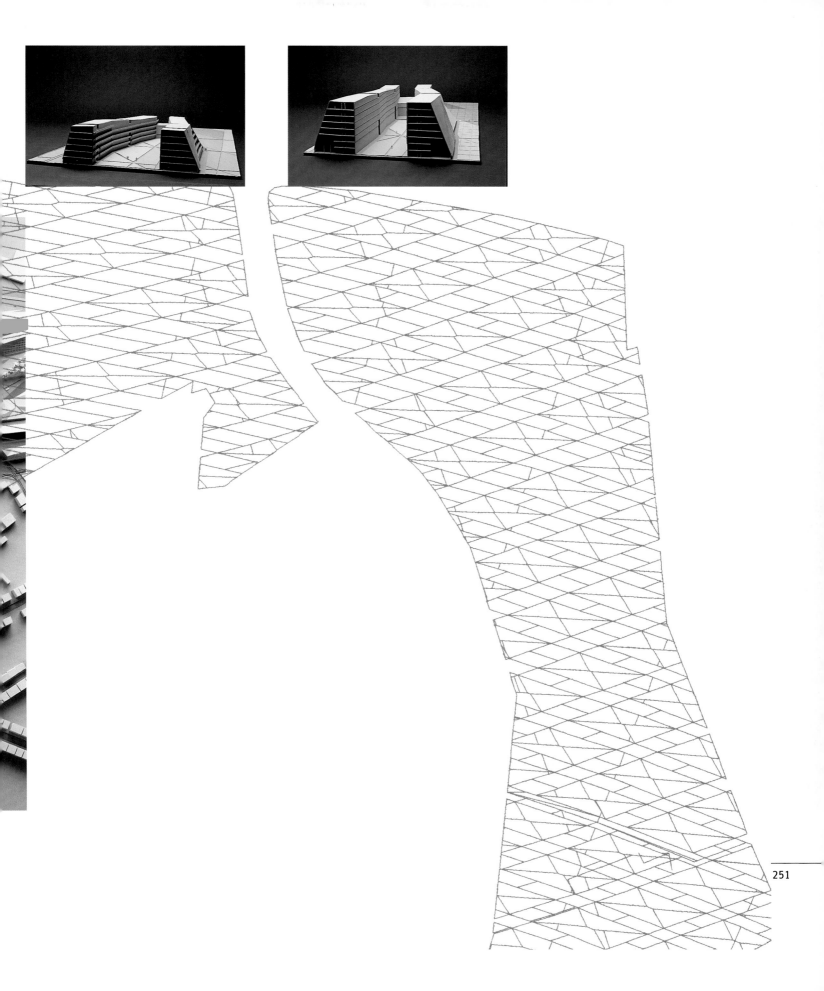

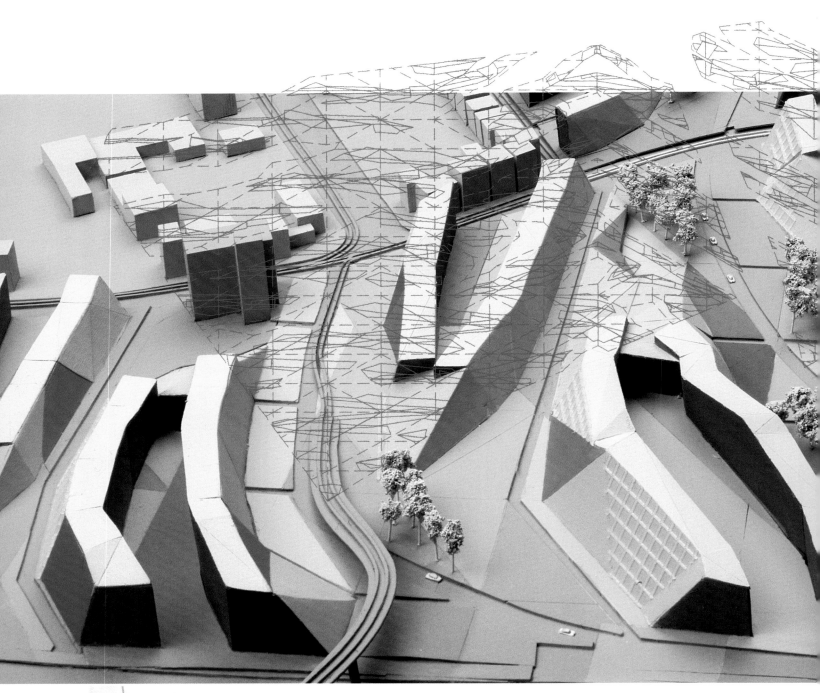

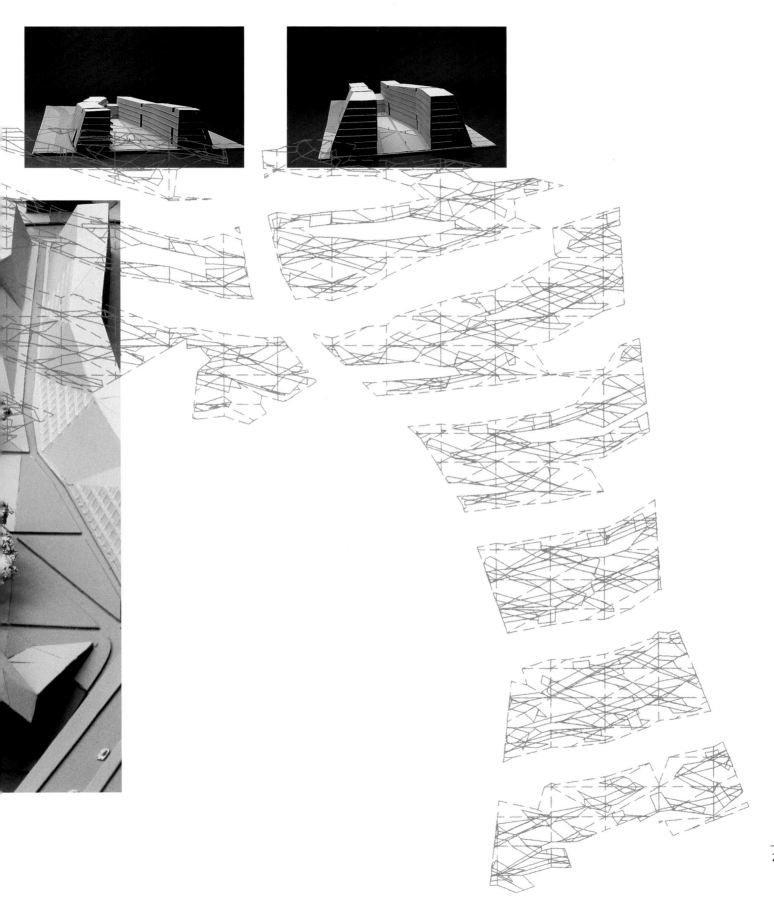

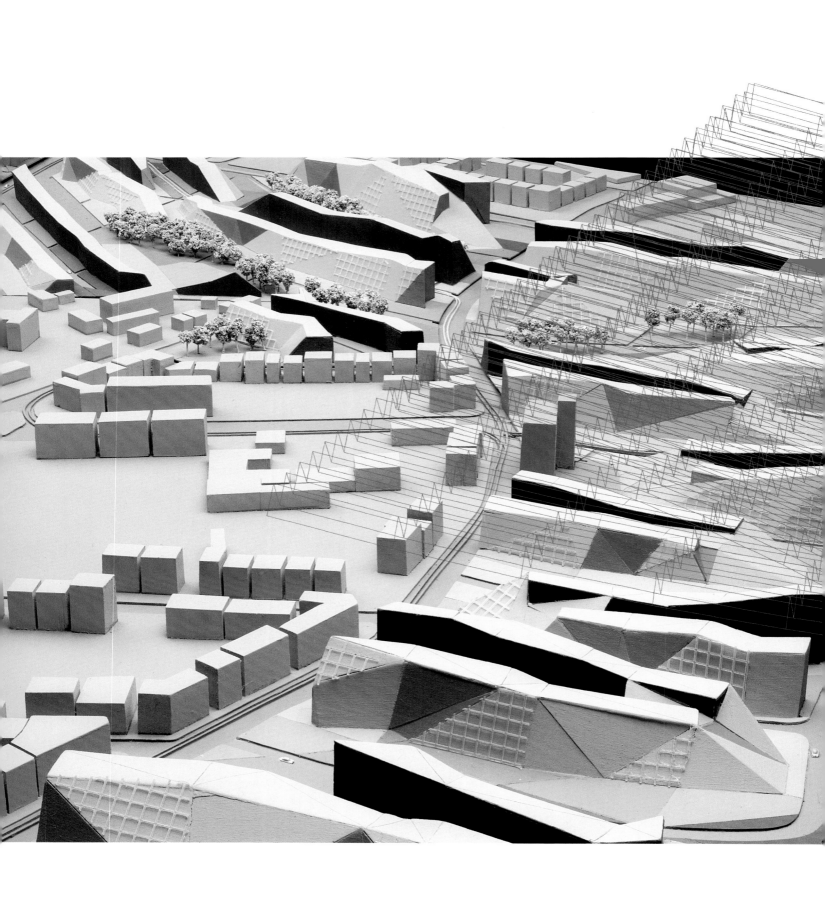

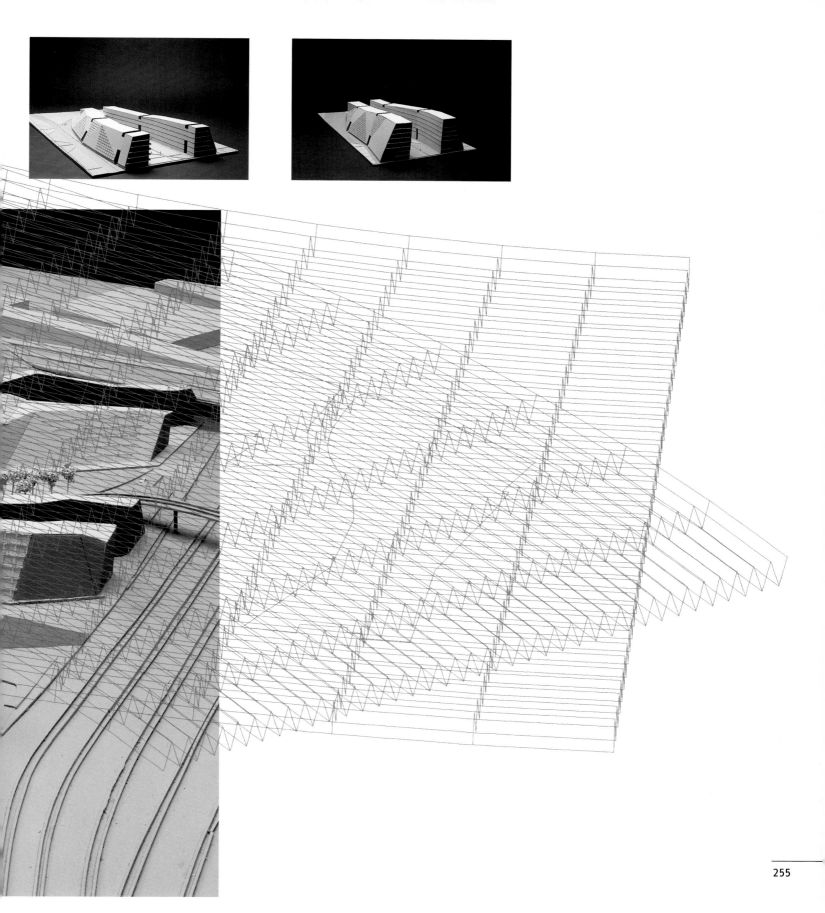

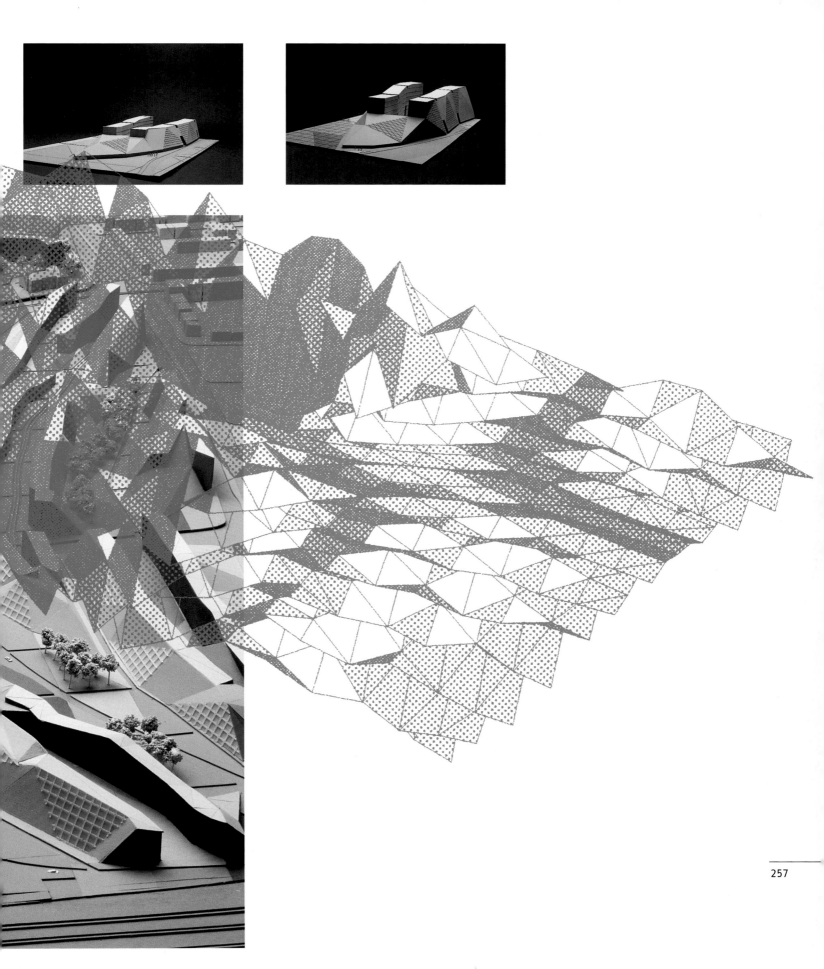

Zones of Undecidability I
The Interstitial Figure:
The Church for the Year 2000

Peter Eisenman

If, as Heidegger suggests, the human being is a place or a zone, then it is also possible to introduce an idea of a body not as a human subject or an architectural object but as the idea of an embodying object. Ever since Vitruvius said that architecture was essentially commodity, firmness, and delight, architecture has faced the question of representation and, because of its particular condition of presence – the sign of a column and the column being one and the same thing – embodiment. In this sense, Vitruvius did not mean that architecture should stand up (firmness), since to be architecture it must already stand up, must resist gravity. Rather, and importantly, architecture must look like it stands up. Thus architecture has always been both being and a representation of that being, both the sign and the signified in the presence of the sign itself. Jacques Derrida has consistently attempted to demonstrate that in language the sign and the signified are a heterogeneous, enfolded structure. Architecture, however, presents a different condition of the sign: while the sign and the signified may be enfolded, they are also always embodied; the column is always the sign of the column as well as, say, the sign of an upright tree or human figure. As Derrida has said, architecture will always mean, even though it is a weak sign system. Therefore, to question architecture's condition of representation is to question its embodiment. It is not a question of denying the function and meaning of the object, but rather an attempt to question the legitimacy of the formal decisions made in their name. This idea is argued by Rosalind Krauss and Yve-Alain Bois in *The Formless: A User's Guide*. They state that to preserve the singularity of objects today we must cut them off from their previous modes of legitimation. From this perspective, it is possible to speculate that a primary objective of architectural theory could be to propose some alternative to the legitimacy of previous notions of architecture's embodiment.

Since the 16th century, architecture has assumed that the Vitruvian dictum was not so much a convention as it was natural to its discourse. This led even Mies van der Rohe, whose tenet "less is more" was a significant attempt to undercut the legitimacy of embodiment, to make a fundamental change in his architecture: at the Alumni Hall building on the Illinois Institute of Technology campus, he added what looked like structure to what actually was structure to express the fact rather than to be a fact.

Clearly the representation of function has always been architecture's primary form of embodiment. Such things as metaphor and symbol also speak about embodiment.

Embodiment in architecture can thus be defined as the codification of form as it has been legitimized in time by function, aesthetics, and meaning. But while architecture will always embody its meaning, this does not mean that this representation of function or meaning should be used as a form of legitimacy. The question that must be asked is, how can architecture be a function without using that function to legitimize its form?

In his book *Francis Bacon: Logique de la sensation,* Gilles Deleuze proposes an idea that might be useful in this context: a difference between figuration and the figural. For Deleuze, figuration is an embodiment of the figural; it is narrative and illustrative. He suggests two ways to escape figuration: one is to move toward pure form or abstraction; the other is to move toward the purely figural. While abstraction characterized an aspect of modernism, one of its problems was the failure to realize the need for the figural. Nietzsche says in *The Will to Power* that figuration is a primary drive of humankind. The difference between figural and figuration is important because it clarifies a problem of embodiment in architecture, for in Deleuze's sense, the figural in architecture has also always been lodged in the figurative.

Figure in architecture has traditionally referred to a condition of formed presences, as well as to the corollary idea of ground; that is, figuration presumed the ground to be a nonfigure but to have no less a presence. This embodiment of figure and ground present in figuration is one of the primary conditions that has historically legitimized architecture. The legitimacy of the figure/ground relationship was being questioned by Piranesi as early as the mid-18th century, particularly in his drawing of the Campo Marzio, in which he operated on two conditions. First, he obliterated the relationship of figure to ground by producing a plan of only figures, a figure/figure urbanism in which the ground is only an emptiness outlining the filigree of the figures. Second, and more important in this context, he inserted in the leftover voids between the figures additional figures, which can be called *interstitial figures.*

Traditionally, the interstitial in architecture is seen as a solid figuration generally known as poché, which is an articulated solid (usually a wall or facade) between two spaces; these walls can be either between exterior and interior spaces or between two interior spaces. While the interstitial is a containing presence that is figured or articulated, it is also primarily inert or static. This traditional context of the interstitial can be considered figuration in the Deleuzian sense, because it already embodies its content as a container that encloses, shelters, and has an aesthetic.

In order to see the interstitial as something other than an articulated yet inert presence between two spaces, its status as an embodied figure must be changed. This change in status could initially be proposed as an absent presence within an absence (a kind of double absence). In this sense, the interstitial proposes a dissonant space of meaning; it becomes an autonomous, figural matrix of forces. This idea of the interstitial is distinguished from previous conditions of the interstitial in architecture by three characteristics. First, it will be seen to be the result of a process of extraction that produces a figural as opposed to a formal condition of embodiment. As Deleuze writes, in order to reach the figural, it is necessary to extract it from the figurative. Second, this idea of the interstitial will exist as a condition of spacing as opposed to forming, as an absent presence in an absence, that is, between two conditions of figure as opposed to a condition of figure and ground. Finally, this idea of the interstitial as an absence is no longer seen as forming, containing, or inert. It is as if the voids that are the spaces and rooms of any building are now seen as balloons filled with water or sand and are acted upon by the interstitial voids, which are now no longer inert but are exerting a pressure back on and into the spaces.

This idea of the interstitial as a critique of embodiment was first proposed in the competition project for the pilgrimage Church for the Year 2000 in Rome. The question was whether the church could be a critique of both representation and figure/ground at the same time. That is, could the figure of the church, which is one of the most embodied architectural icons, be extracted from its figuration, and also, could that figuration become interstitial, that is, not only deny the ground but also deny the tradition of the interstitial as it has existed in architecture? In this context, to produce a condition of the interstitial would preclude traditional representation as the end product.

The tradition of the pilgrimage church centers on the issues of proximity and distance. Often such churches had no nave but were merely markers along a route. The ideas of proximity and distance, of route and no center, and thus the idea of the transgression of type and function, became a critique of embodiment. This critique produced an object that was neither figure nor ground but rather could be considered interstitial – figure *as* ground.

The extraction of the figural was attempted by imposing an external diagram of a liquid crystal onto a diagram of program and site. This new diagram was to act as an index of a condition between proximity and distance in the pilgrimage church. The liquid crystal itself is a condition of between, a state of suspension between a static crystalline form and a flowing liquid state. The liquid crystal is also a basic element of visual media today, a fact that was important in the development of the specific form of the church. When superposed over the diagram of function and site, the liquid crystal diagram began to blur the legitimating function of that diagram but without compromising its function. The overlay of the two diagrams attempted to produce a form that would embody neither the first nor the second diagram. Instead, this overlay reproduces the gradual distortion of the original liquid crystal phase to a between state of flux. In the form of the church, the multiple layers of the overlays of the diagrams become deformations of the former solid/void, figure/ground relationship of the container.

In this sense, the church is literally figured out of a ground of the molecular order of the liquid crystal. The traditional forms of authority and embodiment associated with the pilgrimage church, or simply the church itself, are displaced and deformed by the introduction of the diagrammatic overlay. This extraction of the figural from the figurative does not necessarily produce a condition of interstitial void. Another important step is necessary, one in which the material structure no longer envelops the contour in order to develop the figure. Rather, here the interstitial figures pass through the contour in order to dissipate into material structure. Thus the contour, no longer dormant between exterior and interior, assumes a new function.

The facades of the church in the Middle Ages were a form of media. The facades of the Church for the Year 2000 become an other form of media, one between the diagram of the liquid crystal and a large-scale liquid crystal screen, now transformed from an outer layer to the interstitial void of its inner layer. Here new media and new architecture are enfolded to deny the former embodiment of the image of the church. In an age of media, embodiment is further problematized as an aspect of architecture by television's ability to make images more quickly than architecture can. If television, media, and virtual reality make the images that were formerly the domain of architecture, how is architecture to return to a discursive possibility? There seem to be two possibilities. The first is to return the affective body of the subject to architecture. The space of the church project has an affective relationship in its physical form to the human body. It asks critical questions about the relationship of the body in space. The second is to question the figure/ground relationship. The embodiment of ground is associated with a basic human desire for ground. In this context, it might be possible to mediate between the desire for ground and an affective condition of space. Affective space becomes the virtuality of the interstitial.

CHURCH FOR THE YEAR 2000   ROME, ITALY   1996

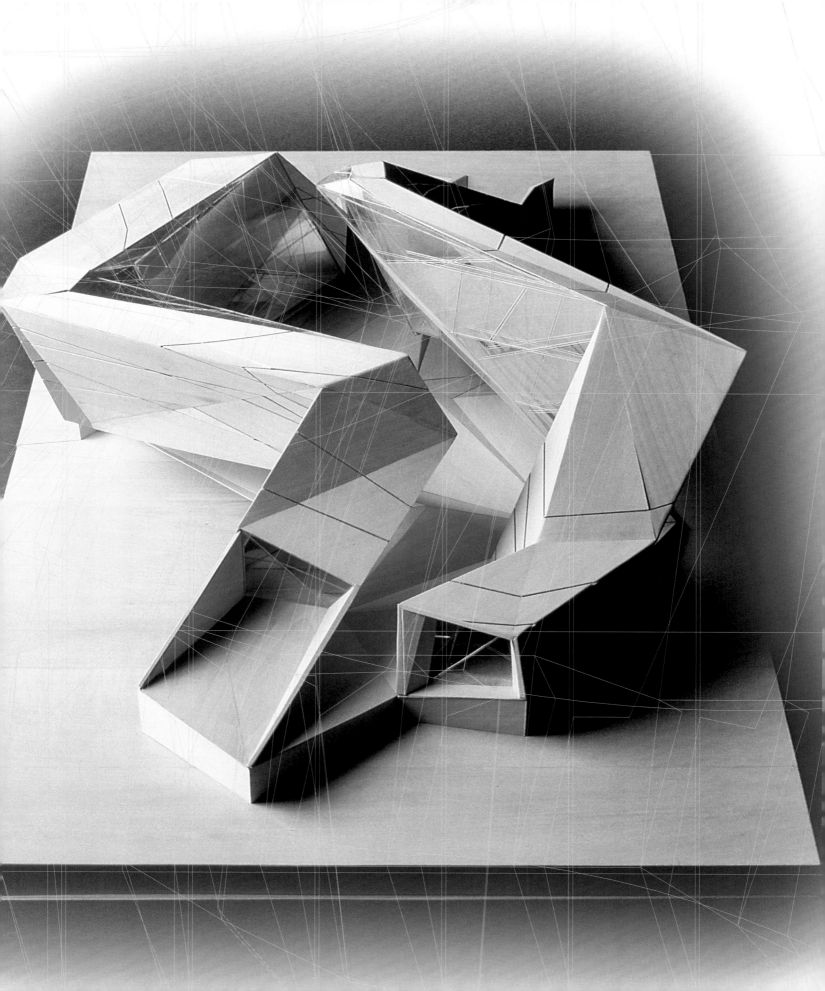

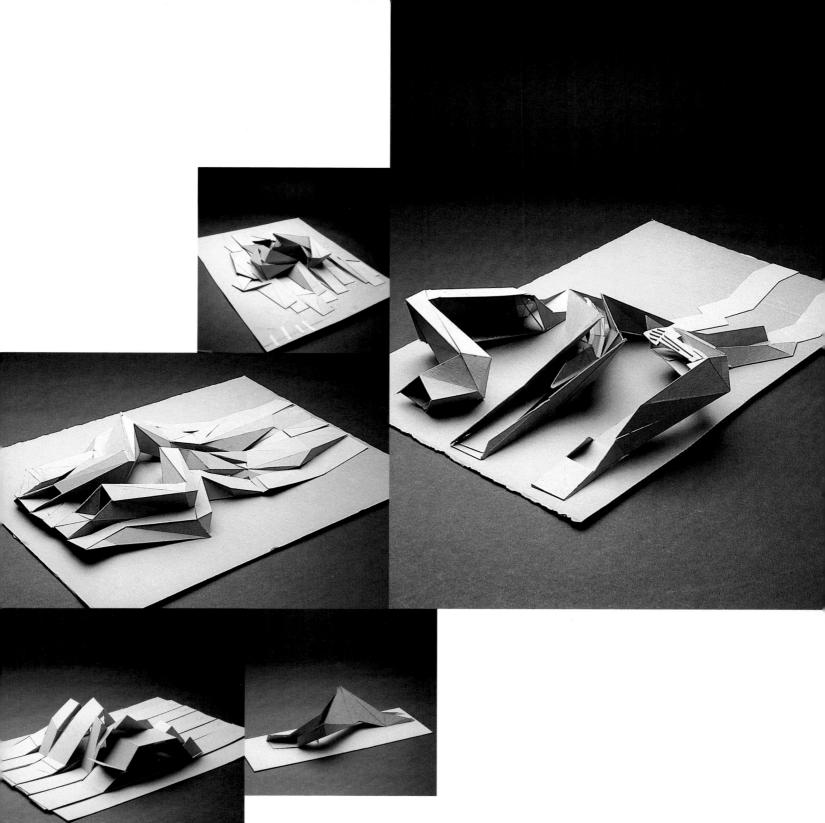

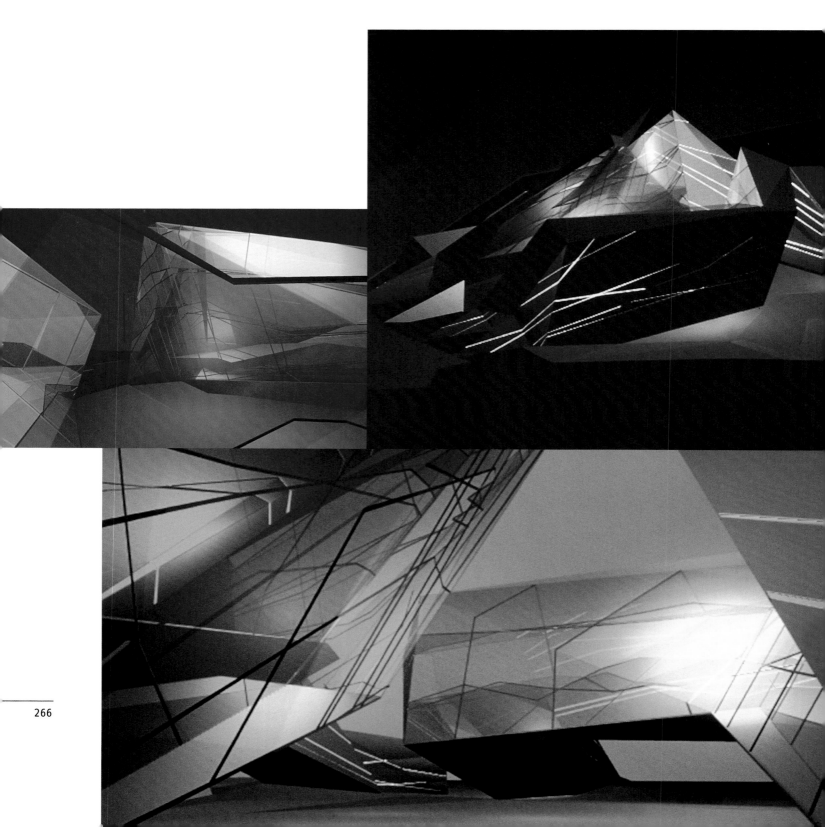

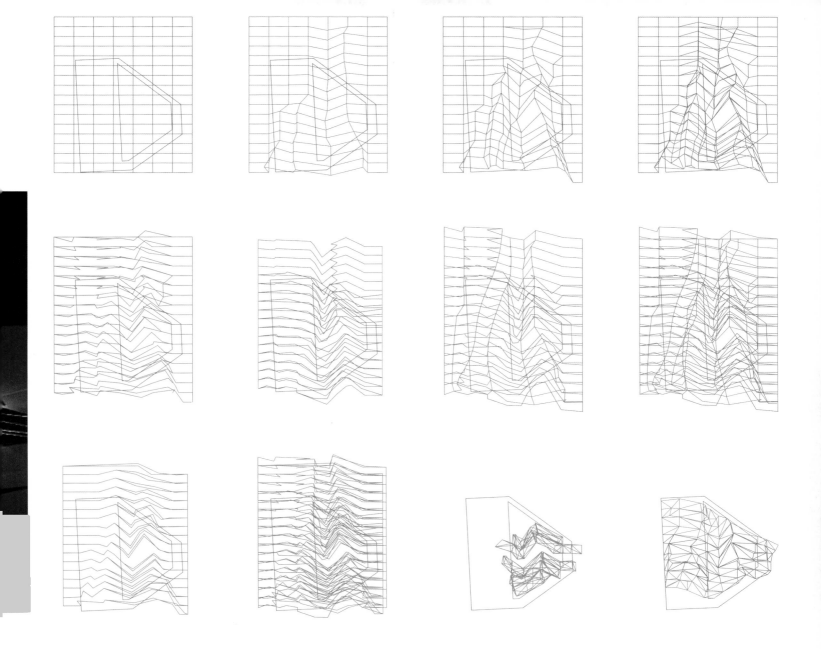

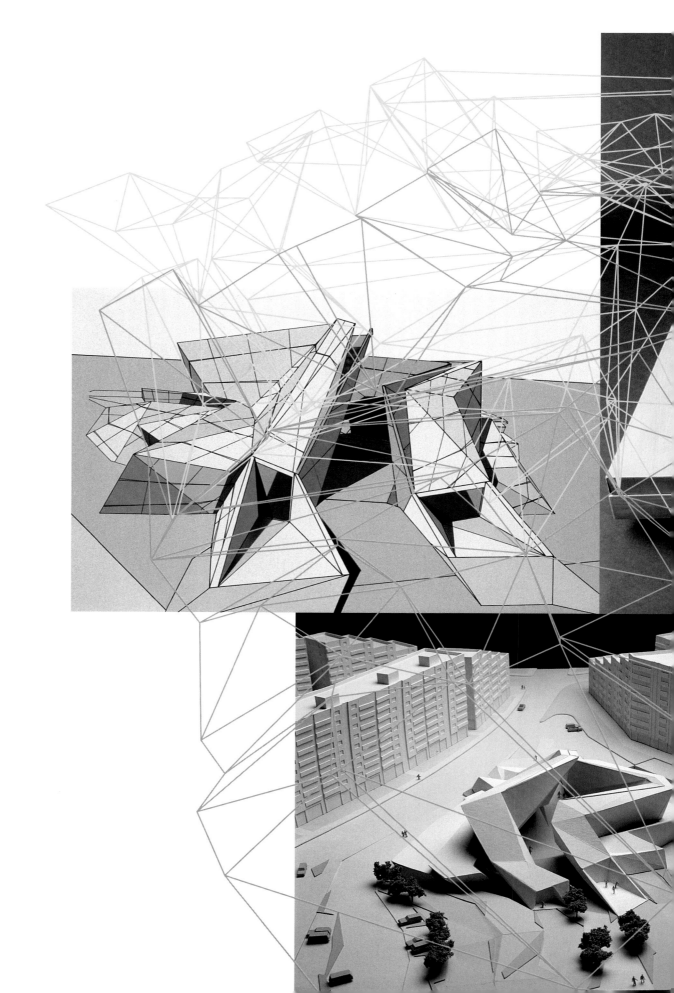

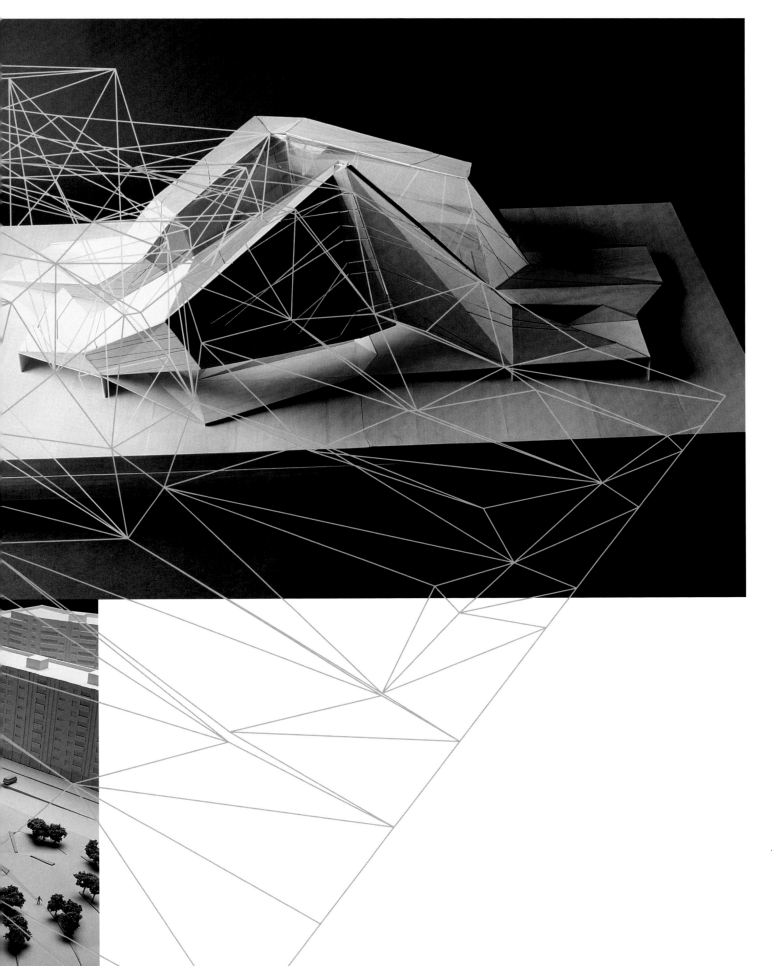

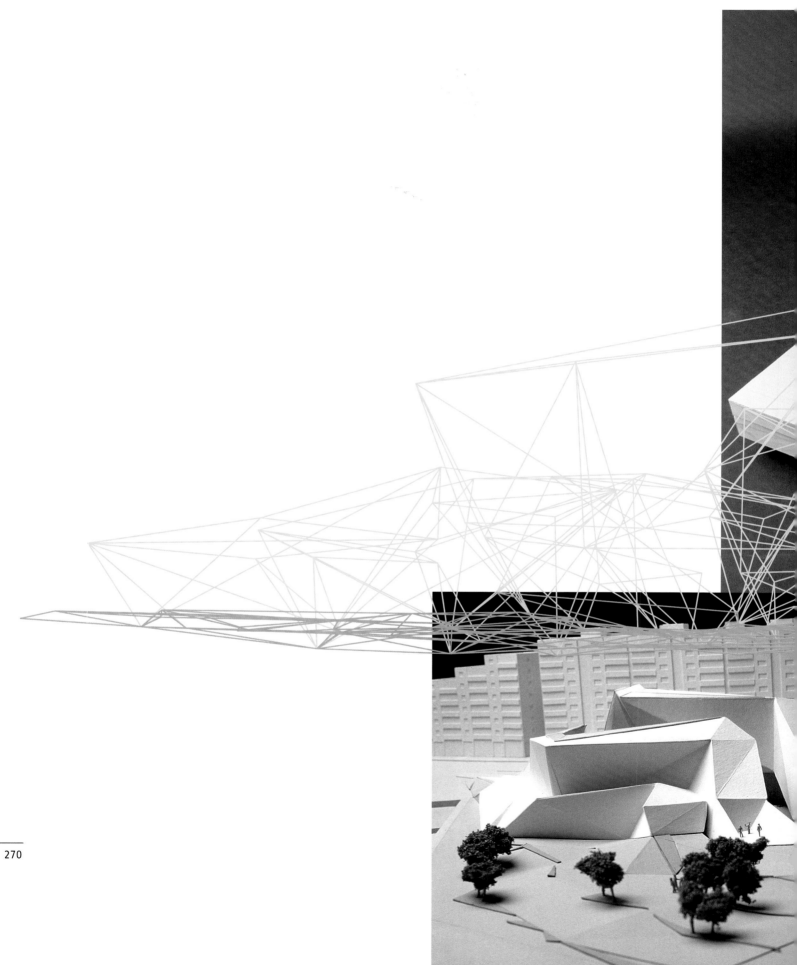

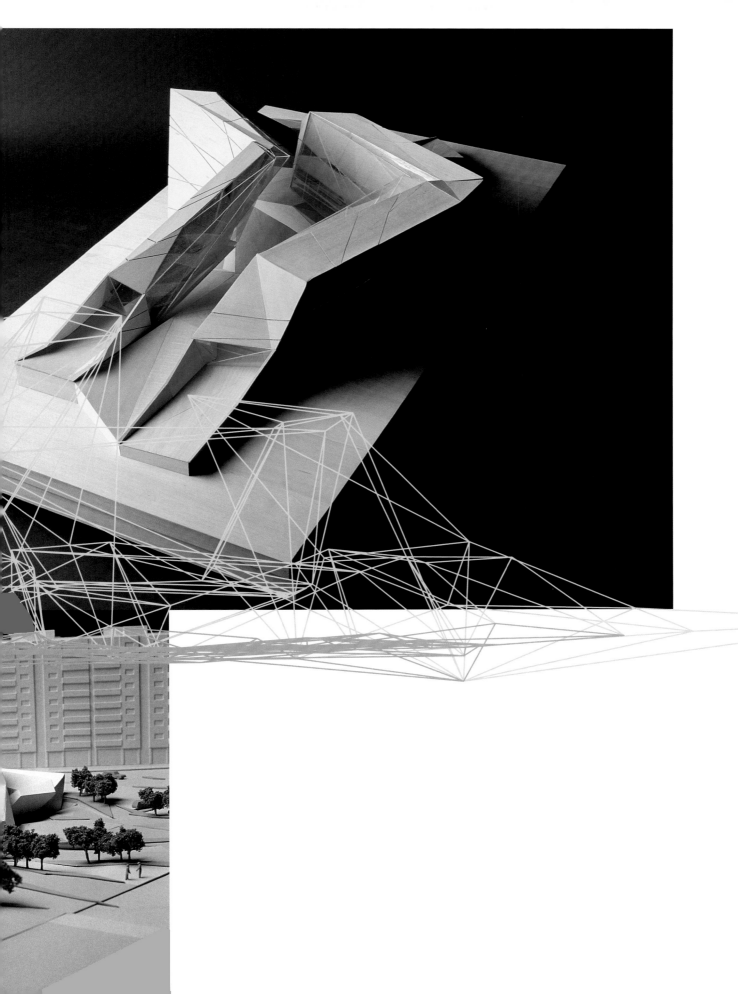

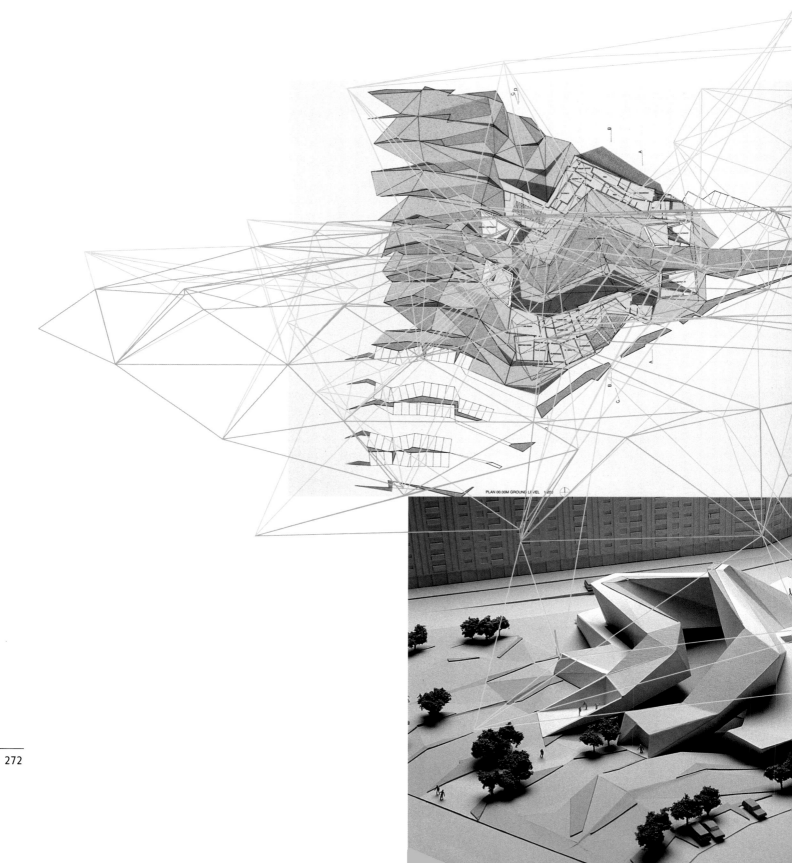

PLAN 00.00M GROUND LEVEL 1:400

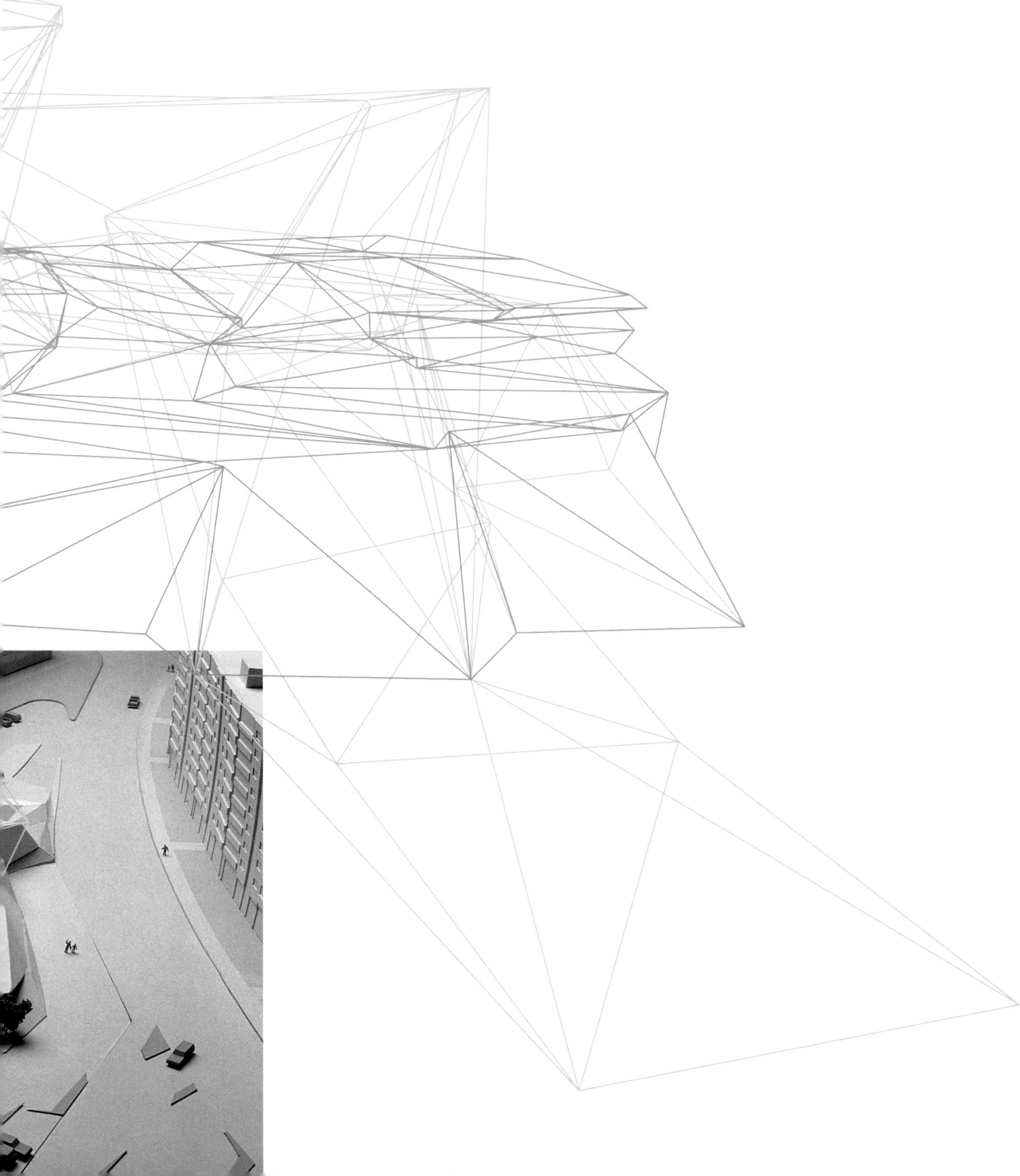

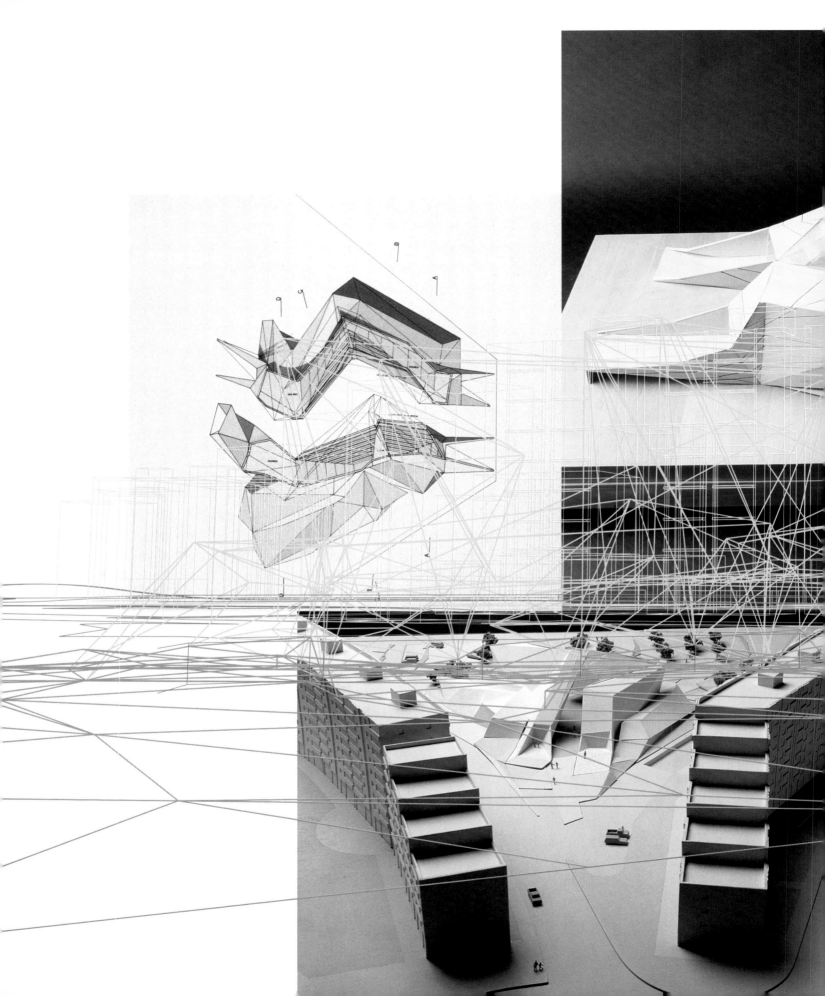

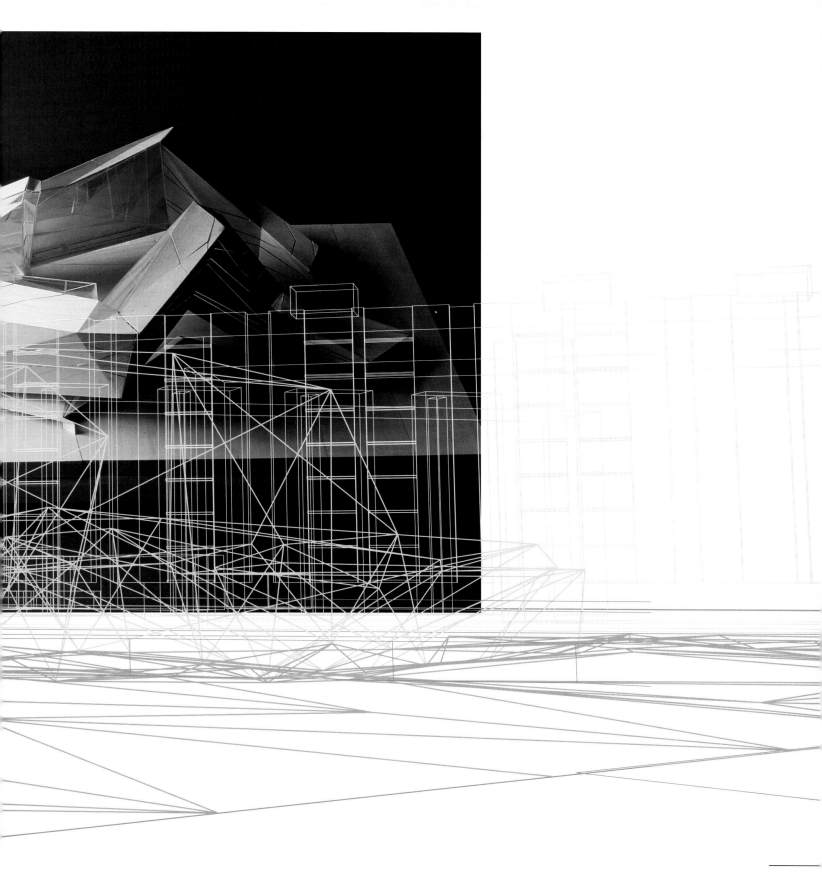

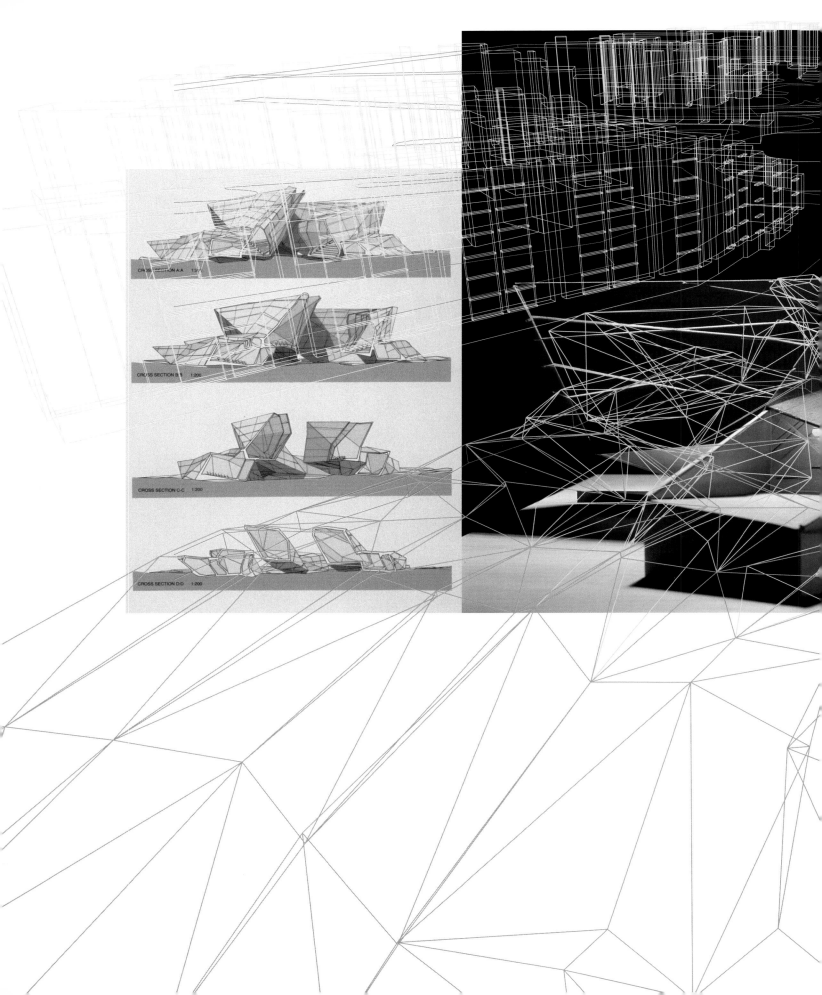

CROSS SECTION A-A 1:200

CROSS SECTION B-B 1:200

CROSS SECTION C-C 1:200

CROSS SECTION D-D 1:200

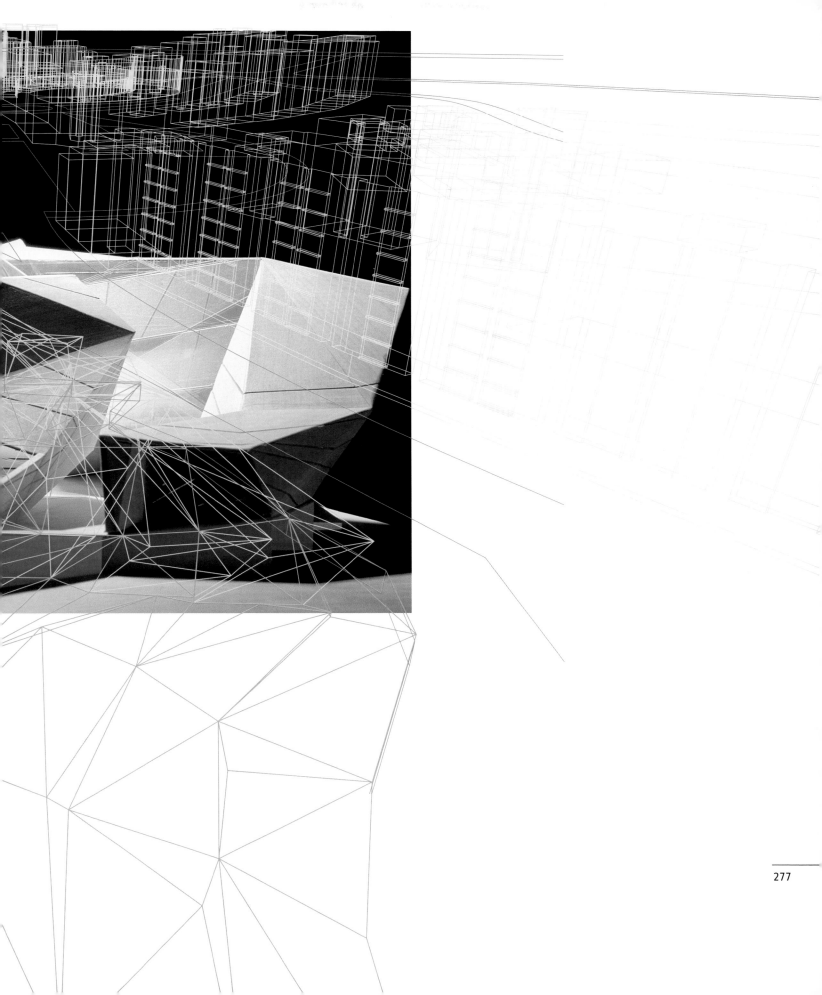

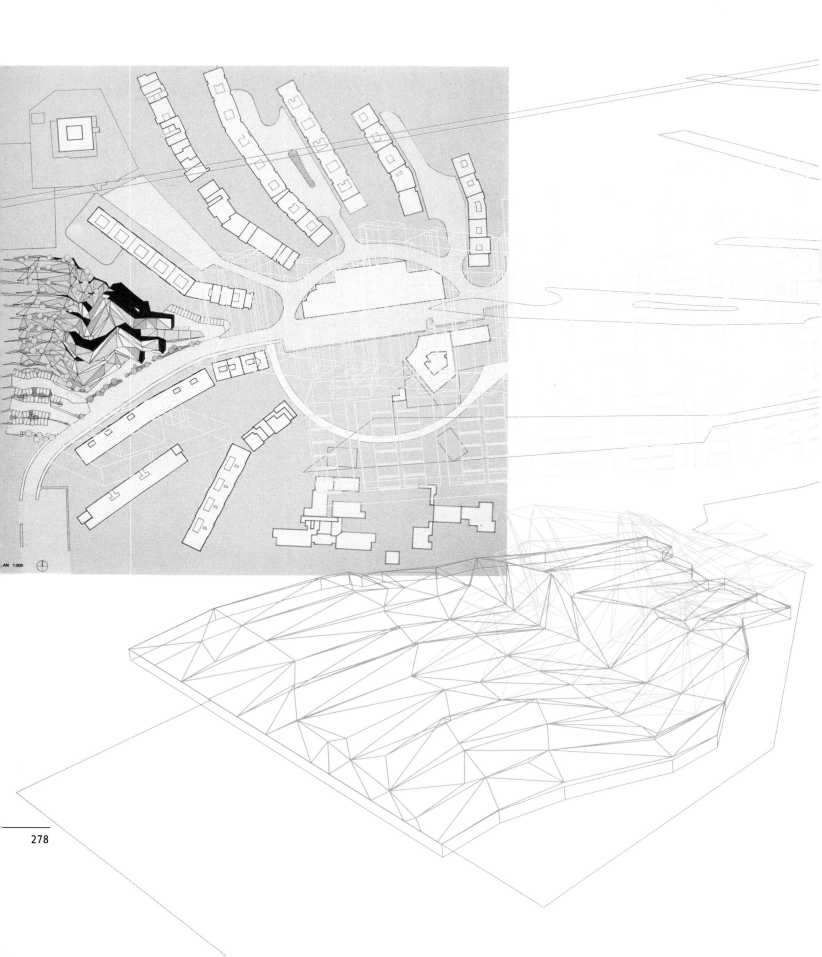

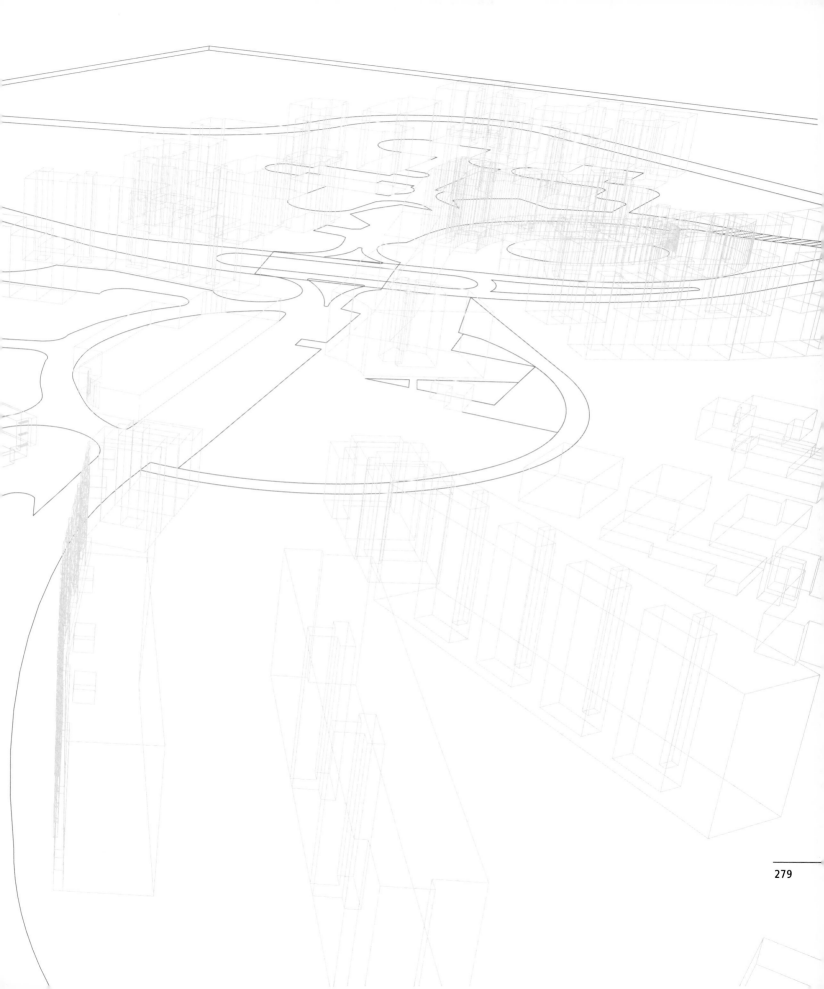

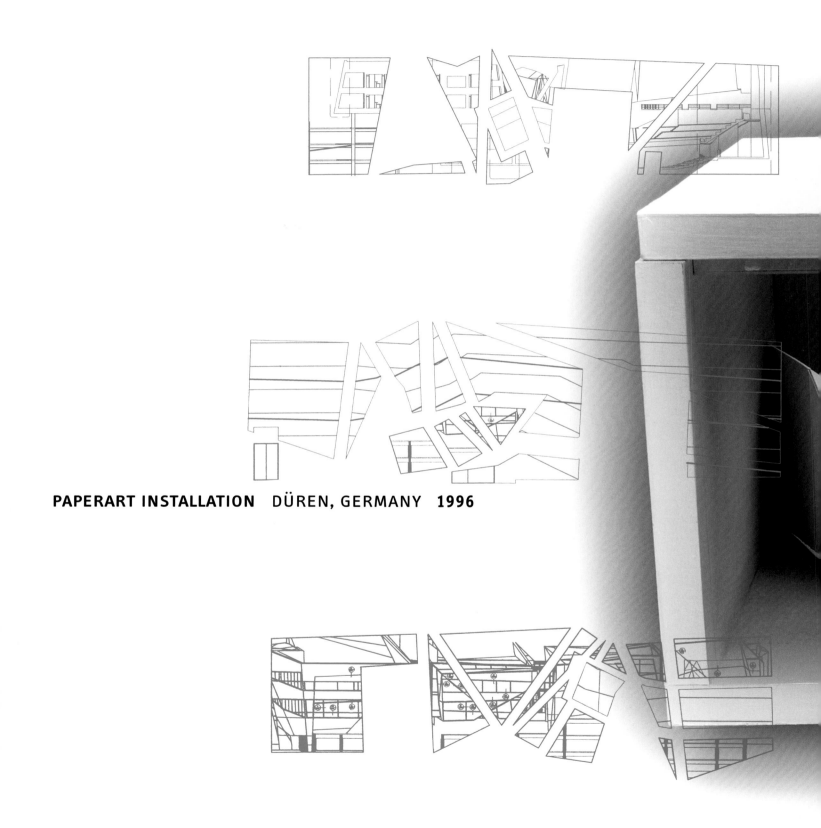

PAPERART INSTALLATION DÜREN, GERMANY **1996**

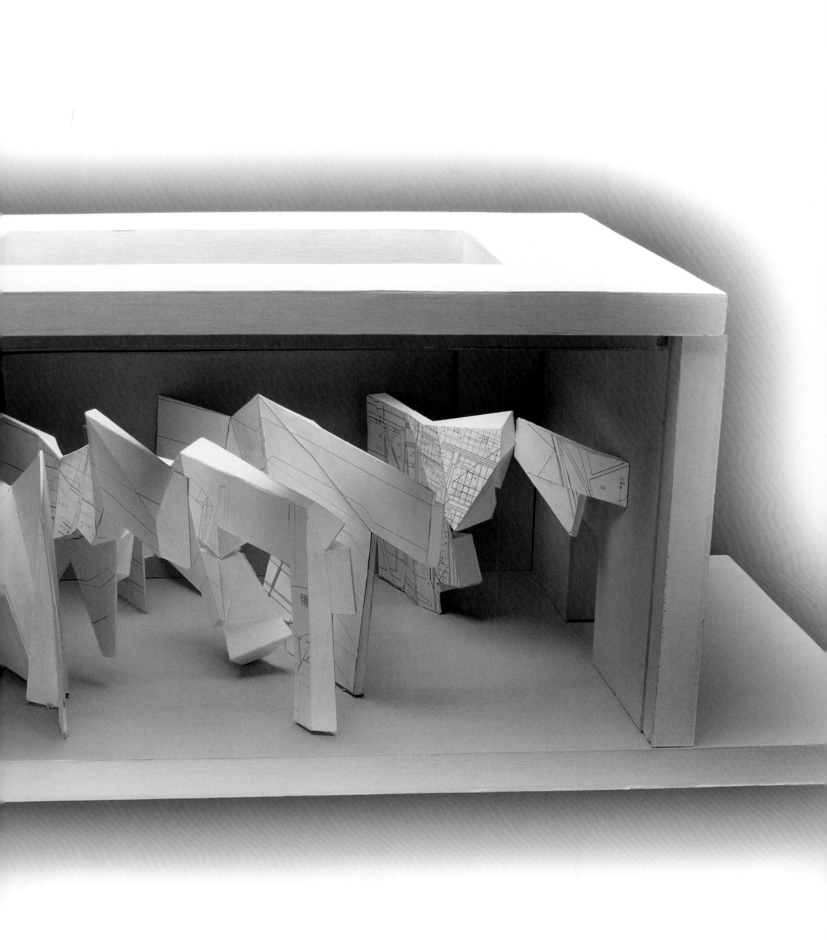

Zones of Undecidability II
The Processes of the Interstitial: Destabilizing Tropes

Peter Eisenman

In conversation one day, the architect Harry Cobb said, "There is a difference between design and architecture. Design is about giving satisfaction and architecture is about subversion." This statement is all the more interesting because Cobb is a partner in one of the most prestigious corporate architectural firms in the world, Pei Cobb Freed & Partners, which may be perceived to be more in the business of satisfaction than subversion. However, the difference between satisfaction and subversion may not be as great as it initially seems, for subversion is also often a form of satisfaction.

One idea of subversion in an architectural context exists in a purely theoretical and perhaps political sense. A second idea, more relevant to this discussion, is the possible subversion of our preconceived notions of what constitutes real space and time in architecture. This suggests that there are other possible conditions that in some way are suppressed by what is assumed to be the factual condition of architecture. Since architecture's structure cannot be subverted because it must always stand up, subversion must deal with what can be called architecture's rhetoric. Such a condition of rhetoric is ultimately different from the idea of literary rhetoric. This is particularly true when it comes to the issue of the architectural trope. Jacques Derrida

would argue that spatial, or architectural, metaphors cannot be found in what he calls "literary ideality." Unlike in literature, where the trope begins to define literature, the trope in architecture could be a condition of excess, those conditions that are not necessary to structure. When most people think of rhetoric in architecture they think of visual metaphors, such as a house that looks like a ship, or a classical facade that looks like a bastion of democracy. Even Le Corbusier's "a house is a machine for living" has more to do with a visual image than it does with processes. This is because it is thought that tropes attach themselves to stable conditions, which are necessary for any image. However, when it comes to the physical conditions of solid and void, metaphors are active in a different way. Metaphors such as "carving away solid" are just that, metaphors. There is no actual carving, but because of the articulation of the container, the space is made to seem that way. The appearance of carving away is not in itself destabilizing. Rather, destabilizing occurs when such metaphoric "carving away" produces a condition that can no longer be read as simply carving away, that is, when the reading becomes blurred or multiple. Such a condition would confound any one stable reading where the metaphor is destabilized by its own processes. And further, the trope of carving away would become an active process of destabilization or subversion in architecture.

Tropes are conditions of architecture that have existed since the time of the Renaissance, that is, from the time when architecture became representational of the relationship between a newly conceptualized subject and the architectural object, and thus became something more than mere structure and use. While clearly any form of representation is some form of metaphor, not all of these metaphors are subverting. Early Christian, Romanesque, and Gothic architectures are metaphoric, yet the intention of these metaphors is hardly subverting. Tropes perhaps became subverting starting in the Renaissance, when architecture first attempted to overcome the present (that is, the Gothic) with a conscious use of the past as a form of subversive representation. For example, in Alberti's facade of San Andrea in Mantua, two historical tropes, the triumphal arch and the Greek temple front, are superposed, draining them of their historical meaning and creating an entirely new idea of "church" facade. While this transformation of historical precedence was not subversive of the idea of church – in fact, it was done to reinforce that idea – it was subversive of the original condition and meaning of those two formal constructs.

The trope in architecture is commonly used to distinguish the discourse of one architect from another. The way a facade is developed or a plan is organized can define differences in what is traditionally referred to as the style, or "signature," of an architect. Equally, tropes also define how architecture is commonly perceived and experienced. For example, space is usually deployed and understood though a narrative continuity or sequence, usually around an axis of circulation. Such organizations have come to be seen as natural, as opposed to merely conventions, and are rarely challenged. But in fact their possible transgression and subversion not only define differences from one architect to the next, they also provide for the possibility of change in the discourse of architecture itself.

In order to understand how tropes operate in architecture to destabilize, it is possible to examine a fundamental condition of architectural space, that is, the relationship of solid to void, of structure to space, in order to illustrate the operation of a trope as subversive of such a normative condition as container to contained. The relationship of solid and void is not a trope as such; trope is how this relationship is both presented and represented in a building.

For example, it can be argued that Alberti's interpretation of Vitruvian *firmitas* had nothing to do with the firmness or stability of structure, but rather suggested that what is stable in architecture should look like it is stable, that is, the rhetoric of the structure is what represents stability. Thus from Alberti's idea of *storia,* architecture became representational in a way that it previously had not been. *Storia* is the narrative that is necessary to situate a trope in a historical context. Because the rhetoric of a trope was considered excessive, it had to be located in some historical contexts. Often the way these narratives were made manifest became destabilizing tropes of architecture. This can be seen in the development of the relationship of solid and void in Brunelleschi's San Lorenzo and Santo Spirito churches in Florence and Bramante's Pavia Cathedral and St. Peter's projects. Here the evolution of a trope concerning solid and void, in particular in relationship to the development of what is now called poché, can be seen.

In Brunelleschi's San Lorenzo, the structure is articulated as a regular bay grid not very different from the structure of Gothic cathedrals. The difference, however, is important, in that the solid material of the columnar profile is organized to clearly define a perspectival depth down the side aisles and the main nave. At Santo Spirito there is another change in the profile of the solid columnar material, which does not so much reflect a structural change as it does a rhetorical one. Here the profiles are articulated to create a layering across the aisles, establishing a continuous series of frontal, or picture, planes as the subject proceeds from the front of the church toward the transept crossing.

Trope then is the conscious deployment of an excessive device, an effect, to heighten the affect in space of the subject. Affect can traditionally be heightened through the confrontation with expectancy.

In both churches there is the presence of solid material in excess of what would have been necessary or usual in a Gothic columnar structure. This acts rhetorically to subvert both the clarity of structure and the narrative conditions of space present in late Gothic structures. It is not so much that the structural columns themselves are different from Gothic structures; rather, their rhetorical deployment as manifest in an excess of solid material has changed.

This is also true of Bramante's cathedral project for Pavia, which in this context must be seen as a transitional work. Here the solidity of the piers begins to articulate an entirely different concern, one that has less to do with the perspectival subject in space and more to do with an autonomous relationship between the solid articulation and its effect on the spatial articulation. This autonomous relationship becomes more apparent in Bramante's first project for St. Peter's, where an entirely new relationship between solid and void is proposed. No longer are the solids seen as poché, as structure, or as enclosing. Rather the solids now appear as a molten mass imbricated with the space in such a way that the outline of the space has lost the clarity of its definition between structural solid and void space, and thus the relationship between the two has lost its iconic content as symbolic of structural form. Instead, there is a lack of definition of what is structure and what is not. This unclarity led to a traditional consideration of such poché as defining a gestalt phenomenological figure/ground reversal. But the issue of a figure/ground dialectic between solid and void had yet to become a conceptual issue at St. Peter's, that is, it remained untheorized. (It would only become so with Serlio and others.) Indeed, something else is at work. First, Bramante's organization of space and structure moves from the mechanism of structure to the organism of successive scales of solid and void integers as they nest within one another. Second, the iconic qualities of circle and square have been reduced and subverted by these new quasi-amorphous relationships of solid to void. Thus for the first time a rhetorical form has been turned into a condition that approaches matter, or pure material, through a subversion of what is normally indicated by the structure or the container. In this context, normal vision also has to be subverted to be able to reconceptualize the architectural elements. This transformation of what could be called poché from an inert mass between

forms, or as something from which void space is cut, to something deformed, highly mobile, and volatile can be seen to be a subversion of the form of both traditional solids and their traditional organizations in space. This modification of the material condition can be given a new name: *the interstitial*.

The interstitial must be theorized differently from the idea of poché, which presumes a base condition where the solid preexists the void. In the interstitial there is no necessary primacy of origin of either solid or void. Where poché is the result of a mute solid being eroded by an active void, in the interstitial, solid and void are active simultaneously. This modification of solid, it can be argued, is achieved through the presence of a rhetorical trope rather than through the modification of a structural organization. While rhetoric is always active in the definition of any artistic act, it is not always acting transgressively or else there would be no continuity in any discourse. However, when tropes act to displace continuity, they can open a discourse to new conditions of its being. What Bramante did was to articulate something that had never been previously conceptualized as the interstitial. The interstitial as a tropic process of displacement has been used from the time of Bramante to the present. This trope does not produce stable images but rather ones that change and deny their stability throughout different periods of time. The suggestion here is that this transformation, or more precisely, deformation, brought about by the processes directly related to the trope of the interstitial might still provide the same possibility as it held for Bramante: for looking at architecture again – not abandoning architecture, as others have suggested, but in fact looking at what has been previously repressed in its received history.

This brings the argument to the idea of zones of undecidability, or the processes of the interstitial. This idea of the interstitial is different from and subverts Bramante's interstitial. It is a condition between form and space, between figure and ground, between an affective and a mental experience of space. The processes of the interstitial do not begin from either a container or a contained, even though all architecture is in some way traditionally legitimated by functional containers. This is not to say that there is no container or contained, only that these terms are no longer used to legitimate the work. Instead, it is possible to think of a container that is more amorphous and mutable, like a series of balloons filled with sand that can both conceptually push into space and be pushed into. These zones of alternation or pulsation produce an interstitial condition that is neither all solid nor all void but rather something that contains both. While ultimately stable in real space, this condition produces a disjunction in narrative time. It is no longer experienced in continuous time; it is understood as a nonvisual sensation that also introduces an other condition of the affective body in space at the same time that it begins to question the hegemony of visual representation in architecture.

The project for the Bibliothèque de l'IHUEI of the United Nations in Geneva is an example of how the interstitial can be used as a trope to destabilize the traditional spatial organization of a library. The process initially begins with an attempt to destabilize the idea that buildings are containers of meaning, structure, and function, and as such are dependent on them for their visual recognition. While these conditions will always in some way exist, they are not necessarily the only conditions that legitimate their being.

The process is similar to the one for the Church for the Year 2000. It uses a diagram external to architecture and chosen because it would not produce in real space and time a recognizable image. Such a diagram could perhaps reveal in its internal structuring alternative spatial possibilities. For the United Nations library, the process began from a diagram that had no immanent relationship to the program of a library but rather depicted a moment of neurological activity, illustrating a combination of individual synaptic movements separated from each other in space. A membrane recording movements of this was superposed on the first diagram, deforming itself to accommodate the height differences of each individual synapse. As the neurons were pushed past their thresholds, the membrane recorded these as height differentials to be incorporated in the project. The resultant diagram was separated into two frequencies, which recorded the traces of their individual activity. The relationship between trace and frequency was then interpreted in a three-dimensional solid/void relationship. This relationship produced a series of overlaps that twist through the initial matrix, producing, at an arbitrary moment in the time of this activity, a series of potentially interstitial conditions that could be assigned library functions. The result is neither programmatically based nor an object of personal expression, but rather produces in its processes a series of formal structures that have the potential to become interstitial yet are different from previous incarnations of the interstitial.

The resultant three-dimensional matrix is composed of four linear elements that act like the balloons filled with sand. The voids between these elements then participate in a process of evolution leading to a complexity where they are no longer either solid or void. Lateral sections of these voids were then compared to some normative condition of solid and void. These sections between the voids and the normative conditions were seen as different stages in the development of an interstitial condition containing a fluid relationship between solid and void, their figural qualities containing little resemblance to any known figuration. At any moment in the process, the voids could be frozen in space and time, thus engaging the form of the original solid components. Each of these frozen stages could be superposed on each other to produce the resultant interstitial condition as an overlay of both solids and voids.

Thus from seemingly value-free or arbitrary origins, a series of interstitial conditions was produced that contains both a memory trace of their processes as well as an object, the final form of which could not have been predicted from the process. Here the ground no longer frames the object but becomes part of the object itself, thus transgressing the conditions of container and contained. The result is not so much a recognizable "building" as it is an experience of space and time, which would produce in the subject an affective bodily experience. This matrix is the result of a process that produces a figural condition of figure/figure, one that involves the transformation and recording of vectors – energy flows that have a mass and a density – in a way that produces not a container and contained but a series of interstitial membranes from the periphery to the interior.

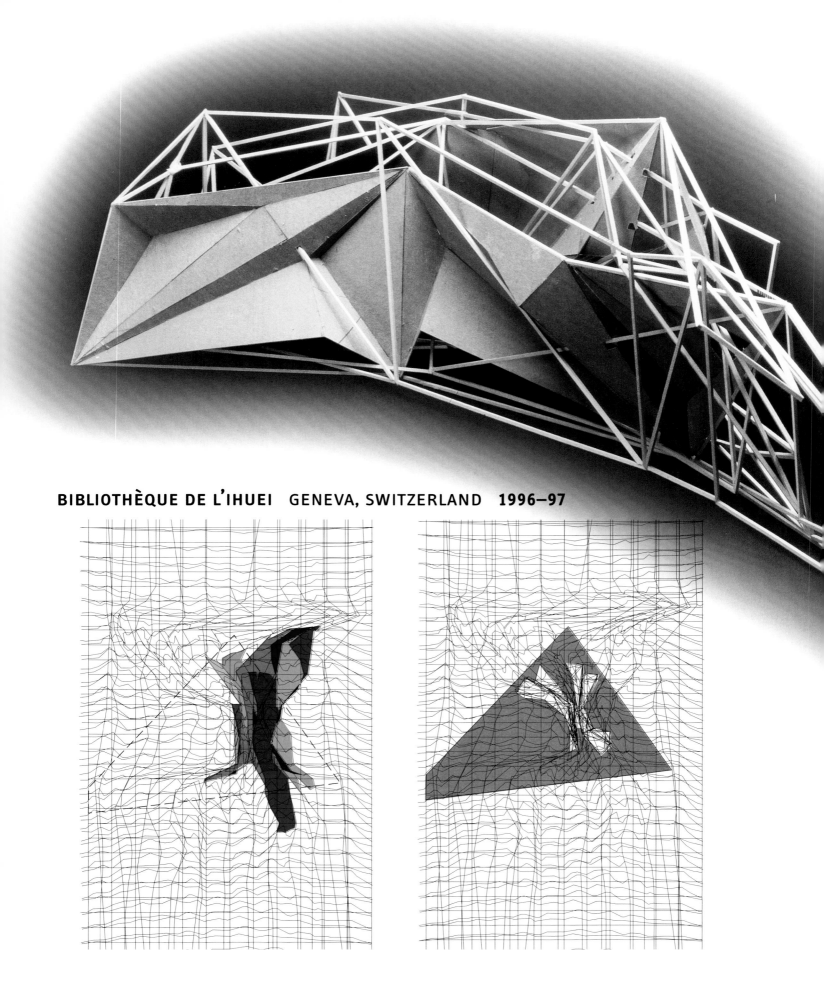

BIBLIOTHÈQUE DE L'IHUEI   GENEVA, SWITZERLAND   **1996–97**

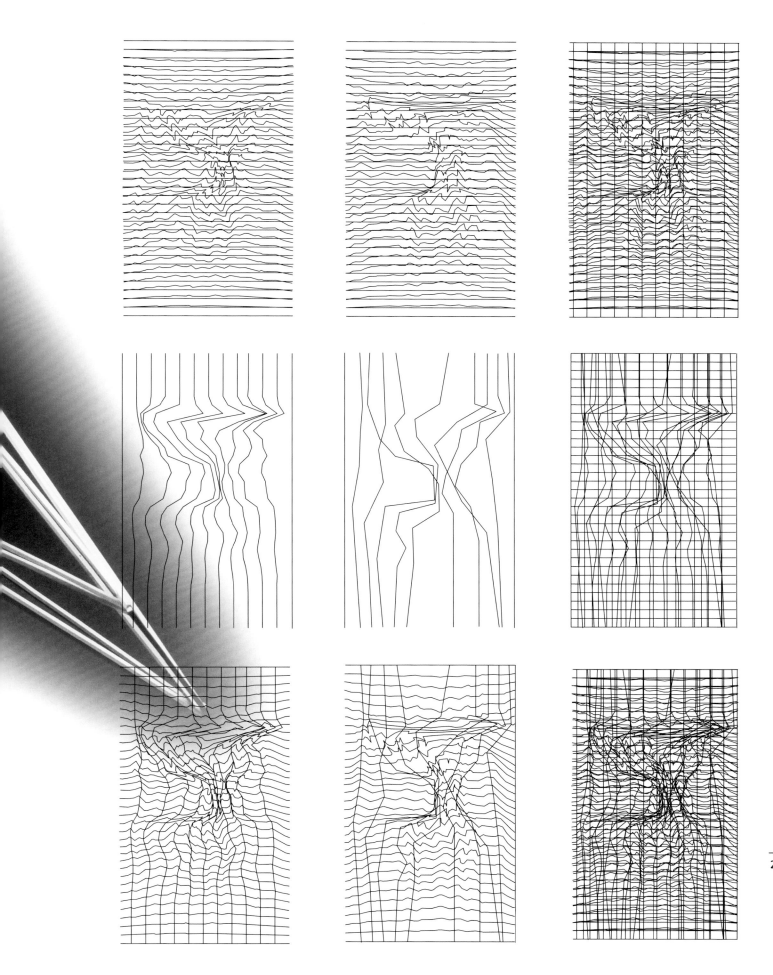

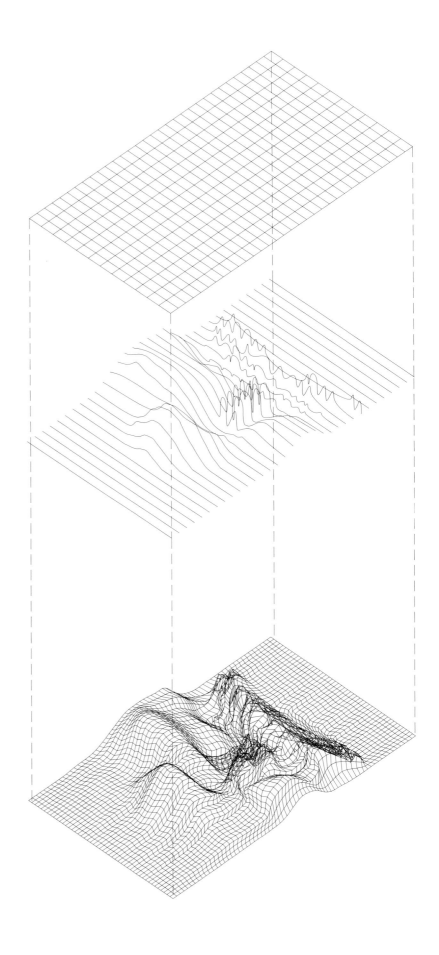

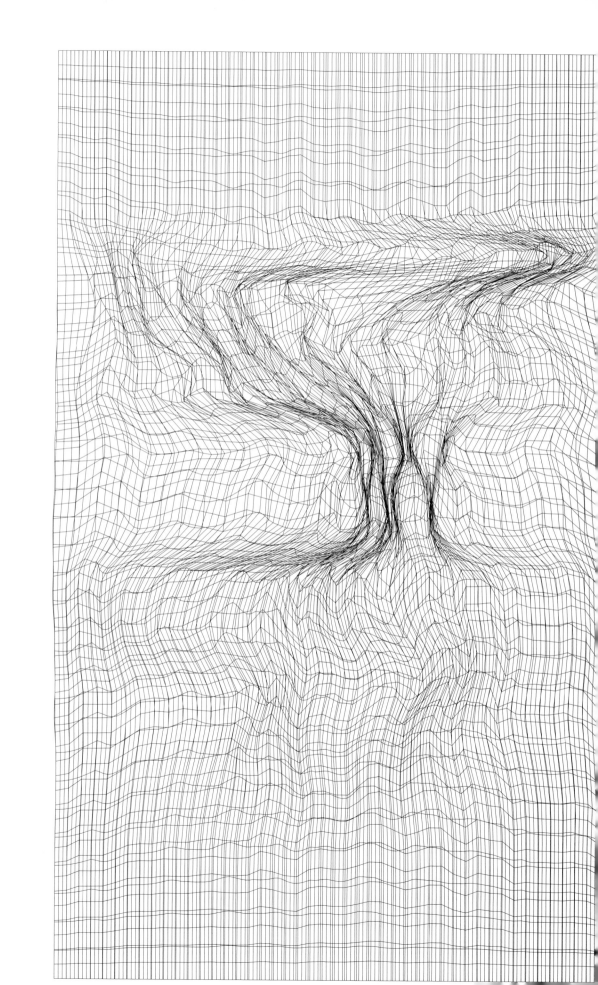

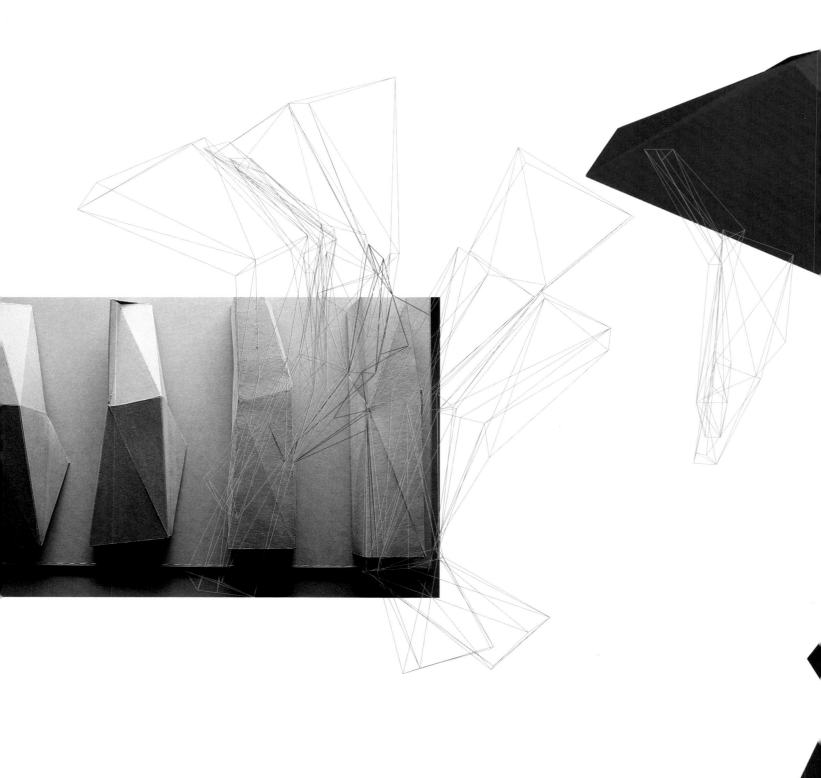

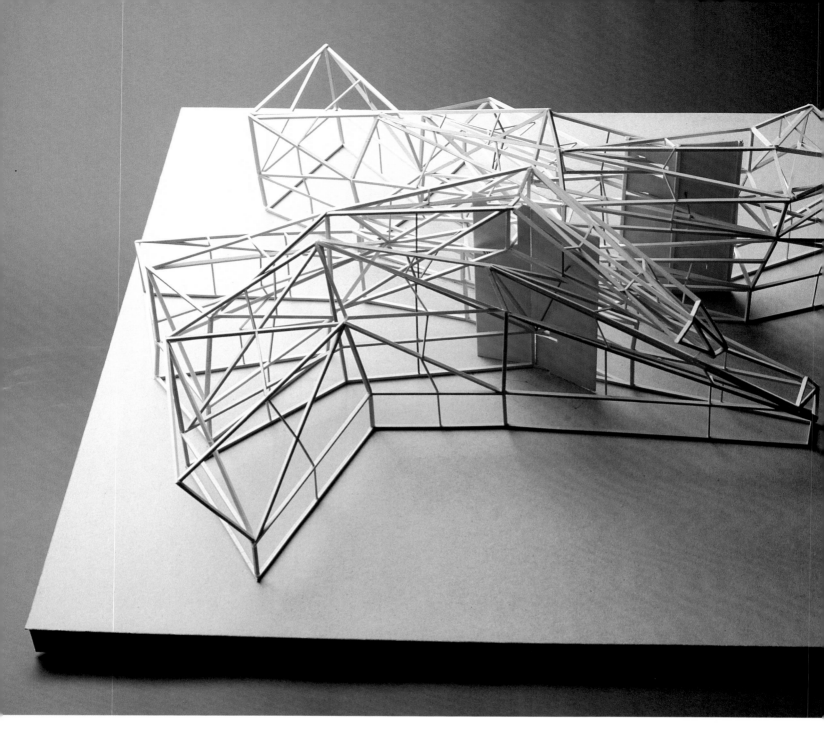

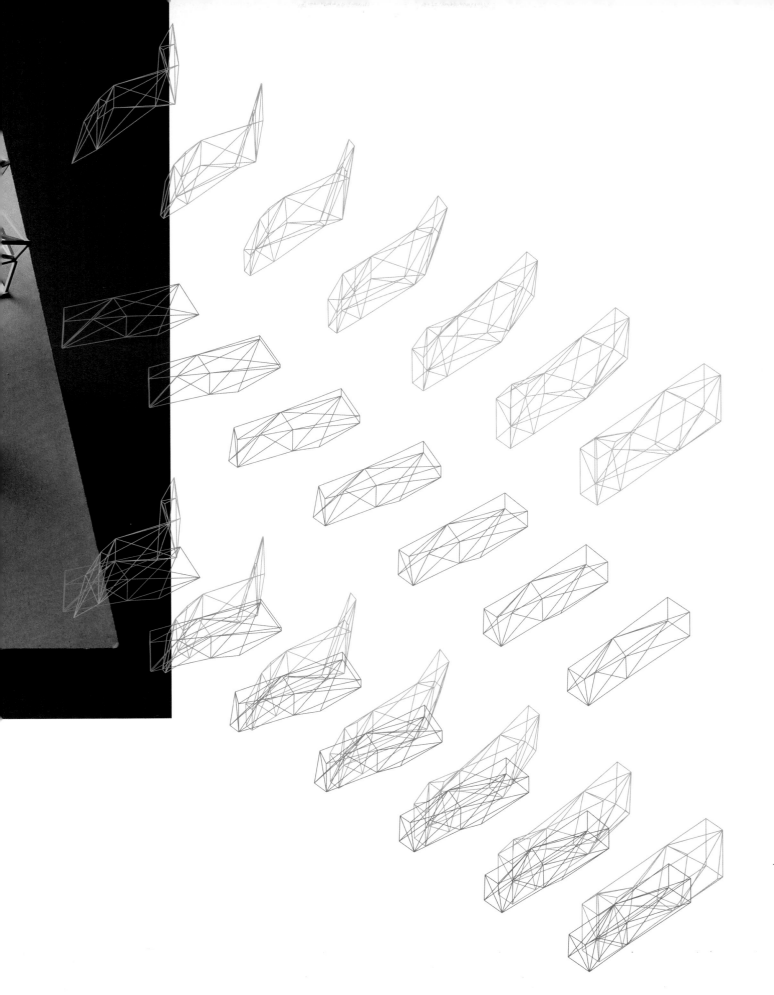

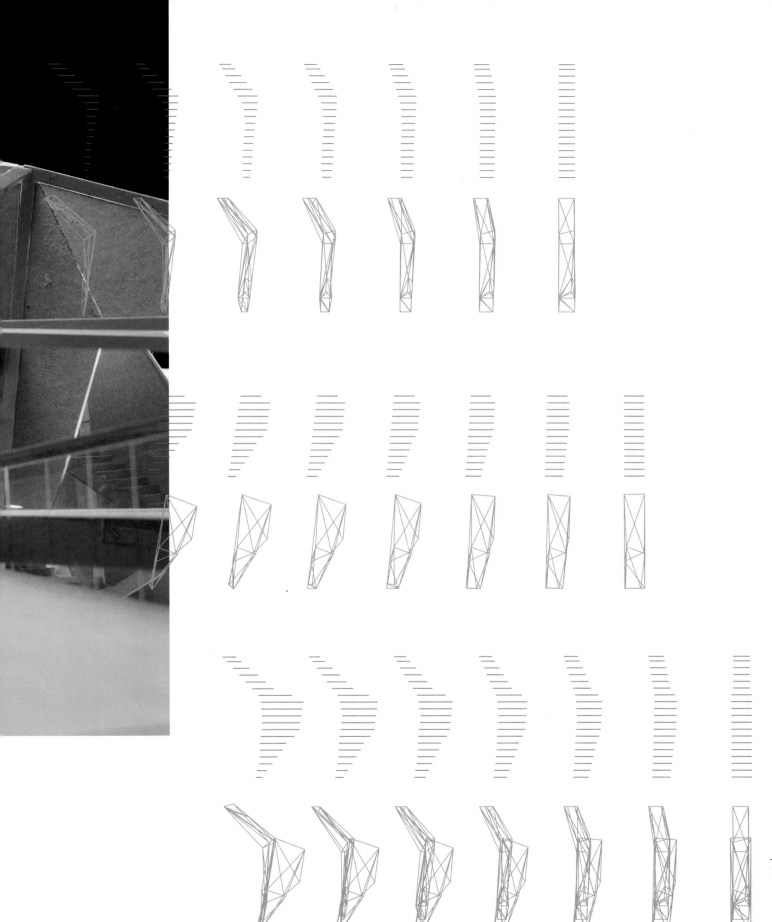

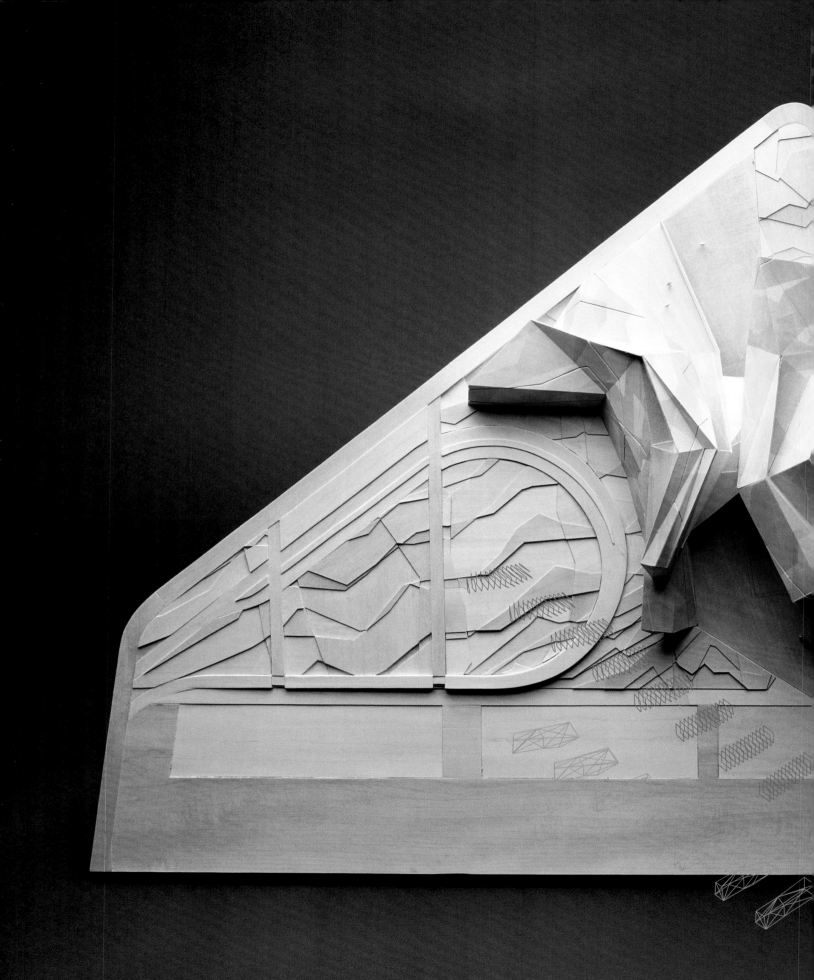

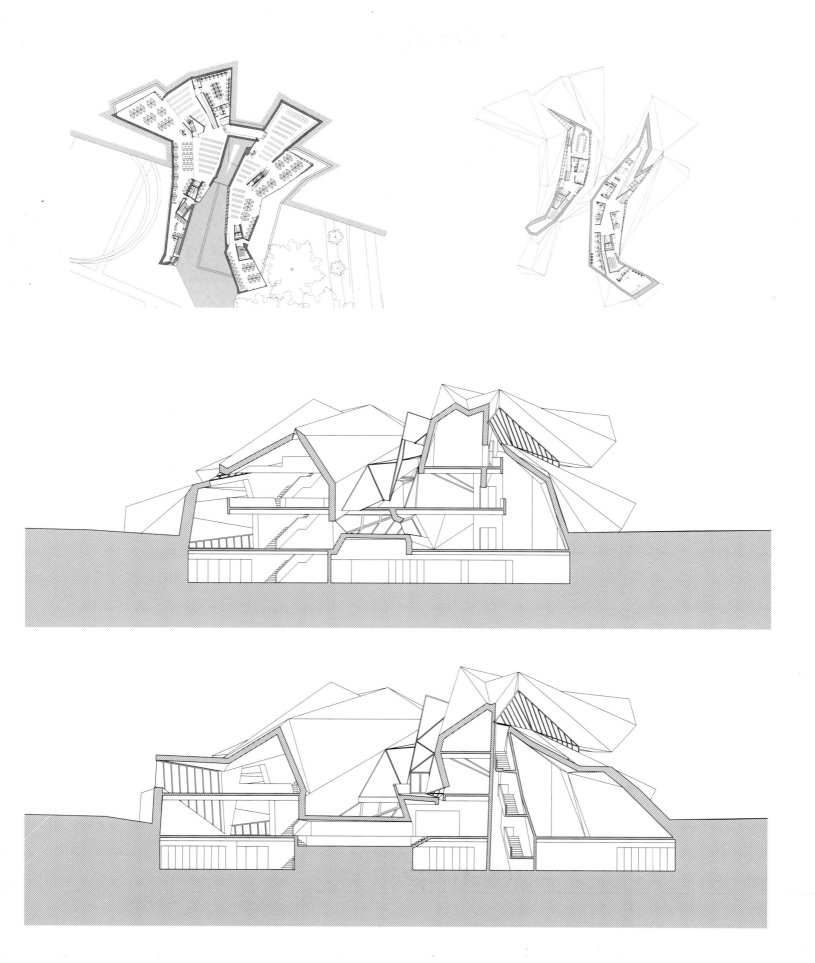

Opening the Interstitial: Eisenman's Space of Difference

Andrew Benjamin

Two possibilities for architectural thinking arise from the writings of Georges Bataille. These possibilities are of central importance not only because they open up different conceptions of the architectural, but also because in their difference lies the distinction between a philosophical or theoretical definition of the architectural on the one hand and the development of architectural theory on the other. The first leads to an investigation of architecture as symbol and thus as the conveyor of meaning. The second, while not precluding this dimension, is concerned with the generation of form. It also opens a way into the recent architectural concerns of Peter Eisenman, in particular how the internal generation of form presents different ways of understanding the theoretical demands stemming from Eisenman's use of the terms *blurring* and *interstitial*.

Eisenman's own distancing of a concern with meaning and his incorporation of the interstitial as, in Bataille's terms, a productive negativity or destabilizing rather than a given reiterate the movement from architecture as symbol to the presence of *l'informe* as a productive destabilizer in Bataille's own writings. This is not to say that Eisenman's recent theoretical work is a simple application of Bataille's work to architecture. Rather it is to argue that a concern with destabilizing and interiority is linked to the

impossibility of escaping the need for form. This reiterates Bataille's explicit commitment to materialism on the one hand and implicit use of an ontology of becoming on the other. For both Eisenman and Bataille, the relationship of materiality and becoming yields the theoretical problem of accounting for the "event" of plurality within architecture. This point must be approached in a three-stage move: first, to note the role of architecture as symbol; second, to allow for *l'informe* as destabilizing – though the very nature of the production in question brings with it a necessary criticality; third, and only then, to pursue the question of destabilizing as *l'informe* in architecture. This is the question, it will be argued, in relation to the idea of blurring in architecture that is central to any analysis of Eisenman's recent theoretical work.

One of the most important instances in which architecture takes on the role of a symbol, Bataille argues, was during the French Revolution, when the revolutionaries struggled against the symbolic power of the Bastille. Its destruction was the destruction of a symbol. It is impossible to argue that the Bastille did not work as an organizing symbol. The question that arises is, how did its internal organization of space – an organization that contained and divided the people from their potential or actual leaders, for example – aid or facilitate the operation of the symbol? It is possible to argue that at the outside there is a relation of indifference between these two aspects. The internal configuration and its operation as a prison allowed the Bastille to figure as a symbol; however, the symbolic function of the building was not a reflection of the way it worked as a prison. Its field of operation – both as symbol and as prison – indicates the two dimensions proper to building. Only the latter – which is concerned with the organization of space and the operation of a regime of incarceration and imprisonment – falls directly into the realm of the architectural. This latter dimension is a concern with the generation and effective organization of space. It assumes that some level of analysis is involved in the way in which the building constitutes space as an activity.

In the place of the symbol there is work as process. In its relationship with stasis and concern with meaning, the symbol is counterposed to activity and thus to process. The latter arises when in the place of an ontology of stasis there emerges an ontology of becoming. It is at this juncture and with a division of this type – i.e., an ontological divide – that *l'informe* can be situated. Bataille's delineation of what can be described as a productive negativity, productive in the sense that it resists its own negation, occurs in his writings on poetry. But precisely because this negativity is not posed in his writings on architecture, the question of the architectural must be posed. What, then, is *l'informe* in architecture? Any attempt to answer this question has to begin with *l'informe*'s utility. It works. It works to undo a particular given formal determination that leads not to simple formlessness but to another formal possibility. As such, *l'informe* has to be thought in relation to a certain architectural practice, to account for the place of *l'informe* as a destabilizing agent.

In this context attention should be paid to the consequence of this process of undoing, moving, and repositioning (recognizing the difficulty of translating Bataille's term *déclasser*). Moreover, it is a theme that is repeated in Eisenman's use of the term *destabilize* in his description of his Bibliothèque de l'IHUEI project in Geneva. All

such terms pose the same problem; i.e., they have to be present within and as part of the building's realization as a building. The task at the theoretical level is to account for the nature and consequence of that presence. On a descriptive level there has to be a way of accounting for the specific work of destabilization.

One direct and important consequence of the movement marked out in Bataille by the use of the term *déclasser* (literally, to lower in status) and in Eisenman by the term destabilize is that both result in an opposition between form and the formless (or that which could be counterposed to form). This is no longer an appropriate way of accounting for form. The presence of form (or its opposite – the so-called formless) is not central. The more demanding problem is to account for a destabilization in the generation of form, the movement from what is – i.e., the givenness of a form – to what becomes or to what is generated. This is also the consequence of the movement from symbol to generation as process. Finitude, or stasis, yields its place to a specific modality of becoming. However, because the structure of the dialectical either/or has also been displaced – which would have been present in the opposition form/formless – finitude and becoming are not mutually exclusive. As a consequence, two interrelated tasks arise. The first concerns the presence of the absence of the oppositional; the second concerns the nature of the copresence of finitude and becoming. In sum, pursuing these tasks involves recognizing that what is at work here is a conception of the ontological in which the productive presence of a founding complexity has to be taken as the point of departure. This is not complexity as understood in Leibniz's "infinite folds of the soul," but one in which the origin is understood as the productive copresence of ontological registers that are irreducible. Production is linked therefore to the anoriginal presence of a differential ontology. Production is the measure of the work of such an ontology. Allowing for the productive interplay of finitude and becoming opens up the need to describe what is being staged within such a setup. Their copresence is partly what destabilizes homological relations between form and function. More significantly, that disruption introduces the quality of the yet-to-be determined. In poetry, this registers as much on the level of meaning as it does on the level of form. In architecture, the yet-to-be is present as a formal possibility and is explicable in terms of program. The question that has to be addressed concerns the relationship between l'informe and the already present, and thus materially maintained, yet-to-be.

In general theoretical terms the demands made by Bataille's formulations enjoin a task that necessitates a philosophical thinking that begins with *origins* as an event of plurality. Eisenman's description of the internal spacing of the Aronoff Center can be rearticulated in terms of the destabilizing copresence of finitude and becoming. It is at this precise point that it becomes possible to detail the way this concern with the critical within the operation of *l'informe* – understood as that which is at work in the movement of undoing, an undoing always linked to a doing – is also at work in Eisenman's discussion of blurring and the interstitial as critical and destabilizing pluralities.

Speaking of Bramante's project for St. Peter's, Eisenman reformulates Bramante's transformations of formal qualities in terms that concentrate on "modification." He says that a transformation of what could be called poché from an inert mass between forms, which is something from which void is cut, to something highly mobile and volatile can be seen as the subversion both of the form of traditional solids and of their traditional organization in space. This modification of the material condition can be given a new name – the interstitial.

Here the interstitial is both the condition of the between – a spacing – and the consequence of a particular process. As such it could be described as both process and effect, but it is not one and the other – process and effect – as though they could be separated. Here the inscription of an element whose work is both process and effect is present, and its presence can only be explicated in terms of *particularity*. This description needs qualification. What are these transformations? There is no suggestion that any transformation would only involve a reiteration of maneuvers similar to the one enacted by Bramante. Such a move would only reintroduce an envisaged homological relation between form and function. Even though a great deal is

to be learned from a detailed study of such transformations, the point remains that it is essential not to see transformation as literal. Eisenman's point is that the history of architecture can be read in terms of transformations on the level of formal possibility. More significantly, in this instance, the design consequences arise from pursuing the interruption and displacement of the conceptual oppositions – the tropes – through which architecture works. Eisenman is after the interstitial as the generative between. To arrive at this, he must blur or destabilize form/function to arrive not at the formless but the formed.

Eisenman claims that the aim of his Bibliothèque de l'IHUEI project was to deploy the interstitial – understood as the *twofold* of process and effect articulated through architectural tropes – "to destabilize the traditional social organization of any program." The initial object, he says, was "to destabilize the ideas that buildings are containers of meaning, structure, and function, and are dependent on their visual recognition as such."

Initially, the key term in this passage is *dependent*. There is no attempt to undo the presence of either structure or function, which in fact are given central access. What is destabilized is the homological relation between form and function. The interstitial works to break that homology. The break is not the move from form to the formless. Rather, it reintroduces into the presence of form an indeterminate quality that alters the perception and practice of the building, while at the same time allowing for programmatic possibilities that were not determined in advance. What is of concern is how in this context the interstitial is established. Fundamental to this is Eisenman's argument that the object is structured through a transformation of the conventional oppositions given to architecture. Transformations are both internal and yet constitutive of the internality itself.

Eisenman's own description of the interstitial is of great significance. Within it there is an important gesture to what could be described as arguments central to Bataille's concept of *l'informe;* it is also the case that this interior spacing involves the active presence of time. Allowing for that activity means that spacing takes on a workful, as opposed to meaningful, quality. What persists is the central question concerning the nature of that work. Eisenman writes: "My recent work has been involved in an attempt to understand how . . . changes in spatial organizations affect our understanding of time and place. My work deals with how this internal time-space relationship affects how we understand buildings and, more particularly, how we make plans and facades. Specifically my work addresses the space of difference between the exterior and the interior and the space of difference that is also within the interior. The term that we use . . . for that space is *the interstitial*."

From his description of the United Nations library, the interstitial is constitutive of internality in its displacing of structures of recognition, which allows an object to take on different temporal possibilities. Explaining those possibilities demands that an attempt be made to link what has been identified as the yet-to-be and *l'informe*. As has been suggested, central to the operation of *l'informe* is its utility. It works to destabilize. What is undone is the homological relation between form and function. In other words, *l'informe* works to undo an envisaged one-to-one relationship between a given function and the form it takes. The homology of the pregiven is destabilized by this operation. However, this is no simple undertaking; it is one that would define the limit condition of architectural practice. The relationship between the form and function dialectic can be understood as the repetition of certain fundamental structures within architectural practice and thus in terms of architecture's expectations and the expectations held for architecture. The site of intervention is therefore a structure, or concatenation of structures, of expectation. This becomes the site and the possibility for criticality. Eisenman's description of the United Nations project is precise. What would have become impossible within its actual realization was an identification of place and thus an identification of program as given by an immediate awareness of a position within the building.

What does Eisenman mean by "the space of difference"? From the above citations the differences in question pertain to the relationship between exterior and interior as well as to differences within the interior. The nature of this difference is the question. Obviously there is a difference between exterior and interior; they are different by

definition. What more is being adduced in Eisenman's formulation? Answering that question necessitates recourse to a specific project.

The Aronoff Center at the University of Cincinnati involves an addition to an existing building. It is also the addition of a new building insofar as elements of the new building are distinct from the old. Nonetheless, there are points where what is central to the building's operation is the way it negotiates the addition. Eisenman describes the negotiation as a blurring. He writes: "Our addition created an interstitial space between the existing building and the new building, so as to blur the boundary between the two. A contrasting curved form was initially placed next to the existing volumes in order to activate the interstitial space between the new and the old, capable of pressing into both. The expression of that pressure would be manifest on the exterior surface and the new interior surfaces of the old."

A third condition was generated by the addition. It emerged as something that could be reduced neither to the presence of the old nor to that of the new. It arose from within their relation. The spacing that both divides and relates the exterior and interior is such that in this instance it generated another possibility – a possibility without material presence. This occurred because of the nature of the relationship between an existing exterior space that came to be incorporated and an interior space that was properly that of the addition. Here terms such as *exterior* and *interior* lose their hold if taken to define in an absolute sense the occupation and programmatic effect of the building. (In part, these terms can no longer be defined literally; that possibility is not architecturally present.) Displacing the opposition exterior/interior does not mean the object vanishes, however. On the contrary, the insistence of its immaterial presence demands a reconfiguration, and thus theoretical reexpression, of its constitutive elements. That reconfiguration occurs here due to the way the spatial elements are brought together.

In Eisenman's formulation a similar state of affairs occurs in regard to the opposition between new and old. It is essential to note the way a certain utility is being attributed to "interstitial organization." This gives rise to two demands: that an account be given of both this utility and its work of blurring. He says that the proposed spatial organization blurs the distinction between new and old, where new pushes into old and old into new. The different energies that move from these spaces are marked on the interior surface and inserted between the old and the new.

What is being staged here is straightforward. The interstitial as the space of difference operates by undoing the tropes, usually present in terms of binary oppositions, through which the conventions and expectations held for architecture operate. The space of difference is no longer that of literal differences but one in which the hold of the literal has diminished in such a way that exterior/interior and old/new can be rethought.

What this means is that the interstitial understood as the space of difference has an effect. It is not a simple "between"; it disrupts expectations. The essential point is that in disrupting the homology of form and function, the quality that is produced – the third term that is the unpredictable consequence – cannot be determined in advance. It is not empty space awaiting programmatic injection. Rather the complex activity of blurring produces the yet-to-be determined. In the case of the Aronoff, it is not in the addition itself but in the way the addition causes a destabilization of the determinations of exterior and interior. Thus another condition has to be added. Once it can be assumed that what is at work is a relationship between a certain sense of determination, and thus the allocation of programmatic elements within a building with an explicit function, then the yet-to-be, while defined in relation to program, introduces two complicating elements. The first brings a certain sense of plurality into play. The building takes on the quality of both the determined and the yet-to-be. Indeed, this has to be the case. Once the homological relationship between form and function is broken, then instead of an architecture of prescription, what occurs is the inscribed presence of a future operating in the present.

The already determined and the yet-to-be cannot be reduced to each other. The terms of ineliminable plurality – an anoriginal irreducibility – are that the building can only take on the quality of a plural event. The second complicating element is that the interplay between determination and the yet-to-be staged by the building means that it is then defined by the interplay of finitude and becoming. Finitude is the attribution of content and programmatic specificity. Becoming is at work both in the continuity of the realization of the finite and, more importantly, in the maintained presence of the yet-to-be, which is understood as the continual opening within the building's work.

Eisenman's formulation of the interstitial brings these two different elements into play. The first is the disruptive and destabilizing. In destabilizing, the functional and programmatic elements are retained, but retained in their transformation. This brings the second element into play. The interstitial causes terms such as interior, exterior, surface, new, old, void, etc., to break the hold of the literal and thus operate in different ways. Again, these differences cannot be determined in advance. In addition, these two senses of destabilization preclude the possibility of reading the building from its surface. Instead it becomes a series of layers opening out, holding, yielding, and waiting. No longer simply between, the interstitial is now concerned with forming the between. Indeed, it is within this formulation that it becomes possible to trace Bataille's *l'informe* as a concern with the generation of form.

Once architectural concerns are delimited by the generation of form and the maintained presence of the critical, then there has to be both a productive negativity and a disruption. In Bataille, the latter is the practice and work of poetry. Equally, it would be what other possibility there was for the work of *l'informe*. For Eisenman, criticality in eschewing the prescriptive has to allow for the integration of alterity into the building's work. Alterity and the critical are always marked by a present futurity. This becomes part of the complex processes of blurring and the interstitial.

Andrew Benjamin is a philosopher and has taught at the Architectural Association in London. This essay was written for **Blurred Zones** in June 1999.

MEMORIAL TO THE MURDERED JEWS OF EUROPE   BERLIN, GERMANY   1998

Architecture is about monuments and graves, said the Viennese architect Adolf Loos at the turn of the 19th century. This meant that an individual human life could be commemorated by a stone, a slab, a cross, or a star. The simplicity of this idea ended with the Holocaust and Hiroshima and the mechanisms of mass death. Today an individual can no longer be certain to die an individual death, and thus architecture can no longer remember life as it once did. The markers that were formerly symbols of individual life and death must be changed, and this has a profound effect on the idea of both memory and the monument. The enormity and horror of the Holocaust are such that any attempt to represent it by traditional means is inevitably inadequate. The memory of the Holocaust can never be a nostalgia.

The enormity of the banal is the context of this monument. The project manifests the instability inherent in what seems to be a system, here a rational grid, and its potential for dissolution in time. It suggests that when a supposedly rational and ordered system grows too large and out of proportion to its intended purpose, it loses touch with human reason. It then begins to reveal the innate disturbances and potential for chaos in all systems of seeming order, the idea that all closed systems of a closed order are bound to fail.

In searching for the instability inherent in an apparently stable system, the design begins from a rigid grid structure composed of some 2,700 concrete pillars, or stelae, each 95 centimeters wide and 2.375 meters long, with heights varying from 0 to 4 meters. The pillars are spaced 95 centimeters apart to allow only for individual passage through the grid. Although the difference between the ground plane and the top plane of the pillars may appear to be random and arbitrary, a matter of pure expression, this is not the case. Each plane is determined by the intersections of the voids of the grid of pillars and the grid lines of the larger site context of Berlin. In effect, a slippage in the grid structure occurs, causing indeterminate spaces to develop within the seemingly rigid order of the monument. These spaces condense, narrow, and deepen to provide a multilayered experience from any point. This agitation in the field shatters any notions of absolute axiality and reveals instead an omnidirectional reality. The illusion of the security of order in the internal grid and the frame of the street grid is thus destroyed.

Remaining intact, however, is the idea that the pillars extend between two undulating grids, forming the top plane at eye level. The way these two systems interact describes a zone of instability between them. These instabilities, or irregularities, are superimposed on both the topography of the site and on the top plane of the field of concrete pillars. A perceptual and conceptual divergence between the topography of the ground and the top plane of the stelae is thus created. This divergence denotes a difference in time, between what Henri Bergson called chronological, narrative time and time as duration. The monument's registration of this difference makes for a place of loss and contemplation, elements of memory.

In a prescient moment in **Remembrance of Things Past**, Marcel Proust identifies two different kinds of memory: a nostalgia located in the past, touched with a sentimentality that remembers things not as they were but as we want to remember them, and a living memory, which is active in the present and devoid of nostalgia for a remembered past. The Holocaust cannot be remembered in the sentimental, nostalgic mode, as its horror forever ruptured the link between nostalgia and memory. Remembering the Holocaust can therefore only be a living condition in which the past remains active in the present.

In this context, the monument attempts to present a new idea of memory as distinct from nostalgia. We propose that the time of the monument, its duration, is different from the time of human experience and understanding. The traditional monument is understood by its symbolic imagery, by what it represents. It is not understood in time, but in an instant in space; it is seen and understood simultaneously. Even in traditional architectures such as labyrinths and mazes, there is a space-time continuum between experience and knowing; one has a goal to work one's way in or out.

In this monument there is no goal, no end, no working one's way in or out. The duration of an individual's experience of it grants no further understanding, since no understanding is possible. The time of the monument, its duration from top surface to ground, is disjoined from the time of experience. In this context, there is no nostalgia, no memory of the past, only the living memory of the individual experience. Here, we can only know the past through its manifestation in the present. —P.E.

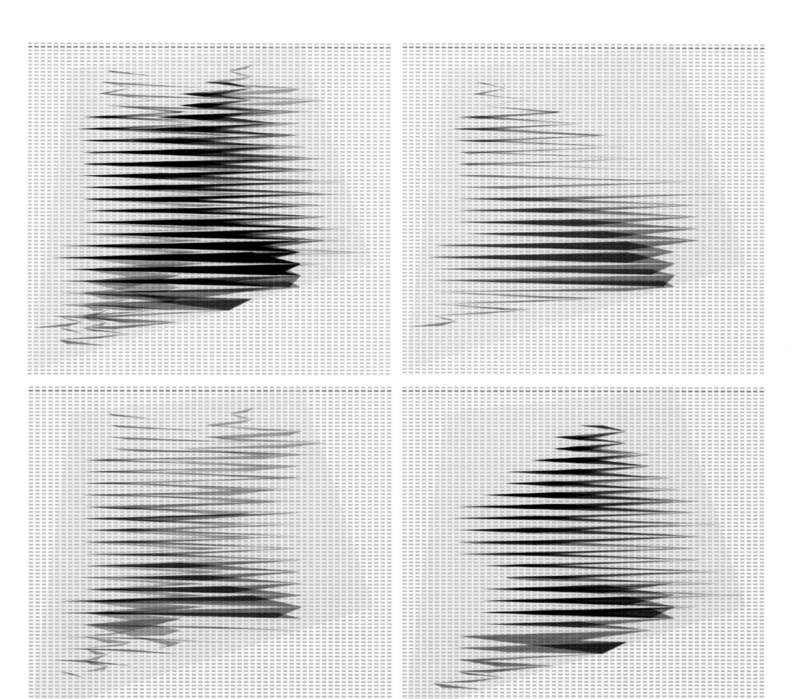

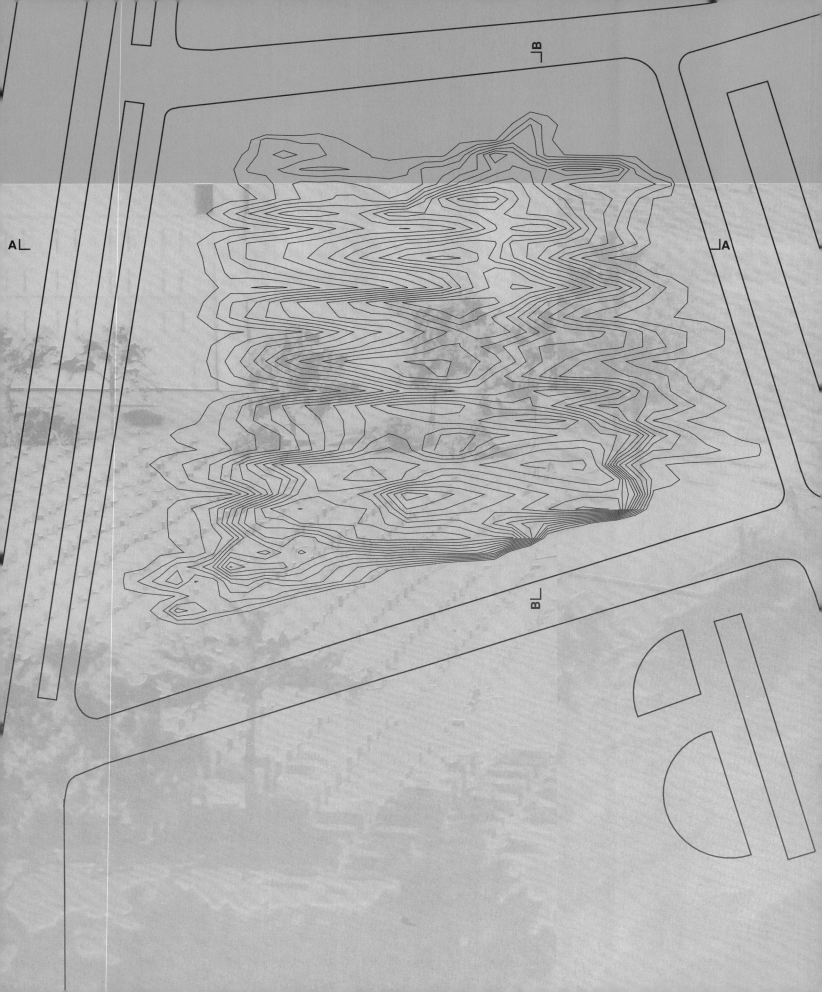

A

B

A

B

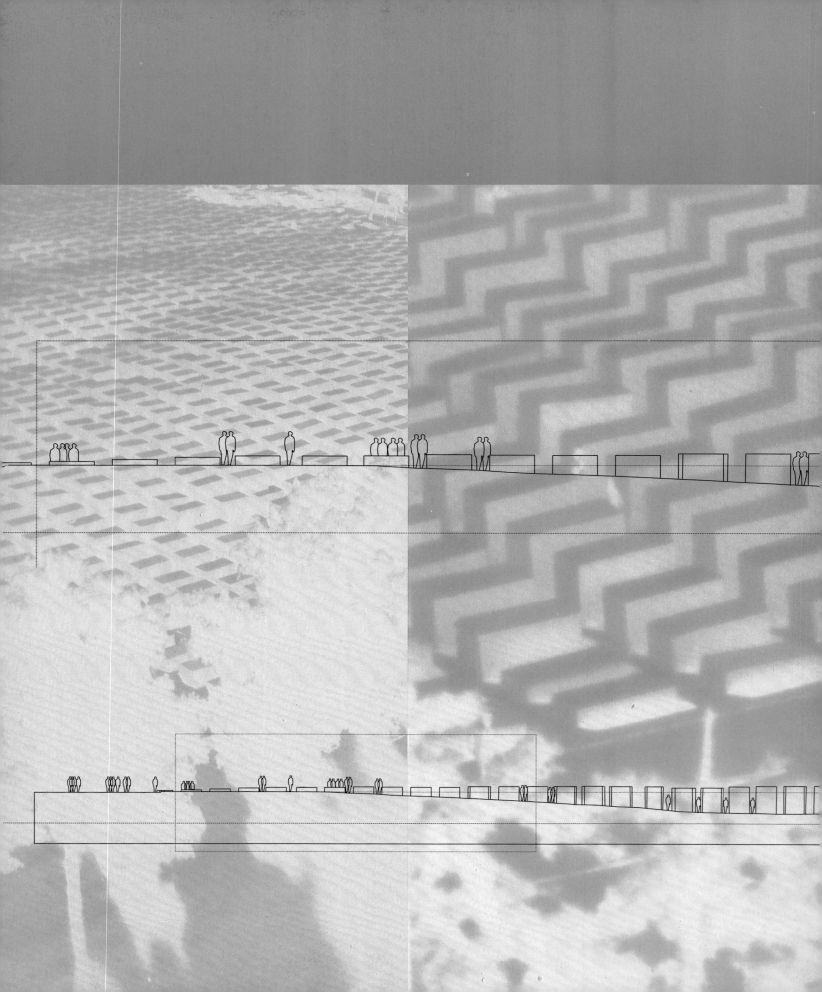

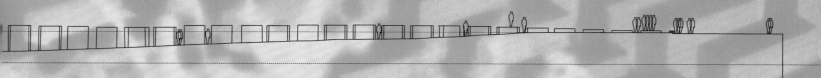

Germania Remember: Berlin's Memorial or Eisenman's Danteum?
Luis Fernández-Galiano

To build, or not to build – that is, well, the question. If it is built, the Memorial to the Murdered Jews of Europe will become part of the symbolic history of humanity, a tourist destination and a haunting landscape in the heart of Germany: Berlin's Memorial; if it is not, it will be the most moving project in the career of its author, a fascinating scheme and a black-and-white photograph of the model in architectural history books: Eisenman's Danteum.

Suffering the slings and arrows of outrageous opinions, the fate of the memorial has not yet been settled; but if the sea of troubles ends up sinking the vessel, the architect will not be on board: at risk will be the German past and the European future. Moving the capital back to Berlin without the liturgy of repentance is a disdain of protocol that would be resented even by those who advocate amnesia; and to do so dismissing a proposal of such blinding drama and violent beauty would only pile aesthetic miscarriage on top of political misjudgment. But this would hardly affect an author whose main purpose is to fade.

Landscape and landmark, the haphazard perfection of the memorial defies authorship. As in popular poetry or vernacular design, the mixture of effortless ease and sharp definition makes origins redundant. When form is both obvious and exact, it becomes self-explanatory, and the author recedes, exiting the stage. Robert Rauschenberg exhibited an erased Willem de Kooning, but here Eisenman offers an erased Peter Eisenman. And while it may seem paradoxical that a signature architect should erase his identity, it is even more perplexing that a blurred landscape should become a sharp landmark, precise and unexpected.

A BLURRED MONUMENT

In the beginning, this blurred monument was a rather recognizable combination of the heavy materiality of Richard Serra and the geometric complexities of Peter Eisenman. But as time wore on, the same form started acquiring a life of its own, and the traces of its makers became fainter. Under the resilient light of public scrutiny, this frozen sacred forest stirred to independent existence, and very soon it was impossible to imagine any other memorial. The more evident it became, the more blurred its authors, who were bound to abandon their autonomous offspring. So exit Serra, and – with the tentative green light – exit Eisenman.

Only if left unbuilt would the architect retain ownership, and critics would interpret it from the formal mores and ideological ritornellos of his biography. The unstable grid would be understood as a representation of the angst of a cosmopolitan Jew, split between Enlightened repetition and Romantic difference; the undulating surfaces would be referred to as an obsessive syntactic game that benefits from digital draftsmanship; and the narrow labyrinthine passages would be perceived as a stubborn effort to excavate an artificial order: an anxious artifice for solitary pleasure, crafted with playful geometries and sterile dexterity.

But the memorial is half-built already, having taken such deep roots in the public imagination, and thus the author is almost absent and the critic is replaced by the historian. The historian knows that the sagging grid expresses the perverse rationality of the Holocaust, the mass production of murder; that the undulating shapes evoke at the same time open fields and war cemeteries; and that the oppressive passages force upon the visitor the individual experience that conventional monuments neglect: under a peaceful, ordered, and reassuring landscape, a hundred narrow paths descend to a familiar hell.

A LANDSCAPE OF FEAR

This landscape of fear is a landscape of remembrance. Square and monument, field and figure, urban and architectural, this cross between landscape and sculpture is really an excavated installation, which forces upon the visitor the oppressive experience of disorientation and loss. Stranded in a grid, and trapped in an open passage, the visitor feels anxiety through order and claustrophobia without closure. So drama is not so much remembered as perceived through the senses, and the body is subjected to a performance that frightens and hopefully reminds of the latent presence of evil in our landscapes of order.

Within this silent theater, a thousand simultaneous individual plays are performed, but none of them is playful. It is a serious game, and the erased designer of these blurred fields of anxiety was aware of the stakes. In an installation by Ulay and Marina Abramovic, visitors were invited to enter the exhibition space by slipping between the naked bodies of the artists; here, clothed bodies are invited to bare their symbolic skins by slipping between concrete blocks that shape a maddening labyrinth

of order, fluid like a gridded field of cold volcanic lava, and making their descent into a clean, precise, and oppressive underworld.

And though many will be tempted to relate the experience of walking between close and heavy geometrical bodies to works of Serra, like *Snake* in Bilbao or *Torqued Ellipses* at the Dia Center – where one passes between huge thick plates of steel that menace the senses and shatter the spirit – and many more will relate the waving bands and gridded furrows to works of Eisenman, like the Greater Columbus Convention Center or his repeated excavations – which challenge perceptions, twisting conventional order – in the end this memorial does not lead back to particular artistic biographies but leads forward to the universality of human experience.

AN ERASED MEMORIAL

To descend into a netherworld is indeed a representation of death, but this rite of passage cannot be separated from its material and symbolic complement, birth, and the memorial thereby becomes the site of both emotional annihilation and spiritual rebirth. Climbing a mountain is associated with the exhilaration of ascent, which leads to spiritual lustration and the command of a wide panorama; in our inverted mountain, the views of the urban surroundings are closed as one enters deep into the geometrical forest and very soon only the sky can be seen, smaller and farther away as the monoliths grow taller and thicker around us.

The memorial is made all the more haunting by the contrast between the harrowing experience of entering and the amiable image it offers from afar, where it appears as soft ripe waves that break on a geometrical beach, gently fusing with the sidewalks as their pattern blurs and peters out into the neutral surface of the city. At the same time, this fading of the boundaries makes the memorial unlimited, extending it below the pavement and presenting the visible rectangular fraction as a tiny ripple of the immense sea of tombs and pain that lies under Berlin: a subterranean aquatic underbelly of inconceivable evil.

This unspeakable terror cannot be represented, and perhaps not even hinted at. Words fail, and so do forms.

Here again the memorial dutifully erases itself into flat silence and scattered ashes. Having allowed the authors to blur and fade, now it is the work that blurs and fades into the impassive skin of the city, annihilating itself with the violent eloquence of a mute gesture. Docile and rebellious, archaic and unworldly, this tenacious memorial is both a machine *à émouvoir* and a spinner of metaphors, ambiguous and unsettling as only very few products of the human imagination ever manage to be.

THE DREAM OF GERMANIA

This blurred field of sharp pain will become – if built – the spiritual heart of the new Berlin. The fall of the Berlin Wall did not absolve Germany, and the mythological nature of this sham metropolis needs a precinct of integrity that will hold the ground for historical truth. When Culture Minister Michael Naumann proposes to build a research center instead of a memorial, he may think his option is closer to the Jewish centrality of the book than to the Greek or Gentile preference for architecture; but he is in fact diluting the symbolic meaning of a gesture of repentance and removing it from the public realm in a city where no urban decision is innocent.

Devoid of gravitas, transformed into a mediathèque linked with Spielberg's Shoah Foundation, this reminder of history would be as harmless as Goering's Aviation Ministry refitted with Eames chairs. But this is exactly what has been done to house the Finance Ministry, so there can be no doubt about the direction of the wind in this republic of Berlin, which has Schroeder at the helm. The last gust blew from Frankfurt, and Martin Walser sent a shrilling black swan to stir the waters of the mourners of Auschwitz. And if the Book Fair preaches amnesia, Duisenberg will soon replace Adorno on the intellectual coat of arms of the city.

The dream of Germania is still alive in the upsetting beauty of Leni Riefenstahl's pictures of Potsdam, and Berlin awaits the future shrouded in its past. But amnesia demands expiation, amnesty demands repentance, and the metropolis on the Spree cannot walk into the next millennium without looking back. If it does, the storms of history may throw it backward into the future like Klee's *Angelus Novus*. Building the expiatory monument, Germany will deprive Eisenman of a Danteum, but will endow Berlin with the memorial demanded by sense and sensibility when faced with an abyss of horror. " 'Tis a consummation/Devoutly to be wish'd."

Luis Fernández-Galiano is a teacher and editor of **Arquitectura Viva** in Madrid. This essay was written for **Blurred Zones** in January 1999.

**Eisenman Architects
1988–1998**

Francesca Acerboni
Barbera Adabauer
Karina Aicher
Emmanuela Alessandri
Ted Arleo
Tracy Aronoff
Philip Babb
Donna Barry
Hans-Georg Berndsen
Federico Beulcke
Hervé Biele
Armand Biglari
Andres Blanco
Lawrence Blough
Pornchai Boonsom
Massimiliano Bosio
Joachim Bothe
Sergio Bregante
Marc Breitler
Andrew Burmeister
Gustavo Calazans
Yolanda do Campo
Kristina Cantwell
Juliette Cezzar
Chi Yi Chang
Robert Choeff
Mina Mei-Szu Chow
Adriana Cobo
Rosa-Maria Colina
Vincent Costa
Lise Anne Couture
Edgar Cozzio
Brooks Critchfield
John Curran
Cornelius Deckert
Michael Denkel
Jon Dillon
Angelo Directo
Stanislas Dorin
Winka Dubbeldam
Daniel Dubowitz
John Durschinger
Michael Eastwood
Mats Edlund
Peter Eisenman
David Eisenmann
Ramon Jose Farinas
Abigail Feinerman
Martin Felsen
Begoña Fernandez-Shaw

Lars Filmann
Jean-Cédric de Foy
Reid Freeman
Luca Galofaro
Marco Galofaro
Carolina Garcia
Chris Garcia
Sigrid Geerlings
James Gettinger
Diana Giambiagi
Brad Gildea
Tom Gilman
Jorg Gleiter
Nazli Gononsay
Felipe Guardiola
Christophe Guinard
Nicholas Haagensen
Judith Haase
Jan Henrik Hansen
Silke Haupt
Jan Hinrichs
Bart Hollanders
Matthias Hollwich
Robert Holten
Norbert Holthausen
Kelly Hopkin
Martin Houston
Chien-Ho Hsu
Simon Hubacher
Lloyd Huber
Timothy Hyde
Claire Hyland
Diana Ibrahim
Lewis Jacobsen
Nikola Jarosch
Sang-Wook Jin
Rasmus Joergensen
David Johnson
Jan Jurgens
John Juryj
Annette Kahler
Keelan Kaiser
Patrick Keane
James Keen
Gwendolyn Kerschbaumer
George Kewin
Brad Khouri
Jörg Kiesow
André Kikoski
Robert Kim
Jan Kleihues
Selim Koder
Yvhang Kong

David Koons
Justin Korhammer
Bernard Kormoss
Rolando Kraeher
Richard Labonte
Abhijeet Lakhia
Oliver Lang
Scott Larsen
Joseph Lau
Maria Laurent
Thomas Leeser
Vincent LeFeuvre
Dirk Lellau
Fabian Lemmel
Jorg Lesser
Luc Levesque
Alexander Levi
Frédéric Levrat
Stephano Libardi
Alexandra Ligotti
Ingel Liou
Jung Kue Liou
Peter Lopez
Gregory Luhan
James Luhur
Claudine Lutolf
Greg Lynn
Greg Mahnke
Jon Malis
Dean Maltz
Mari Marratt
Hiroshi Maruyama
Anne Marx
Nuno Mateus
John Maze
Mark McCarthy
James McCrery
Lawrence McDonald
Michael McInturf
Gregory Merryweather
Kathleen Meyer
Steven Meyer
Will Meyer
Magdalena Miladovski
Pierre-Olivier Milanini
Gianluca Milesi
Edward Mitchell
Sebastian Mittendorfer
Philipp Mohr
Julien Monfort
David Moore
Antonio de la Morena
Michael Morrow

Max Muller
Michael Muroff
Maureen Murphy-Ochsner
Karim Musfy
Corrine Nacinovic
Jean-Gabriel Neukomm
Yasmin Nicoucar
Alex Nussbaumer
Yayoi Ogo
Elisa Rosana Orlanski
Debbie Park
Celine Parmentier
Boris Paschotta
Maria-Rita Perbellini
Daniel Perez
Matteo Pericoli
Astrid Perlbinder
Anne Peters
Sven Pfeiffer
Bernd Pflumm
Marco Pirone
Karen Pollock
Christian Pongratz
Tom Popoff
Silke Potting
Hadrian Predock
Christi Raber
Axel Rauenbusch
Ali Reza Razavi
Mirko Reinecke
Tilo Ries
Stefania Rinaldi
Giovanni Rivolta
Heather Roberge
Ingeborg Rocker
Luis Rojo
Richard Rosson
Lindy Roy
David Ruzicka
Claire Sà
Patrick Salomon
Antonio Sanmartin
David Schatzle
Dagmar Schimkus
Michael Schmidt
Olaf Schmidt
Stephan Schoeller
Rainer Scholz
Joe Schott
Oliver Schütte
Chiara Scortecci
Jerome Scott
Mark Searls

Raquel Sendra
Setu Shah
Jody Sheldon
Julie Shurtz
Donald Skinner
Tod Slaboden
Giovanni Soleti
Angelika Solleder
Madison Spencer
Lucas Steiner
Jon Stephens
Andrea Stipa
Urban Stirnberg
Bettina Stolting
Marc Stotzer
Susanne Sturm
Matthias Suchert
Masahiro Suzuki
David Swanson
Ilkka Tarkkanen
Thor Thors
Lisa Torris
David Trautman
Martin Ulliana
Henry Urbach
Weiland Vajen
Erin Vali
Helene Van gen Hassend
M. Magdalena Velez
Kiran Venkatesh
Irina Verona
Maximo Victoria
Anton Viditz-Ward
Mauricio Virgens
Paul de Voe
Selim Vural
Benjamin Wade
Marcus Wallner
Joseph Walter
Mark Wamble
Janine Washington
Benjamin Wayne
Karen Weber
Lois Weinthal
Ian Weisse
Robert Wetzels
Jim Wilson
Brad Winkeljohn
Jason Winstanley
Markus Witta
Corinna Wydler
Evan Yassy
Leslie Young